MOSES

MOSES

by Elias Auerbach

Translated and edited by
Robert A. Barclay and Israel O. Lehman
with annotations by Israel O. Lehman

WAYNE STATE UNIVERSITY PRESS   DETROIT   1975

Auerbach, Elias, 1882-1972
  Moses.

    Bibliography: p.
    1. Moses. 2. Bible. O.T. Pentateuch—Criticism, interpretation,
      etc.
BS580.M6A813   222'.1'0924   72-6589
ISBN 0-8143-1491-0

This translation from the German of Elias Auerbach, *Moses,* Amsterdam, G.J.A. Ruys, 1953, has been made by permission of Elias Auerbach.

Contents

Introduction: Sources and Method

The remarkable figure of Moses, standing at the inception of the history of Israel, has fascinated poet and scholar again and again, but neither one has ever been able to do justice to him. His achievement is so great and his influence so far-reaching throughout the centuries that only a truly great poet might be able to comprehend and depict him. In the gray outlines of early history and against the shadowy background of legend, his figure is so indistinct that it confronts the historian with great difficulties. Our understanding of this great hero has been made difficult mainly because those two approaches have been confused. But we must decide in favor of one or the other — either for poetic imagination or for critical historical research.

If we follow the second method of critical investigation, we must first form a clear idea, as in all historical research, of the kinds of sources that are available to us about Moses and about their value to us historically.[1]

Our sources are exclusively biblical; nothing is known about Moses from any other source, such as Egyptian. The attempts made by Robert Eisler and Hubert Grimme to derive contemporary testimonies about him from the Sinai inscriptions are discarded nowadays as imaginative failures. Therefore, only the biblical narratives remain. They, however, cannot be used for historical research in their present state; indeed, they present peculiar difficulties.

The literary testimonies which may be ascribed with any degree of certainty directly to the time of Moses are very limited in number and extent. Essentially, only the Ten Commandments (Exod. 20:1-17 and Deut. 5:6-21), the Song of Miriam at the Sea of Reeds (Exod. 15:21), the sayings about the ark (Num. 10:35-36), and the Song of Sihon (Num. 21:27-30) are known. These pieces are sources of first-rate importance for understanding the personality of Moses and for interpreting the external and internal history of his time. All other accounts about him exist in the form of legends and miracle stories which were composed much later.

They were revised, enlarged, and altered many times, and this process did not end even when the definite form of the biblical narratives was determined. The Talmud and Midrash contain numerous Moses legends that, obviously, do not go back to an old legendary tradition but are products of later, freer poetical expression. The same, indeed, applies to the later strata of the biblical accounts about Moses. It becomes clear in all instances that these later strata are totally dependent on an older account and are inconceivable without it. In details they at times contain genuine old data, particularly in cases where the oldest account has not been preserved. But they are not pertinent for making historical deductions from which concrete facts regarding the personality of Moses may be ascertained, because they are too far removed from the oldest sources and reflect their own much later period, and not the time of Moses.

Our first task in all the sources is to penetrate to the oldest accounts in the Mosaic legends. After achieving that goal, however, we must not expect to find historical reports about Moses, since, strictly speaking, no such reports have been preserved. Scholars are in about the same position here as they would be concerning the Homeric poems, if nothing else were known about the most ancient history of the Greek tribes. Yet even then Homer would be a mine of historical information, not so much for the understanding of single events and of the people actually taking part in them as for the geographical, political, social, and cultural background of that bygone period which, due to archeological investigation, has come to life once more in a way which confirms Homer time and again.

In many respects the oldest account about Moses, usually called the Jahwist(J), in its relation to an individual historical character, is even nearer to reality than is Homer to Greek prehistory, because of its specific character. It appears in written form about the time of David, that is, some two hundred and fifty years after the time of Moses. It originated in the circle of the priests of Shiloh, who in all probability were direct descendants of Moses. It therefore contains family traditions with numerous individual features that would presumably have been lost in any other traditional account. Only this account can bring us near historical reality.

Beside it in the Mosaic accounts we find two further sources, usually designated as Elohist (E) and Priestly Code (P). Both are later than J. The Elohist is only a little later, but the Priestly Code in its extant version is much later. Both essentially use J for a basis and are totally dependent on it. Here and there, it is true, they have a genuine old tradition, but on the whole they are secondary throughout and hardly to be used as sources of information for ancient historical conditions.

Even the oldest account has to be used with the greatest caution if the recovery of a historical portrait of Moses is to result. All that we learn about Moses is clothed in the form of legends and miracle stories. Not one word of these stories goes back to Moses himself. Scholars are, in fact, in a similar position when, on the basis of the Gospels, they want to build up a historical picture of Jesus. But in the case of Jesus, there is a foundation of sayings and parables that no doubt do go back to him. Moreover, the Acts of the Apostles can in part refer to the statements of contemporaries. Neither applies to the Moses stories: not one word handed down from Moses, not one contemporary report leads back to him directly.

Since this is so, our historical insight of the legends has to be utilized with the greatest methodical rigor. Legends are connected either with localities or events. Place legends are practically timeless and with the change of epochs may be transferred from one person to another. Their value is based on their knowledge of the historical background. Legends which center around events or persons, on the other hand, have almost always some sound historical substance. They are sometimes transferred to other places, but they still retain essential elements of historical events or of personalities taking part in them. They constitute the form in which history is related in the most ancient period. The distinction between these two kinds of legends is therefore of fundamental importance, and, as far as possible, must be recognized throughout.

Consequently, events must not be considered as unhistorical because they are given in a legendary form. Rather, for the ancient historical narrative of the East, this *is* the given form of presentation. King Sargon of Akkad, although his birth, youth, and rise to royal dignity are related in the form of a legend, is a historical personality. Moses is just as much so, and the same pattern of legend is applied to him. The characteristic deviations from the pattern of the legend contain the most valuable historical material. Thus they are not simply legends; they are *historical* legends. Since it is clear that they contain some sound hist, rial substance — otherwise they could not have come into being — everything depends on ascertaining what this is. That is done by establishing the locality to which they belong and what circumstances they presuppose. Accounts that have been handed down orally for two-and-a-half centuries can render no more than a distant echo of the events and persons about which they tell us. We have to realize clearly that the figure of Moses stands, and always will remain, not in the limelight of history but in semidarkness. Nevertheless, it is surely worth while to follow all the clues and to advance historical knowledge with all the means at our disposal, as far as the oldest preserved accounts render this possible.

Only two serious attempts have been made so far to undertake this task: Eduard Meyer, *Die Israeliten und ihre Nachbarstämme* (1906,) and Hugo Gressmann, *Mose und seine Zeit* (1913), both brilliant works.

With the vision of a historian of genius Eduard Meyer discovered new territory and laid a new basis for further investigation. His studies have achieved more of a real historical understanding than all the critical literature before him. Though in fact the Moses legends occupy a preeminent place in Meyer's work, they are part of it only. For this reason sufficient attention has not been paid to the precise connections between Moses and his work. Meyer's skepticism about the figure of Moses, understandable though it is in a historian of his strict training in method, definitely goes too far. The result is that the insight which might be gained becomes limited.

Gressmann's work is devoted throughout to the investigation of the Moses legends. But he is mainly interested in problems of literary history, the origins and development of the legends as such. The various accounts are for him instruments of equal value for the elucidation of the history of legends. The fundamentally different position of the oldest account compared with the later ones is therefore not emphasized. Moreover, in the evaluation of the material, Gressmann gives weight to general "laws" in the development of legends, which surely is not always deserved. He has the same somewhat dogmatic attitude in drawing up laws of development in the history of religion; he thereby prejudices an unbiased estimate of Moses' achievement and his genius. Contrary to all "laws of development," however, there is one historical fact, namely, that the early achievements of genius emerge spontaneously in the gifted nations of antiquity. This is so with the Egyptians, Sumerians, Babylonians, and Greeks as much as with the Israelites. In the beginning there was the deed, and the theory has to adapt itself accordingly.

Both Meyer and and Gressmann have felt and repeatedly stressed the special significance of Kadesh in the life and work of Moses. But the full importance of this fact, the central role of the oasis of Kadesh in the religious and historical development of that time, still needs a fresh presentation. Here lies the key to many problems which so far have remained unsolved. It is remarkable, in spite of the wide range of theological literature by Jews and Christians, that a full critical evaluation of the Ten Commandments has not yet been made from the point of view of history and comparative religion. This is partly because of the mistaken notions which scholars have about the religious conditions existing in the environment of the Decalogue and partly because this document, connected inseparably with the political work of Moses—the creation of the coalition "Israel"—, has not been understood with sufficient clarity. The division between religious and profane history, as Gressmann tries to trace it in the conclusion of his book, is no more possible here than in the foundation of Islam by Muhammad.

The reader who is anticipating an interesting essay about Moses will be disappointed. Rather, his painstaking cooperation is expected. And one thing more: he must entirely discard cherished ideas and allow himself to be influenced only by the material which is to be presented to him here. Only in this way can a truly historical insight be gained. It is a migration through the wilderness, but its goal is the burning bush.

1

Account of Moses' Youth

Exposure and Discovery of the Child Moses

The legend of the persecution, exposure, and rescue of the hero-child has been treated many times. First and foremost, Gressmann (in *Moses und seine Zeit*) compiled the numerous parallels and showed the general motif. In the Jewish field alone there are at least four parallels: (1), the biblical account in Exodus, chapter 2; (2) the birth-story of Moses in Josephus; (3) the legends about the birth of Abraham; (4) the birth-story of Jesus in the New Testament.

In addition, there are other than Jewish parallels: the birth-story of Sargon of Akkad;[2] Oedipus; Cyrus; Romulus and Remus; the birth-story of Gilgamesh found in Aelianus. A common legendary motif underlies all these parallel stories. But not one of them contains all the features of the motif; each shows some variation in individual features. The full development of the motif as such has not been preserved in our literature. If reconstructed, it would, roughly, look like this: by divination the king learns that in his country (or through his daughter) a hero-child will be born who will become a danger to his throne. He gives orders to seek out the child and kill it (or all the children in question). Through the deity's wonderful intervention, the child is saved and grows up (in hiding or even at the king's court) and finally fulfills his destined mission.

Individual elements are subsequently taken from these legendary motifs, which are found in several nations, and are used to elaborate the accounts about the youth of the different heroes. The legendary character of this pattern is perfectly clear. This does not, of course, imply that the figure of the hero himself is legendary. Sargon, Cyrus, and Jesus are definitely historical personalities.

Now this also holds good for Moses. Primarily we shall have to consider those features as historical which contradict the general pattern of the legendary motif and can only be explained separate from it; as there was a firm historical tradition here, they could not be passed over in the shaping of the story. Before we investigate the Mosaic problem from this angle, we must first try to trace the form of the oldest account as faithfully as possible.

The oldest account, which is added at the end of the book of Genesis, begins with Exodus 1:6: "And Joseph died and all his brethren and all that generation." 8. "And there arose a new king over Egypt who did not know Joseph."

From this it follows clearly that the storyteller has only a short sequence of generations in mind, by no means the four hundred thirty years which a late source (Exod. 12:40) gives as the duration of the Israelites' stay in Egypt.[3] Rather, the conception of this source is roughly the following: the king, under whom Joseph held office, dies, and probably his son also, who must have known Joseph and his merits. His grandson is then the pharaoh of the oppression, and he again is about a generation older than Moses who was born under his rule. We have then before us a total of four generations, of which one generation is that of the immigration, and one that of the exodus, with the result that the extent of the stay in Egypt has to be estimated at about two generations, that is, fifty to sixty years. The original reckoning by generations, found even in the late P source (Exod. 6:16-20), fully agrees with that, though it is artificially lengthened by enormous life spans.[4] We find also a total of four generations:

Levi (generation of the immigration)	Generation of the 1st pharaoh
Kehath	Generation of his son
Amram	Generation of the oppressor
Moses	Generation of the exodus.

Here the two lines of tradition agree with each other and with some measure of certainty we can regard as historical the assumption that the Israelites were in Egypt for some fifty to sixty years.

This account then continues: 9. "And he [the king of Egypt] said unto his people, Behold, the people of the Bne Israel are more and mightier than we. 10. Come, let us deal wisely with them, lest they multiply, and it come to pass that, when there breaks out any war, they also join themselves unto our enemies and fight against us, and get them up out of the land.''

The intention of the plan is to limit the increase of the people. This makes it certain that the next verses, 11 to 14, do not belong to this source. For these verses report the oppression by forced labor, but forced labor is not a means of limiting the increase of the population. This second source, however, is later and dependent on the first; for, contrary to its own wording, it takes up the motif of the limitation of the increase, which does not fit at all, by stressing (v. 12) that the people increased in spite of the compulsory service — which is understood.

But this second source, though its redaction is later, also contains reliable ancient information. It mentions the important fact that the Israelites built two store cities for the pharaoh, Pithom and Ramses.[5] Here is a sound historical recollection, for both cities are situated in the eastern province of Goshen, which had been assigned to the Israelites as pastureland and, according to Egyptian testimony, served also for the accommodation of Bedouin tribes. Both places have been rediscovered by excavations, and inscriptions have shown their builder to have been Ramses II (1290-1224),[6] implying that he was the pharaoh of the oppression. The forced labor is likely to be a sound historical recollection too, for, in fact, the Egyptians made use of Bedouin tribes[7] who entered their territory for such labor. The older source is also likely to have known about the forced labor, though it does not mention it, for the king of Egypt wanted to prevent the Israelites from leaving the country because he did not want to lose his workmen.

To return to the king's plan in the first account. 15. ''And the king of Egypt said unto the Hebrew midwives,[8] 16. When you serve as midwife to the Hebrew women, look at the sex organs;[9] if it be a son, then you shall kill him; but if it be a daughter, then she shall live. 17. But the midwives feared God and did not as the king of Egypt commanded them, but let the male children live. 18. And the king of Egypt called for the midwives, and said to them, Why have you done this and let the male children live? 19. And the midwives said unto Pharaoh, Because the Hebrew women are not like the Egyptian women; for they are like the animals and are delivered before the midwife comes to them. 22. And Pharaoh charged all his people, saying, Every son that is born you shall cast into the Nile, but every daughter you shall let live."

Here is the means proclaimed for the reduction of the people of Israel: the killing of the newly born, at first by means of a ruse and then by brute force. One point, however, immediately strikes us: why are the girls spared? It would suit the purpose better if *all* children were slain. Only one explanation is possible here: it reflects the general pattern of the legend, which has nothing to do with the special case of the Israelites. What is to be prevented is the birth of a particular boy who is going to become dangerous to the king; and that is also made evident by the continuation of the story. Although the motif is covered up, it emerges clearly, as in the murder of the boys at Bethlehem. Here it is shown unmistakably that a matter which originally belonged to a different sphere, namely, the suppression of the Israelites, is related according to the pattern of the legend about the birth of a hero-child.

Only now, after the general milieu has been outlined, does there follow the account of Moses' birth (Exod. 2:1-10). We now quote from the oldest document (J). 2:1 "There went a man of the house of Levi and took to wife a daughter of Levi. 2. And the woman conceived and bore a son; and when she saw him, that he was a goodly child, she hid him for three months. 3. And when she could no longer hide him, she took for him an ark of bulrushes and daubed it with slime and with pitch, and put the child in it, and laid it among the reeds by the bank of the Nile. 5. And the daughter of Pharaoh came down to bathe in the Nile, and her maidens walked along by the bank of the Nile; when she saw the ark in the midst of the reeds, she sent her maid to fetch it. 6. She opened it and saw the child, and beheld a boy that wept. And she had compassion on him, and said, This is one of the Hebrews' children. 10. When the child grew, she brought him to the court of Pharaoh,[10] and he became her son. And she called his name Moses, for she said, Because out of the water I drew him."[11]

In this story, which comprises the kernel of the legend describing the birth, exposure, and rescue of the hero-child, there is a series of important pieces of information. First, we are informed that Moses belonged to the tribe of Levi. That agrees with all the other information we have about Moses and can be considered as a historical fact.

Second, the name of his father is not given; he is simply "a man of the house of Levi." Nor is his mother's name given; she is simply "a daughter of Levi," a Levite. The names Amram and Jochebed, made known in Exodus 6:20, belong to a very late source. Whether they are right or wrong is not important; but it is important that the oldest account knows nothing of them.

A third important fact is that according to the precise text of verses 1 and 2, Moses is the oldest child of his parents and no others are mentioned. The later sources tell of an older brother Aaron and a sister Miriam who is usually identified with the sister introduced here in verse 4. The Aaron and Miriam problem will be discussed later. Here, however, it must be stressed that this passage not only does not mention other brothers and sisters but, indeed, makes their existence very improbable.

This also is the most important reason why we regard verses 4 and 7 to 9 as a later supplement and embellishment of the situation. The motif thereby introduced, that the hero-child is actually suckled by its own mother, is a piece of genuine legend. It is used in even greater detail in the Moses story of Josephus: after the child has refused, by his crying, all attempts to give him an Egyptian wet nurse, he is immediately delighted to take his mother's breast when she is brought to him, and thus he proves his Israelite origin.

If verse 10 is taken as a direct continuation of verse 6, as is done here, it yields important additional information about Moses. In that case *wa-yigdal* does not mean that Moses is a child of one or two years, just weaned, but is a rapidly growing lad. At this age the Egyptian princess takes him to her father's court, where he obtains further education, an Egyptian education. At this period the princess adopts him as a son and only in becoming her son does he receive his historical name, Moses.

What has been written about this name is sufficient and indeed conclusive. The name is certainly Egyptian and means child, son (as in the royal names Thutmoses and Ramoses). The Hebrew interpretation that is given here, as in most such explanations of names in the Bible, is philologically untenable. We have to acknowledge that the hero of the people of Israel bears a non-Israelite name.

Moses in Midian

The oldest account about the story of Moses' birth and

youth ends with Exodus 2:10. Another source begins with Exodus 2:11, the same which in the first chapter reported about the forced labor of the Israelites. The beginning of the new source is recognizable because it relates once more that "Moses grew up" (which has already been stated in verse 10). It then relates how Moses killed the Egyptian who slew the Israelite.

At first sight, then, verse 14 seems to form the direct continuation: the pharaoh hears of Moses' manslaughter and wants to kill him; Moses flees to Midian.[12] Since, however, the account about Moses in Midian undoubtedly belongs to the older J report, we have to scrutinize more closely this connection with the second source. It is rather striking that the killing of a subordinate Egyptian should give the pharaoh cause to intervene and threaten Moses with death. In fact, verse 15 is the direct continuation of verse 10 and contains the resumption of the legendary motif, relating the persecution of the rising hero by the king who feels threatened by him. This connection, which in our text is blurred, is clearly worked out in the account given by Josephus. He does not relate the episode of the killing of an Egyptian at all. The cause of the persecution and threat to Moses by the king is rather the old prediction that Moses would become dangerous to the king. The account of Josephus indeed looks as if he had seen the older account only (which of course is not the case!). When verse 15 is joined directly to verse 10, then the words *eth ha-dabhar ha-zeh* in verse 15 do not mean that the pharaoh has received news of Moses' manslaughter of the Egyptian, but that he has received information about the Hebrew youth being brought up by the king's daughter (he would naturally hear of it through a prediction saying that he was in danger) and thereupon he has decided to kill him.

The text continues. 15. "Now when Pharaoh heard this thing, he sought to slay Moses. But Moses fled from the face of Pharaoh and went[13] to the land of Midian: and he sat down by a well. 16. Now the priest of Midian had seven daughters: and they came and drew water, and filled the troughs to water their father's flock. 17. And the shepherds came and drove them away: but Moses stood up, helped them and watered their flock. 18. And when they came to Re'uel, their father, he said, How is it that you have come so soon today? 19. And they said, An Egyptian delivered us out of the hand of the shepherds, and also drew water for us, and watered the flock. 20.

And he said unto his daughters, And where is he? Why is it that you have left the man? Call him that he may eat bread. 21. And Moses was content to dwell with the man: and he gave Moses Zipporah, his daughter. 22. And she bore him a son, and he called his name Gershom: for he said, I have been a stranger in a strange land."

We learn nothing about the reason Moses turned to Midian. But the fact that in the later accounts the figure of the Midianite father-in-law is inseparably linked with the figure of Moses makes it reasonable to consider Moses' stay in Midian as historical. That belongs to the facts which a tradition cannot invent. In our account Moses' father-in-law is called merely "the priest of Midian." His name is not given (v. 16). When he is given the name Re'uel, it is certainly a late addition; for afterwards, in verse 21, where the name should without question be repeated, he is simply called "the man." Actually, the later tradition about this name varies to an unusual degree, making the man famous because of his many names.[14] He is called in Exodus 2:18, Re'uel; Exodus 4:18, Jether; Exodus 3:1, Jethro; Judges 1:16, Cain; Judges 4:11, Hobab; Numbers 10:29, Hobab ben Re'uel, the Midianite. Just this multiplicity of names is the surest indication that in the oldest account the man was nameless. If he had been named here, no later source would have dared to alter it. Whether the name of Moses' wife, Zipporah, is original or added later can hardly be decided; but the name appears again in the very old legend 4:25 and in this way is supported. The name of his son, Gershom, appears in Judges 18:30 which proves it to be historical.

Historical Conclusions
from the Account of Moses' Youth

There can hardly be any dispute about the general character of the accounts handed down to us about Moses' youth and early manhood. These accounts are not what would be commonly described as historical. Historical accounts as such describe events which are known, more or less accurately, to the informant who is the source, either from his own experience or from a reliable primary source. That is not the case here. Just as with all the great figures of the older periods of history, so in the case of Moses, at best we know historically the work which he created as a mature man. Tradition can take note of him and become a part of the legend about him only when he begins to create history. His life up to this point gains interest only when his work suggests to people that they look back in the mood of later generations. Then, when it is too late, will tradition make an effort to collect information about the days of his youth. But what it knows can be related only as legend or saga. At most, tradition can actually know only single basic facts and circumstances from the hero's youth. It weaves them into a narrative context by combining the hero's life with the familiar resources of a legend.

Our most important task is to pick out those single basic facts and circumstances from the account of Moses' youth which may be considered as historical tradition. To be sure, the account of his youth, in the form in which it is told here, is largely legendary and, as we have seen, shows numerous connections with related legends. But it is not legend altogether. It has a number of features which contradict the motif of the legend, features which no tradition can invent; they are faint but genuine recollections of actual historical facts. These features are the basis for the most important outlines in reconstructing a picture of the real Moses. We can hardly do more than guess from them whence he came, who he was, and how he became what he has become in history.

Is Moses a Historical Figure?

There can be no doubt whatever about the historicity of Moses' personality, certainly no more than about the historicity of Buddha or Jesus. I am not proposing to go into the general historical and philosophical reasons for drawing conclusions about the creator of the work from the work itself; this consideration alone would be sufficient to prove his historicity. In the course of our investigations we shall come across literary remains which can be traced back only to Moses, but for the moment we will not consider them. We are, however, going to show episodes in the account of Moses' youth which are of so individual a character that they point to a definite personality.

Do we possess any historical testimony about Moses? We have none; neither from Egyptian nor from Israelite sources is there historical testimony about him. There are stories dealing with him; but that is not the same thing, for those stories were written down much later. The oldest account, which we shall try to trace and present here, was at the earliest drawn up some two hundred years

after Moses. We do have, however, one certain proof of his physical
existence: Moses left descendants. Quite apart from the Moses
stories, a grandson of his, the Levite Jonathan ben Gershom, is
attested in Judges 18:30. The Eli family of Shiloh also can very likely
be traced back to Moses. That it will ever be possible to find any
further testimony[15] is very unlikely, nor is it of decisive importance.

Was Moses an Egyptian?

The suggestion has been repeatedly made that Moses was
an Egyptian. In recent years Sigmund Freud devoted an entire book
(*Moses and Monotheism*, [1939]) to this problem. But with all due
respect to Freud's genius it must be said that here he has applied his
psychological method to a subject which is not suitable for this kind of
treatment. Psychoanalysis can unravel psychological phenomena
and developments, but it cannot uncover historical facts. It would
require very strong evidence to prove that a nation's hero, who had
not only marked the first great turning point of the nation's development but had also given direction to this development over enormous
distances, was not a son of his own people. How many difficulties and
improbabilities oppose such an assumption! What should have induced an Egyptian to leave his own people and become the leader of a
foreign and much lowlier people? How is it conceivable that Bedouins
should accept the foreigner not indeed as a guest seeking shelter,
which occurs frequently (see the Egyptian story of Sinuhe[16]), but as
hero and leader who gave them an entirely new style of existence?
How is it possible that the spiritual creation of this foreigner should be
so fully accepted by the soul of his adopted people and become so
thoroughly incorporated that it became the foundation of their culture
and outlasted its creator by millennia in a continuing living development? How is it possible that not the slightest recollection of this
man's foreign descent remained but, rather, the contrary was reported about him? Very strong, overwhelming evidence would have
to be adduced to brush aside all these doubts. Actually, however, the
only "proof" that Freud can cite in support of the Egyptian origin of
Moses is his name, his Egyptian name. This evidence is not sufficient
to support a thesis with such far-reaching consequences.[17] A man's
name is first merely a reference to the cultural milieu in which it was
given. In most cases that will be the milieu of his own people, and only
to this extent does the name point to his descent. But it may also be

the result of cultural assimilation, and in many instances that is the case.

The Jews in their eventful history supply thousands of examples of just that. In the Bible itself we have a case which provides an exact parallel to that of Moses. The Israelite Joseph goes to Egypt, there becomes an "Egyptian," and receives the Egyptian name Ṣaphenath-Pa'neah (Gen. 41:45). It is in this respect immaterial whether we consider the figure of Joseph, his name, and this account in the Bible as truly historical or not; the only fact which matters here remains in any case conclusive. In later times, owing to cultural assimilation, foreign names appear in Jewry in large numbers. Some biblical examples are: King Jehoiachin calls one of his sons Sin-bal-uṣṣur (Sheshbassar); a pious Jew in Susa is named Mordecai (after the Babylonian god Marduk), his niece Esther (Ishtar); a priest of Jeremiah's time Pashḥur. In Hellenistic times thousands of Jews adopted Greek names and some of them are held in favor with the Jews to the present day, like Alexander, Phoebus, Isidor. In modern times this phenomenon has become so common that we are no longer astonished. A historian living two thousand years hence, who does not know the background, would surely think a man bearing the two thoroughly German names Sigmund Freud to be of German descent — to the detriment of the Jewish people, which is proud to reckon him among its own.

In the case of Moses we are faced with the second possibility, namely, that this man was an Israelite bearing an Egyptian name. We would then have to assume that by environment or education he was Egyptian by assimilation. That is in fact how the biblical account represents it, and in this it is eminently trustworthy. A people, unrestrained by a firm tradition, would not relate that at an early time its ancestors were slaves[18] in Egypt, nor would it recount that its leader and hero was "half an Egyptian," unless it was obliged to do so by a reliable tradition.

But if this man Moses had been a real Egyptian, then our account would have quite a different shape. Corresponding to the general primitive form of the legend, it would report that there was born to the king of Egypt (or his daughter) a child, who was persecuted and saved and in the end became a grave danger to the kingdom owing to the liberation of the Israelites. The biblical report deviates from this pattern of legendary style in many characteristic details, although it clearly makes use of the motif of the hero-child's birth and salvation. From a historical point of view these deviations are more important by far than the agreements, showing as they do in which points the account was connected with a definite and specifically Israelite tradition.

Contrary to the pattern of the legend, Moses does not come from the king's circle, is temporarily in the lower sphere of the common people, and then returns to the circle of the king; but he emerges from the lower sphere of the suppressed people, appears temporarily in the sphere of the king, and then returns to the sphere of the people. This then must be a tradition which is strong enough to lead to a complete reconstruction of the legendary account. We are therefore entitled to draw the conclusion: *Moses was not an Egyptian but an Israelite*. His Egyptian name shows that he was assimilated into an Egyptian environment and returned from it to the Israelites. The representation given in the biblical account about these principal points is for internal reasons the most probable. Whether or not he had special relations to the royal court can in this respect be entirely ignored.

The biblical account describes one special and important detail about Moses' descent: Moses belongs to the tribe of Levi. This piece of information cannot be freely invented by tradition any more than can Joshua's and Samuel's membership in the tribe of Ephraim and Deborah's in the tribe of Issachar. At this point we cannot discuss the special position of the tribe of Levi toward the priesthood, but for the moment we can accept it as an established fact. It will then be clearly seen that all the information otherwise found about Moses agrees that he is a Levite and the founder of the Israelite priesthood. As Moses' historical existence is witnessed by the descendants left by him, so is his Levitical descent by the Levitical status of his descendants and the cultic institutions he has left. Among the latter is the Ohel Mo'ed ("tent of meeting"), which remains in the hands of the Levites of Gibeon, and in the oldest narratives, which we will discuss later, is always traced back to Moses. The ark which we find with the Levitic priests of Shiloh, goes back to Moses, and the two sayings spoken over the ark are its oldest testimony (Num. 10:35-36). The oracular vessels of the Urim and Thummim are with special emphasis traced back to Moses (Deut. 33:8); later they are in the possession of the Levites of Shiloh. Finally, there is in the (Levitic) Temple of

Jerusalem the brazen serpent whose origin is likewise expressly reported as handed down from Moses. All these facts, with complete certainty, characterize Moses as a Levite. They are totally independent of the narrative in Exodus 2. This in turn proves the note about Moses' descent to be a genuine and reliable historical tradition, occurring as it does within an entirely legendary account of his birth and exposure. It does not lose its great historical value by being connected with legendary elements of the account.

Moses then was a Levite. How he came to Egypt and his relation to Egyptian culture are questions which for the moment are not important; we shall return to these problems later.

Moses in Midian

That Moses made a long stay in Midian is reported in Exodus 2:15-22; the question whether or not we may consider this as a historical event can hardly be answered on the basis of that text. Only an argument of a general character could be used in favor of this assumption: it is hard to imagine that such a report could be invented without the existence of some definite tradition. How is it that Midian is the place named? Egyptians avoiding punishment may have fled frequently from Egypt toward the East and sought refuge with Bedouin tribes. A similar situation is presupposed by the well-known story of Sinuhe. He flees to the Bedouins of the Sinai peninsula and from there northward to the district of Hauran. But how would a Moses story hit on Midian? The territory of Midian is situated near the Gulf of Akaba and east of it, and the Midianites do not belong to the Bedouin tribes which maintained a constant connection with Egypt. If then our account names just Midian, that may after all be based on some historical recollection and becomes a certainty when we see that, quite independently of this account of his youth and flight, the later Moses stories repeatedly connect him with Midian.

The man with whom Moses makes contact in our account is the "priest of Midian." This priest of Midian, Moses' father-in-law, appears also in the well-known story of Exodus 18, where he visits Moses after the exodus and offers up the first public sacrifice mentioned in the Moses stories. In Exodus 18 a new organization of Israelite law is also traced back to him. The same man, moreover (Num. 10:29-33), stands in some relation to the introduction of the ark, even if somewhat obscure in our present text. The testimony becomes so frequent that the connection of the two men may be considered as a historical recollection of the Israelite tribes, particularly as no legendary elements whatever are associated with this Midianite priest.

It would indeed be perfectly possible for the Midianite priest and father-in-law of Moses to have been subsequently transferred from these earlier accounts to the story of Moses' youth. That, however, is unimportant in deciding if Moses' stay in Midian is to be considered as historically possible and probable, or if we are confronted here with pure legend. Regarding Moses' later connection with Midian, the flight and his relationship by marriage to a Midianite can be described as being in the realm of historical probability. We have no reason to distrust the account of Exodus 2 in its basic features.

A brief remark in this account is important for us. The daughters of the Midianite priest report to their father that an Egyptian man has helped them. For them the stranger is simply an Egyptian. (It is strange that Freud should have failed to use this important passage for his thesis!) *It may be, it is even most probable, that Moses understands and speaks the language of his people* and that through this medium he can make himself understood to the Midianites who speak in a related language. But in his general appearance and clothing he looks like an Egyptian. We have already explained that it is out of the question that he was a bona fide Egyptian. Here that remark is compressed into *one* word which, very significantly, rounds off the picture that we can draw of Moses. He is for all that so strongly assimilated to the Egyptian way of life that non-Egyptians can take him for an Egyptian. Precisely this intermediate position, his Israelite origin as well as his Egyptian education and culture, qualify him for the great work of liberation.

To consider briefly how things are related to each other in time, we know it is represented in the Bible that, when Moses makes his flight to Midian, he is a youngish man and still unmarried. (Josephus has him marry an Ethiopian shortly before, apparently in reference to Num. 12:1.) He may then be taken to be at most thirty years old. If we accept his life's span as the normal human span of about eighty years (it is fixed at one hundred twenty years only because of the style of the P source), we know for certain that he died before the immigration of the Israelites into Canaan. In between

comes the stay at Kadesh, which perhaps did not last exactly forty
years but, rather, approximately one generation. At the exodus from
Egypt Moses was a man of about forty years. His stay in Midian
therefore lasted a number of years, at least ten, the best years of his
manhood. During this time he is said to have been his father-in-law's
shepherd. He thus lived a solitary life in the immense desert. In any
case, for a man who came from Egypt, this was a quiet time when he
could collect his thoughts.

It is profoundly significant that in the life of great religious
leaders a decade of quietude is by no means rare. We find it with
Muhammad, with Buddha, with Zarathustra, and with Jeremiah.
After a man's spiritual powers have been concentrated in this way,
his great life work begins.

2

Revelation at the Burning Bush; The Name of God

~~~~~~

In the context of the Moses stories the revelation of God at the burning bush[19] means something totally different from the later revelation on Mt. Sinai. It assigns to Moses the task of leading his people out of Egypt, assuring him that the God of his fathers is with him and his work. Following all subsequent dominant traditions, at that particular moment the name of God is made known to Moses, and this true name of God, which until then had been unknown and shrouded in mystery, has remained at the center of religion ever since.

To understand the true meaning of the story and the inner development it has undergone, we must also analyze it — regretfully, we may add — according to all its literary strata in order to establish its oldest form, and to recognize from its transformation what religious components have accrued to it in the course of time.

The beginning of Exodus 3:1 continues the J account of 2:22 "Now Moses was keeping the flock of his father-in-law, the priest of Midian [the name Jethro is an addition and missing in LXX. Luc.]; and he led the flock to the farthest end of the wilderness." Here E adds: "and came to the mountain of God (ha-elohim), unto Horeb."

Before continuing, the very different geographical situations in the two sources must be established. According to J, Moses drives the sheep through the wilderness and "to the farthest end of the wilderness." The wilderness is thus limited by fertile land; here it comes to an end. With Moses coming from Midian, from the southeast, that can mean nothing but the oasis of Kadesh. Here then, on its fringe toward the wilderness, the burning bush is placed by the

Jahwist. The Elohist, however (recognizable by his use of the divine name Elohim), immediately speaks of the mountain of God, the Horeb, which, as will be seen later, is equated with the Sinai; here he locates the burning bush. That does not fit in with the preceding account, for the mountain of God is situated *in*, not at the farthest end of, the wilderness. E then was inconsistent in adapting himself to an account which does not agree with his presuppositions. E is thus shown to be later than J.

The account of J in its context is distinguished, through the use of the divine name YHWH, by the term "king of Egypt" and by the introduction of the "elders of Israel," whereas E uses Elohim, calls the ruler of the Nile country Pharaoh, and speaks of the whole people.

3:2 "And the angel of YHWH [as in v.4; later YHWH himself speaks; the "angel" belongs to a later qualifying revision] appeared unto him in a flame of fire out of the midst of the bush; he looked and, behold, the thornbush burned with fire, and the bush was not consumed. 3. And Moses said, I will turn aside now, and see this great sight, why the bush is not burnt. 4a. And when YHWH saw that he turned aside to see, 5. he said, Draw not nigh hither; put off your shoes from your feet, for the place whereon you stand is holy ground. 6a. Moreover he said, I am the God of your father, the God of Abraham, the God of Isaac, and the God of Jacob. 7. (And YHWH said), I have surely seen the affliction of my people in Egypt and I have heard their cry by reason of their taskmasters; for I know their pains. 8a. And I have come down to deliver them out of the hand of the Egyptians and to bring them up out of this land unto a land good and large, into a land flowing with milk and honey. 16. Go and gather the elders of Israel together and say to them, YHWH, the God of your fathers, the God of Abraham, of Isaac, and of Jacob has appeared unto me saying, I have surely remembered you, and that which is done unto you in Egypt. 18. And they will hearken to your voice; then you shall come, you and the elders of Israel, unto the king of Egypt and you shall say unto him: YHWH, the God of the Hebrews has met with us; and now let us go, we beseech you, three days' journey into the wilderness and sacrifice to YHWH, our God. 4:10. And Moses said to YHWH, O my Lord, I am not a man of words, neither since yesterday, nor since the day before yesterday, nor even since you speak to your servant, for I am slow of speech and of a slow tongue.

THE NAME OF GOD

11. And YHWH said to him, Who has made man's mouth? Or who makes him dumb or deaf, or seeing, or blind? Not I, YHWH? 12. Now therefore go and I will be with your mouth and teach you what you shall speak."

This account by J is composed of a small number of simple elements. At the beginning we are informed that "this place" is a holy place, the seat of YHWH. This place is the thornbush and its environment. The word for thornbush, *seneh*,[20] used for the sacred thornbush only here and in Deuteronomy 33:16, denotes something pointed. The word appears once more as the name of a crag in 1 Samuel 14:4 and is explained by the phrase *shen ha-sela'*. Presumably it is connected with *shen*, "tooth," also morphologically, and therefore "to sharpen," "to point" is expressed both by *shanan* and *sanan*. From *seneh*, "thornbush," the name of the mountain, Sinai, is not to be separated; it may therefore mean "the pointed one," or the one belonging to the thornbush, the mountain of the thornbush. The fact that the name of the mountain in E, Horeb, may have a similar sense, perhaps sword-shaped crag, points toward the first explanation; whereas the second explanation would mean that J locates Mt. Sinai on the border of the oasis of Kadesh.

In this oldest account of J the contents and the circumstances of the revelation are quite simple. The deity informs Moses that it knows the misfortunes of the people of Israel, and that it has decided to liberate the people from Egypt and lead them into Canaan. It is Moses' task to convey this resolution by the God of their fathers to the elders of the people; together with him they will conduct the negotiations with the king of Egypt. Moses' fainthearted objection is that he does not understand how to make a speech (a point made in a similar way by Jeremiah at his call, Jer. 1:6); to this the magnificent answer is given that it is God Almighty who opens and shuts the mouth of man. It remains for man only to obey.

The most astonishing aspect of this original version of the account by J is that there is no word mentioned about a revelation of the deity's name. For J the name of the deity at this point is no problem at all. When Moses is drawing nearer, he learns that it is the God of the patriachs who is speaking to him. That is sufficient; it is of course YHWH. J has always called the deity by this name in the patriarchal legends; for him the introduction of this name does not require any special revelation to Moses.

In this approach of J there is no apparent contradiction that has profound significance. It is precisely J that has handed down to us accounts which have in several places a man who is found worthy of a theophany attempting to learn the name of the deity from the deity itself. This search for the name is obviously based on the age-old magical conception that knowledge of the right name confers on man some magic power, above all, power over the deity. That is why the deity is always evasive and does not give its name, nor will it hand this power over to man. Jacob's fight with the deity is both the best known and the clearest of these accounts (Gen. 32:25-32). Here it is said (v. 30): "And Jacob asked him and said, Tell me, I pray you, your name. But he said, Why do you ask my name? And he blessed him there." This account is still shrouded in the darkness of a mythical dawn of history; in its original form in J, it is by far more rudimentary and mythological than in the final revision. There can be no doubt about the implications of Jacob's question. Here, and often elsewhere, the Jahwist without prejudice gives things their own peculiar coloring; that, as we shall see, is no proof that the Jahwist shares these views.

In the theophany of Manoah[21] (Judg. 13), the course of events is quite similar. Manoah asks (v. 17): "What is your name?" adding, to conceal his proper intention, "When your words come to pass we may do you honor." The deity replies in the same words as in the former account: "Why do you ask my name, seeing it is wonderful? *(we-hu' peli'y)."* Here an important new feature is added to the account: the deity, it is true, evades giving its name but at the same time it surrenders its name in a somewhat veiled form, as in a rebus, comprehensible for one who is clever enough to solve the riddle. For it follows from the subsequent text (v. 19), which unfortunately is slightly corrupt, that at this altar YHWH is worshiped under the name "YHWH, the miracle-worker." The answer of the deity might in fact be translated: "Why do you ask my name? It is surely the miracle-worker."

In the view of people of this ancient time, the name of the deity contained a magic power which man may try to obtain and which the deity tries to withhold from him. This belief in the mystical power of the name forms the basis of the peculiar features of the later development. Misuse of the name is already forbidden in the Ten Commandments (the third commandment can be understood only in

this way). The short story in Leviticus 24:10-14 probably attests to this also. Pronouncing the full name of God without any special cultic purpose is possibly subject to punishment; but that is not certain, because the meaning of the word *naḳabh* here (literally "to perforate," "to bore through") cannot be established beyond doubt. Later the custom spread of not pronouncing the name of God in full (that was permitted to the high priest once a year only, on the Day of Atonement; this stage of the development is, consequently, post-exilic); the name was replaced by circumlocutions. Finally, in later Judaism the mysticism of the name of God, forgotten in its original form, unfolded in new, curious ways in legend and cabala — all of them offshoots of the age-old notions regarding the miraculous power of the divine name.

It is rather striking that the Jahwist in the revelation at the burning bush should not mention a single word about a revelation of the name to Moses, although the Jahwist knew this pun on the divine name and elsewhere in his stories repeatedly made use of it. Only two explanations are possible. Either he did so in the original form of the story but the redactor has eliminated it in favor of the Elohist's version (more will be said about this shortly). Or the Jahwist has deliberately avoided it and that seems more probable to me. For him who in his accounts used the name of God in its full form from the beginning, it would be understood that the hero, Moses, would know this name; a special revelation of the name was therefore not required. Going further we may conclude that this writer, who has handed down to us the ancient legends about the mystical power of the "name," has already risen above this stage of religion. For his purified conception of the universality of the one God, the problem of the name of the deity has ceased to be a problem. We shall see presently that in this detail the later Elohist, as so often happens, is closer to the ancient notions.

It is doubtful whether the two "confirmation miracles" with which Moses is provided belong to the oldest stratum of the J accounts. After the deity has expressly foretold (v. 18) that the elders will believe him, it is preferable to suppose that section 4:1-8 constitutes a later amplification (verse 9 is certain to be a later addition). But this point is not of paramount importance. We will now turn to the revision of the account by E.

At the beginning of the account, E limits himself to small

insertions. We have already seen that in chapter 3:1 he adds the words, ''And he came to the mountain of God, unto Horeb.'' In verse 4b E says, ''And Elohim called unto him out of the midst of the thornbush and said, Moses, Moses! And he said, Here am I;'' in verse 6b E adds the words, ''And Moses hid his face; for he was afraid to look upon God.'' This requires no further comment; it agrees with the Elohist's awe as it were of incarnate manifestations of God.

Then in verses 9-14 the famous passage about the revelation of the divine name follows as a large continuous insertion: 9. ''And now, behold, the cry of the children of Israel is come unto me; moreover I have seen the oppression with which the Egyptians oppress them. 10. Come now therefore and I will send you unto Pharaoh that you may bring forth my people, the children of Israel, out of Egypt. 11. And Moses said unto God, Who am I that I should go unto Pharaoh and that I should bring forth the children of Israel out of Egypt? 12. And He said, Because I shall be with you; and this shall be the sign unto you that I have sent you: when you have brought forth the people out of Egypt, you shall serve God upon this mountain. 13. And Moses said unto God, Behold, when I come to the children of Israel and shall say unto them, the God of your fathers has sent me unto you, and they shall say to me, What is his name? What shall I say unto them? 14. And God said unto Moses, I shall be that I shall be. And He said further, Thus shall you say unto the children of Israel, 'I shall be' has sent me unto you. (15. And God said moreover unto Moses, Thus shall you say unto the children of Israel, YHWH, the God of your fathers, the God of Abraham, the God of Isaac and the God of Jacob has sent me unto you. This is my name forever and this my memorial unto all generations.)''

This passage requires careful analysis, prefaced by a few observations to ascertain its ''meaning,'' that is, the meaning which it has in the opinion of the writer, particularly in its decisive and most obscure part, verse 14 at the end. Over the centuries how many profound, religious-philosophical reflections have been devoted to this passage! They all are justified in their own way, indicating as they do phases of the religious development as it bears upon the Book of Books. But not one has any practical significance for the explanation of this passage, for discovering its original ''meaning.'' The point here is not what to read into or out of this passage; on the contrary, the deeper and more beautiful the philosophical explanation is, the less helpful, in most cases, is it in discovering the intended meaning. Rather, we have to make the attempt to understand what the author of this passage intended to say and why he has said it with these very words. That is why I am not going to undertake a discussion of the numerous explanations and translations.[22] Instead I shall take one typical example of inconsistency to elucidate the difference between it and my method: I am referring to the explanation given by Franz Rosenzweig in his essay, "The Eternal One,[23]" which later served as a basis for the translation of the passage in Buber-Rosenzweig's translation of the Bible.

We will begin with the end of the passage, verse 15. Here it is clearly stated in the opinion of an ancient witness what is the plain sense of the whole section: "Thus shall you say to the children of Israel, YHWH, the God of your fathers, the God of Abraham, the God of Isaac and the God of Jacob has sent me unto you." If that alone were stated in this passage in reply to Moses asking for the name, it would not be necessary to try and solve any riddles. Question and answer plainly correspond to one another. Moses asks what is his name? And the deity replies, "YHWH, the God of your fathers." That is perfectly clear and requires no interpretation. The deity's name is given without any evasion: YHWH. But for this reason, precisely, it is certain that verses 14 and 15 could not have come from the same pen. The second clear answer makes the first, which is obscure and tortuous, superfluous; and the first answer makes the second impossible. Whoever wants to conceal cannot immediately reveal, and whoever wants to reveal need not at the start conceal. As is always the case when two different answers are given, here also they are derived from different sources. The phrase "thus shall you say" is used twice; but Moses can speak only like this *or* like that. The introductory formula too, "and God said moreover," is the usual form in which a duplicate source is inserted. Verse 15 is then the statement of a second writer who, thinking the statement of verse 14 too obscure, wants to give a perfectly clear answer. Indeed it almost sounds like a polemic against the text of verse 14 when at the end he confirms, "This is my name forever and this is my memorial [i.e., the designation under which I am remembered] unto all generations": *this* name YHWH, expressly, and not Ehyeh or any other obscure designation. The significance of verse 15, which did not belong to E originally, is that it makes sure about the contents of what precedes, at least in the opinion of this oldest witness: the promulgation of the divine name.

We now turn to the account proper of the Elohist. The beginning (v. 9) repeats the introduction of J's account (v. 7) in very similar words and thereby proves it is a parallel source. The continuation (v. 10) likewise is parallel to J's instruction to Moses (v. 16 and 18). Also verse 11, Moses' doubt about his usefulness, and verse 12, the removal of this doubt by the deity, have their counterpart complete in J, in 4:10-12.

But here the two sources show characteristic differences, which correspond to the generally different styles of the two writers. J is clear and objective as always; in his reply Moses raises the objection that he is "not a man of words," that he does not possess a rich flow of language like an orator, and that he is "slow of speech and of a slow tongue," that for him the formulation of the right words is difficult. E gives those scruples a general turn: as a personality Moses does not feel worthy of this task. The deity's reply is different too. In J God refutes Moses' objection by stating that it is God who in his omnipotence makes man dumb or eloquent, assuring him that He will put the right words in his mouth (v. 12). In E, God reassures faint-hearted Moses by a general assurance that He will be with him, giving him a "sign" to indicate that it is God who is sending him. (Why did he do that? Did Moses have any doubts about *this* point?) And this sign is curious indeed: when Moses leads the people out, they will serve God at this mountain. This "sign" cannot fortify him for his proper task, as it will become operative only after the task has been performed. Yet here that is unimportant.

We now come to the most important difference between the two sources. At this point in E the question about the divine name follows, but it is completely missing in J.

First we have to exclude any doubt that Moses is really asking for the name of the deity. It may sound strange that such a doubt should be raised at all; but the statement is not superfluous because of the attitude maintained by Rosenzweig and (following him) Buber toward this passage. Both translate *mah shemo*, "and what about his name?" This translation obscures the facts. For it means that Moses is not asking here for a name unknown to him or to the people, but for the meaning and relationship of the name, which is known to him. For Rosenzweig and Buber this slight shift is of fundamental importance because of their interpretation of the reply which follows. This shift, however, is absolutely inadmissible and must be rejected. It is above all excluded by the clear reply given in verse 15, "YHWH, the God of your fathers . . . has sent me unto you." Here lies the great significance of verse 15 for ascertaining the true facts. And, precisely for Buber and Rosenzweig who, in opposition to the documentary theory, maintain the uniformity of these accounts, verse 15 ought to suffice as a decisive refutation of their translation.

Following the clear sense of the words, Buber's and Rosenzweig's translation is untenable. That is shown by the parallel passages. The direct question concerning the name occurs in three other passages in the Bible: Gen. 32:28; Judg. 13:17; Prov. 30:4. The passage in the book of Judges is irrelevant for our purpose as the form of the question here is not *mah shimkha,* but *mi shemekha.* But in the two other cases the form is exactly as in our passage: *mah,* connected by a hyphen (*maqqeph*) with *shem.* In Genesis 32:28, on the other hand, there is no doubt about the meaning of the question. The deity asks Jacob *mah shemekha* and he replies, Jacob. Buber also translates this: What is your name? Who indeed will have the idea to say here: And what about your name? Quite the same applies to Proverbs 30:4. Here too Buber appropriately translates: What is his name, what is his son's name? Following these examples it is quite certain that *mah shimkha* and *mah shemo* are the simple and usual forms of the direct question about a person's name. There is no justification whatever for treating our passage, which is completely analogous to the others, as a mystery by reading anything else into this question. Any attempt of that kind, such as Rosenzweig and Buber make, is not a translation or explanation of the text, but is an alteration and distortion of it. Moses does actually ask for the deity's name.

The Elohist makes Moses ask for the divine name. He thereby shows that in this respect he is closer than the older Jahwist to the old, primitive, magical conceptions. For the Elohist the knowledge of the "true name" means something significant and compelling. The Jahwist indifferently reports this struggle for the name in the legends of remote antiquity, but rises above such an approach in this passage, which is most important from the point of view of comparative religion; the Elohist himself, however, still reflects the stage of the ancient legends. His account of Moses' search for the name is consequently parallel to the tales of Jacob's struggle and the theophany of Manoah. Therefore, our task now is to continue the investigation to see if other characteristic features of these tales are found at other points in the Elohist's account.

It is a peculiar feature of these legends, because of some understandable reserve, that the question concerning the name of the deity is not put in a direct way but, rather, in a roundabout way. This is least clear in Jacob's struggle. But here we have a real struggle between the *heros* and the deity, a struggle in which originally not the deity but the *heros* is victorious. Only when the deity has been paralyzed by Jacob's blow on his hip, thus rendered incapable of fighting on, and has to ask for his release; only after that does Jacob venture to put the question. The course of events is clearer in the story of Manoah. When Manoah asks for the name of the deity, he adds, in order to explain his curiosity and to excuse himself, "So that I may honor you when your word comes to pass." This is plainly a pretext, for he could also honor the deity even if he did not know the name; it is however essential to this story. The same motive is found in the story of Gideon, only here it is obscured by a revision of the text. Gideon asks, "Show me a sign that it is you, who talks with me," (Judg. 6: 17). Who is "you"? In this passage, which makes no sense in the present form, the name of the deity is given. Gideon senses the right name and asks for a sign that his surmise is right. This feature is quite distinct in the Elohist's account of the revelation. Moses does not ask immediately, What is your name? I want to know! But he uses the curiosity of the people as a pretext: "When they shall say to me, What is his name? what shall I say to them?"

He too fights shy of the direct question, but this disguise of his own desire to know is rather transparent. The form of Moses' question is therefore by no means accidental and of no consequence, but corresponds to the approach found in similar accounts. The most important feature of these legends is the second. The deity does not immediately reply to the pressing question about its name, but attempts to evade it in order not to give man power over it by surrendering the name. At the same time, however, the deity gives its reply in a form from which the elect can after all grasp the name. In Jacob's struggle only the first move, the evasion, has been handed down. The deity, although hard-pressed, does not surrender its name, but purchases a release from doing so by giving Jacob a blessing. (An allusion to the name is bound to have existed in an even older form of this legend, for Jacob knows, after all, that he did not strive with a nocturnal robber, but with a deity.) This motif is clearly expressed in the legend of Manoah, as has already been stated. The deity, it is true, apparently evades Manoah's question: Wherefore do you ask after my name, seeing it is Wonderful? In reality, the name thereby is indicated and then remains attached to the altar erected here: YHWH, the miracle-worker.

The playful answer of the deity is described with exquisite art in the Elohist's account of the revelation, and by considering it we reach the essence of the story. To Moses' question the deity replies: *ehyeh asher ehyeh.* [24] Because of the simple wording this may at first be understood as a blank refusal, indeed a rebuttal of the question, For what purpose are you asking? I may be whoever I may be! Or, Whoever I am, what concern is that of yours? But only a dull mind would grasp no more than that from the reply. For Moses and the one who has fashioned this conversation many additional undertones vibrate in the reply. Beneath the surface of the reply there is a game of hide-and-seek with the sacred name, quite similar to that in the Manoah story. Behind the sound group *ehyeh* vibrates the name YHWH, and Moses is bound to hear it emerge and to understand it. The later exegete, who in verse 15 simply wrote YHWH, is pointing to that. But verse 14 itself refers to it by continuing, "Thus shall you say unto the children of Israel, *ehyeh* has sent me unto you." This indicates clearly that in *ehyeh* the name is to be sought and found. Wellhausen has suggested that instead of *ehyeh* the third person *yihyeh* was originally written, and in fact this form, which grammatically is required by the syntax, would come much closer to the name of God; it differs from it in one letter only. This assumption, however, is not necessary. The quibble about the name, even in the form *ehyeh,* is sufficiently transparent for Moses, who is expected to interpret it, and for all later men to whom the divine name is familiar. The deity does not mention its name outright, but allows it to be guessed by hinting at it. Thereby this account of the revelation of the name fits in perfectly with the related accounts.

The formal analysis of the story is thus essentially completed. We now understand why it is told at this point. The revelation of the divine name, which was omitted by the Jahwist altogether, seemed so important to the Elohist that he inserted it between Moses' commission and its execution. By tracing the elements elsewhere, we now understand the peculiar form of the story.

There still remains for us, however, the task of penetrating another stratum of the account, its most profound. Like the sound of an organ a still deeper octave vibrates in the deity's short reply. Why was just *this* form of alluding to the divine name selected? Does that not imply a particular intention, a distinct connotation? Certainly! The author *wants* you to hear this connotation in the answer. In this way he manifestly wants to give an *interpretation* of the divine name YHWH. By God's saying "I am that I am" or "I shall be that I shall be", a statement is made which is intended to explain the *meaning* of the name YHWH. In the Elohist's opinion the name expresses God's eternal existence, eternal immutability, His eternal presence. The words as they stand can be understood in this and in no other way. The translation, or rather interpretation, given by Buber and Rosenzweig ("I shall be present as He who will be present") is by no means demanded and is not even possible by wording of the text. They, however, proceed from the same assumption as the author of the account, namely, that the divine name, YHWH, is to be explained through some modification of the concept of "being."

We are now in the realm of exposition. We can see quite clearly how the Elohist interprets the name YHWH. But there is a different question: Is this interpretation *right*? It belongs to the long series of explanations of names of which numerous examples occur in the Bible. Only those names, of course, are subject to such an explanation in which the interpretation presents certain difficulties and is not immediately clear, names like Yesha'yahu, Abi'ezer, and Deborah.

We may suggest a general law implying that the etymological explanations of names in the Bible, which represent so-called popular etymologies, are, strictly speaking, in no single case correct. All the well-known explanations of the names Cain, Noah, Abraham, Levi, Judah, Ephraim, Moses are, from a scientific point of view, not to be taken seriously. It would be a very strange exception to this law if the explanation of the divine name YHWH given here were right. As a matter of fact, it gives only a rather rough approximation to the sound of the name and is totally inadequate for a real explanation of the form.

That indeed is the reason why time and again many other

explanations of the name YHWH have been attempted. It would hardly be worth while discussing these attempts, for not a single one is really convincing.[25] On the basis of Hebrew and Arabic the name YHWH has been explained as meaning the Eternal One, the One Who Succors, the Blowing One, the Destroyer, the Thunderer, the One Who Roars (in the thunderstorm). These attempts always leave unsolved the problem of the name from the point of view of the history of religion proper.

That being so we may approach the problem of YHWH's name from a new angle. One of the greatest difficulties arises because the divine name YHWH occurs, with the Israelites, not only in the full form of the tetragrammaton YHWH but also as a trigrammaton *yahu* or *yeho*, and a digrammaton *yah* or *yo*. Any satisfactory explanation, therefore, must not only give an interpretation of the full form of the tetragrammaton but must also include the shorter forms and give a plausible presentation of their relationship to the full form of the name. The usual opinion is that the proper, original form of the name is the four-letter one; that the form consisting of three letters evolved from it by popular abbreviation; and from that, through a further abbreviation, the two-letter short form. Accordingly the tetragrammaton would be the oldest form; the others would represent later developments. This view, however, does not satisfactorily explain the facts as we have them.

It must first be stated that a difference of age between the various forms of the name of God cannot be established. The full form of the tetragrammaton goes back to the time of Moses; its oldest witnesses are the Song of Miriam at the Sea of Reeds (Exod. 15:21) and the Decalogue. The question whether or not the name YHWH was known to the Israelites before Moses has no validity because there was not a people of Israel before Moses and literary testimonies from pre-Mosaic times do not exist. Furthermore, the question as to whether the name YHWH originated with the Israelites is misleading not only for historical reasons but also, we shall see shortly, for inner reasons which lay in the genesis of the name. The name arose among the Israelites and, indeed, in the Mosaic period, and the tradition of the Elohist that the disclosure of the name YHWH goes back to Moses is certainly based on good historical tradition. Nor is there any trace of the short forms of the name before Moses. (The occurrence of the name Yo in an inscription from Ras Shamra is most doubtful.)

The short forms are not later, but by the time of Moses are contemporary with the full form. Moreover, as is the case later, they appear as part of personal names, the oldest of which may be Joshua (Jochebed is witnessed by a later source only). It is even possible that the very short form Yah was independently handed down from the time of Moses, if the text in Exodus 17:16 is correctly preserved: *yad 'al kes-yah* (or *nes-yah*), "hand on Yah's chair" (or "banner"). As far as age is concerned, no difference between the divergent forms of the divine name can be established; they all appear at the same time. That makes it difficult to see how the short forms can have developed from an abbreviation of the tetragrammaton. For internal reasons it is also unlikely. How is the abbreviation of a divine name possible and conceivable and where else might there be an example of it? I do not know of any either in Israel or in the Oriental or Greek world. It was merely a mistaken theory of the chronological sequence of the forms of the name which suggested this idea.

From the beginning, however, we can recognize how the divine names are used for different purposes.[26] The full form of the tetragrammaton YHWH is used for religious purposes only, to denote the deity in the ritual and in appeals, oaths, and affirmations. It is never used for profane purposes or as a component of the theophoric personal names. The sphere of the Holy is reserved for the full name of God; that presumably is the meaning of the third commandment in the Decalogue. This peculiarity in the employment of the tetragrammaton explains the growing hesitation ever to pronounce the name in its full form. Its limitation to the sphere of the Holy and to rituals is more and more emphasized in the historical development; in its application it is replaced more and more by symbols (never short forms!) until finally the high priest alone is permitted to pronounce it, and then only once a year in a solemn ritual.

The short forms, on the other hand, are from the beginning used only for profane purposes, as components of names. They are never used to address the deity directly or, more correctly, they are used only in very exceptional cases. Such an exception is the use of the trigrammaton *yeho* in the Elephantine papyri. Special conditions may have prevailed here; perhaps in this far-distant congregation, separated as it was from the religious development, the correct pronunciation of the tetragrammaton was no longer known. Another exception is found in the use of the shortest form Yah in cultic exclamations like *hallelu-yah*, which are already crystallized in formulas.

In personal names the trigrammaton occurs in two forms that basically are identical: at the end of names in the form *yahu* and at the beginning in the form *yeho* (apparently following a change of stress toward the end of the name). The digrammaton too appears in two forms: at the beginning of names as *yo*, at the end of names as *yah*. Probably these two forms differed only orthographically and were perhaps pronounced in the same way, because, as a rule on the seals and ostraca from Samaria, *'zyw, gdyw, shlmyw, 'byw, shbnyw*, etc., are found also at the end. There is no basic difference between the two- and three-letter short forms in their usage in personal names. The same name may be written one time in one form and at another time in another form. Beside *Yehonathan* there is Jonathan; beside *'zyhw* there is *'zyh* or *'zyw*. At most the fuller form has a somewhat more solemn character and is usually found in the literary language, whereas the shorter form presumably prevailed in the spoken language. In later times the shorter form became more frequent. In our tradition the theophoric part of the name has at times dropped out altogether: Hezekiah's father always appears under the name Ahaz, whereas the Assyrian inscriptions always call him Yau-ha-zu. They consequently heard it as *yw'hz* or *yhw'hz*.

In considering these facts Rosenzweig, following several predecessors,[27] has made the fully justified assumption that the oldest form of the name is found in *yah* and *yo*. The trigrammaton and the tetragrammaton, however, are to be considered later developments. The meaning of the original *yo*, he thinks, can no longer be detected, since this name is prehistoric; perhaps it should be interpreted merely as an interjection, a shout. Rosenzweig here seems to me to have come very close to the truth. It is important now to have a better understanding of the significance of that development and to draw conclusions from this approach.

The great turning-point in the history of the divine name is the emergence of Moses. With him—and in this, tradition agrees with all ascertainable sources that possess historical probability—the full tetragrammaton form of the name came into existence as the bearer of a new conception of God. It alone remains the vehicle of the religious movement. Thereby the shorter, older, pre-Mosaic designations of the deity became free for profane use and were drawn upon in the formation of personal names. The saying "hand upon Yah's banner" is the only example of the preservation of the name of God from pre-Mosaic times.

If this assumption is right, what does the development from the simplest to the fullest form of the divine name signify? The simplest and perhaps oldest form, the digrammaton, and the next stage, the trigrammaton, are distinguished by the insertion of the letter *hĕ*. I shall call that a *he emphaticum* (an emphatic *hĕ*). Its insertion leads to a stronger emphasis in the pronunciation of the name by prolonging the breath and by the double ejaculation of the final breath. This insertion of a *hĕ emphaticum* is a purely artificial pronouncing process. There is no change of meaning in the word corresponding to it, and no such change must be sought. The only palpable change is that the word, emphatically lengthened, is lifted up into a higher, more solemn region. This may appear to us to be completely external; for ancient man, however, processes like these were charged with a strong emotional element.

There are several examples of the insertion of a *he emphaticum* in the Bible. The one best known is the lengthening of the name *Abram* to make *Abraham*.[28] Here, too, it is a vain attempt to seek a new meaning for the newly formed name Abraham; there is none. On the contrary, the easily understood old name becomes meaningless. But here too the new, emphasized name is the symbol of a new, heightened phase of life, of a solemn covenant between God and man. Abram, the Chaldean, becomes Abraham, the patriarch. We are again on religious ground.

Perhaps—for no more may be suggested than a hypothesis—the name *Aharon* belongs to this category too. This personality, who, as has been proved, was later inserted into the Moses stories in many places, would accordingly have obtained his name, otherwise inexplicable, through an artificial transformation of the name used for the Holy Ark (*aron*) by inserting an emphatic *hĕ*. That, however, is not certain and therefore may be mentioned only in passing.

The divine name *elohim*, on the other hand, offers a complete parallel in all respects. Discussions about this word usually overlook the fundamental fact that taken as a plural of *el* its form cannot be understood at all. This is not a plural of *el*, for the plural occurs in the Bible repeatedly and is *elim*. Grammatically the form *elohim* can be derived from the singular *el* neither in its consonantal formation nor in its vocalization. And, most important it is still questionable whether we should accept it as plural at all. In this respect the word is in line with a group of others, none of which were plurals originally; because of their form, however, at a later time when people were no longer familiar with their origin, they were taken to be plurals. To this class belongs the oracle *urim we-thummim*, the *terafim*, and other words like *mayim, shamayim,* and *ne'urim*. In the word *elohim* too the linguistic instinct fluctuates between constructing it as a plural or as a singular. But things are by no means as they are often represented, namely, that here an old plural, dating from polytheistic times, is used and later understood as a singular. Rather, the reverse is the case: the grammatical construction of the word in the plural is probably more characteristic of later strata, while the older strata understood and construed it in the singular as "supreme god," "deity." The word *elohim* has no analogy whatever in any other Semitic language.

All these characteristics prove that the word *elohim* is not a natural product of Semitic grammar but a conscious and artificial new formation of a theological concept. It uses the word *el* to evolve a form similar to a plural, but gives it a new level of heightened solemnity by inserting an emphatic letter *he*. The peculiar vocalization is hardly accidental. While hitherto the attempt has always been made to derive the peculiar massoretic vocalization of the tetragrammaton from the vowels of the words *elohim* or *adhonay* (it does not fit either entirely), the actual historical relationship could very well be the opposite: *elohim* is vocalized with reference to the old divine name Yaho or Yeho, adapting it to the normal plural *elim*. Understood in this way, the plural of majesty *elohim* would express some idea like: Yaho is the supreme god, the god replacing all gods. That is exactly what the word *elohim* means intrinsically, particularly when we deduce its meaning from its usage.

It now becomes clearer what was meant above when the name Yaho or Yahu was called an emphasized form of an original *yo*.

We have to go but one more step in the same direction. The tetragrammaton arises from the trigrammaton by emphasizing the already emphasized form *yaho (yahu)* again in its second part by the addition of a *hē*. That is the achievement of Moses who creates a newer and profounder form for his new and profound concept of God, a form of strongest symbolic power and unique solemnity. It lies in the nature of its origin that the second emphatic *he*, like the first, must be distinctly audible and consequently must obtain a supporting vowel. What the vocalization was in its entirety is unknown to us. The development from *yahu* makes it most likely that it was something like *yahĕwehĕ* or *yehowĕhĕ*.

The formation of the tetragrammaton thus conceived best fits the facts. Thus it becomes plausible why this designation of the deity, a new name, remained reserved for the sphere of the holy. In the emphasis twice made lay the character of the most holy. As this is an artificial and conscious new formation, it makes no sense to look for the "meaning of the stem"; there is none. It cannot be deduced from any other word or notion. Precisely for that reason, however, it is capable of any interpretation. When the author of Exodus 3:14 associates it with the notion of existence and an eternal presence, in that too he may very well be following a tradition which goes back to Mosaic days.

3

Liberation of the People of Israel from Egypt

◆❊❊❊❊❊❊❊❊❊❊❊❊❊❊❊❊❊❊❊❊❊❊❊❊❊❊◆

Before continuing the story some difficult questions of textual analysis have to be dealt with. The unraveling of the oldest account, which should give us information about the essential content of the Moses traditions, is perhaps more difficult here than in any other part of the Moses stories. Since the possibility of penetrating close to the Mosaic period is, however, bound up with the analysis of this oldest account, we have to be patient in undertaking this task.

First, it can be stated with a good deal of certainty that the text must be rearranged. We now find the note in 2:23, "It came to pass in the course of those many days that the king of Egypt died," without any continuation of the account. For what follows, "and the children of Israel sighed by reason of their labor," has nothing to do with the king's death and belongs to the second source, which tells us something about the bondage. The revelation at the burning bush follows next in the text. When that is concluded, Moses returns to Egypt (4:18-23). On the way there YHWH assails him in the night, and only by his wife's shrewdness does Moses escape death.

This arrangement is impossible. It is an intolerable thought that the deity should reveal its name to its favorite, Moses, in a grand manifestation, give him his charge, and immediately afterwards, by night, assail him with murderous intent. Rather, the original order is the following:

After the first words of 2:23, the immediate continuation is 4:19-20a (verses 20b-23 belong to another source). That closes with the experience by night, 4:24-26. Then comes the revelation, 3:2-4:17, only part of which belongs to the oldest account (see chapter 2). Now for a conclusion is 4:29-31. With chapter 5 begins Moses' appearance before the king of Egypt. Combining the verses in this order, the text would read: 2:23a. "And it came to pass in the course of those many years that the king of Egypt died. 4:19 And YHWH said to Moses in Midian, Go, return into Egypt, for all the men[29] who were seeking your life are dead. 20a. So Moses took his wife and his son and set them upon an ass, and he returned to the land of Egypt. 24. And it came to pass on the way at the lodging place, that YHWH met him and sought to kill him. 25. Then Zipporah took a flint, and cut off her son's foreskin, and cast it at his feet; and she said, Surely, you are a bridegroom of blood to me! 26. So He let him alone. Then [LXX: therefore] she said, a bridegroom of blood, because of the circumcision." (Here follows the revelation at the burning bush 3:2-4:17), 29. "Then Moses[30] went and gathered all the elders of the children of Israel. 30. And Moses said all the words which YHWH had spoken to Moses (and did the signs in the sight of the people), 31. And the people believed: when they heard that YHWH had remembered the children of Israel and had seen their affliction, then they bowed their heads and worshiped."

We first have to justify the omissions made in order to bring out the old account. After the first words of 2:23a another source clearly appears. It becomes recognizable because it presupposes the forced labor, of which J does not speak, and it uses Elohim for the name of God, while J uses YHWH. Its style of formal solemnity is the style of the late priestly source.

We have begun the continuation with 4:19, because verse 18 is in flat contradiction to it and must belong to another source. Verse 18 runs: "And Moses went and returned to Jethro, his father-in-law, and said to him: Let me go, I pray, and return to my brethren that are in Egypt and see whether they are yet alive. And Jether said to Moses, Go in peace!"

Here Moses decides to return and takes his leave of his father-in-law, while in verse 19, which begins as if verse 18 is not known, he receives only the instruction of the deity to go back. Also, the reason for the return is quite different in the two verses. In verse 19 it is political: Moses' adversaries are dead, therefore he can return. In verse 18 it is private and humanitarian: Moses is longing for his "brethren" and would like to know whether they are still alive. Who are those "brethren"? The people as a whole cannot be meant, for they are of course alive; he can only mean real brothers or friends, about whom we hear nothing elsewhere.

In the continuation of the account, verse 20b has to be omitted. The rod of God, mentioned previously in verse 17, outside the J report, is introduced here once more with reference to this verse only. The sudden appearance of the divine name Elohim shows that the second source is speaking. But the subsequent verses 21 to 23 do not belong to the old account either. In a short survey they anticipate all the subsequent events in a programmatic fashion: the hard-heartedness of the king, the miracles and the plagues, and above all the slaying of the firstborn. J never tells his story so clumsily, destroying the tension.

At the end of this section we learn the outcome of the commission which Moses has received in the revelation scene: to turn to the elders of the people, and make known to them the decree of the God of Israel, that he will liberate his people. Here it is expressed tersely but finely: the people believed. No trace of a doubt is discernible. Verses 27 and 28 do not belong here; they refer to Moses' meeting with Aaron which, we have shown in the revelation narrative, is a later addition. From here Aaron is introduced in verses 29 and 30, where he clearly does not belong. The encounter with YHWH by night comes between and then follows the revelation at the burning bush.

The composition of the account, as it is developed in the J report, is now much easier to understand.

Moses is instructed to return to Egypt and sets out on his journey. One night without realizing it he enters the sacred district in which the deity resides; he almost has to pay for this with his life. But in broad daylight the deity reveals himself to Moses. On his arrival in Egyptian territory—the Israelites according to this source are separated from the Egyptians and are concentrated in the province of Goshen—Moses passes on the divine instruction to the elders of his people.

In the arrangement of the text, as we here postulate it, there is in any case a close local connection between the deity's attack on Moses and the revelation to him. Where is this place to be sought? It is clear from the context of the story that it must be situated on the way from Midian to Egypt. If we apply the concepts of modern geography, it means on the way from the area northeast of Akaba (here lay Midian) to Ismailia on the Suez canal (here lay Pithom, at the entrance to the Wady Tumilat). The same is attested by the second passage, which relates that Moses drove his sheep "behind the wilderness," that is, where the wilderness comes to an end.

A glance at the map shows that only one locality can be meant, the oasis of Kadesh, which is very significant. According to this ancient story, YHWH's residence is in or near Kadesh[31] and Moses received the fundamental revelation of God in or near Kadesh. Here is found the burning bush. At the beginning of Moses' religious career lies his connection with Kadesh, which occupies a central position and affects his entire life, as we shall see.

The Nocturnal Encounter

The very short account, 4:24-26, is one of the most remarkable found in the Bible. Its only counterpart is the story of Jacob's nocturnal struggle at the river Jabbok (Gen. 32:25-32). But it is even more obviously primitive and mythological. While Jacob plays the major part and steps forth as victor from the struggle with the deity, here Moses is a subordinate figure. So much so that the impression is given that only accidentally is the story related to him and to this occasion; the contents proper, however, are entirely independent of Moses. The story stands in its surroundings like an erratic block, and a full understanding of it is important.[32]

During the rest at night YHWH "meets" or "encounters" Moses and seeks to kill him. The word *wa-yifgeshehu* expresses the unexpected, the sudden, and at the same time the hostile. We could almost translate it: "YHWH attacked him" ("YHWH set about him"). It is not that Moses meets YHWH but that YHWH meets Moses. The idea is roughly that at night the deity roams around the precincts of its dwelling to inspect it and discovers the intruder who has camped there for the night. Without a word of explanation it is stated that YHWH sought to kill him. Why? Of what is Moses guilty? His only trespass seems to be his unintentional penetration into the deity's sacred area. Does that deserve death?

We are not dealing here, however, with ethical values and scales. The atmosphere of this story is that of mythical antiquity. The deity is a fearsome demon who roams about at night attacking everything that gets in its way. There is just as little reason here for the attack on Moses as there is a special reason why the god at the Jabbok attacks Jacob. Indeed one may say, it is immaterial who are those attacked; it is mere chance that one story is about Jacob and the other about Moses. In both cases it is above all the peculiar distinctiveness and intangibility of the holy places that should be stressed.

Now comes the remarkable and strange action by which Moses is saved. "Then Zipporah took a sharp stone, cut off the foreskin of her son, cast it at his feet and said, Surely, a bridegroom of blood are you to me!"

"His" feet? Whose? To whom is she speaking? To Moses? That does not make any sense. It can only be the demonic divine being. In fact the text goes on: "So he let him alone." Zipporah thus performs a magic action which pacifies the demon. To understand this action one must proceed from the idea of the "bridegroom of blood."[33] For the woman "the bridegroom of blood" is the man whose sex organ by sexual intercourse with the virgin woman is covered with blood. The blood is the sign of the *prima nox*. Now we understand the words, "she made it [the cut-off foreskin] touch his legs." "Legs" stands here euphemistically for the sex organ; it is similar to what one says for urine, *me raglayim,* "the water of the legs." Since this action appeases the demon, he must have had the intention of being the "blood bridegroom" of Zipporah, and she makes him believe that he is. Consequently the reason for the attack on Moses is the sexual jealousy of the demon, who in his sacred district claims the right of *prima nox* for himself. Deceived by Zipporah's maneuver, he leaves Moses alone. It is quite possible that the son was introduced[34] into the story during its many retellings to make it more relatable. Originally Moses himself was probably circumcised, but that can no longer be proved and is not important.

What is the significance of this extraordinary, coarse, and obscure story? It is meant to relate how circumcision originated and how the custom is to be understood. The explanation is that through the symbolic operation, which was originally performed on the growing young man and later on the little child, the demonic deity's jealousy on the bridal night is turned away from the man. The custom of circumcision is traced back to Zipporah, Moses' wife (of course without justification, as Semitic tribes knew and practiced the custom long before).[35]

We are peering into the deep recesses of a primordial, absolutely mythological religion, which is far older than the time of Moses. Only incidentally and accidentally is Moses, who in this story plays a passive role, connected with it. One could just as well say "a man and a woman" in place of Moses and Zipporah. It is remarkable that this short story found any acceptance in the Moses stories, and that it was not expurgated by later redactors. Its value from the point of view of the history of civilization is so great that we must be thankful for it. The place where it has been related in the oldest account is characteristic, even symbolic; it comes immediately before the revelation at the burning bush. In the darkness of the night a primeval, demonic YHWH attacks Moses; on the following day, in the light of the sun, the God of the burning bush reveals himself to Moses as the liberator of his people, as Lord of all men, a just and compassionate judge of fate.

The Egyptian Plagues and the Exodus

Great acumen and diligence have been applied to the task of analyzing the account of the plagues[36] and separating the different strata of the sources. The result is rather unsatisfactory; it is sufficient to read the revelant sections in Meyer and Gressmann to be convinced of that. The reason is that this section (Exod., chaps. 5 to 13) has been revised and enlarged again and again until the simple underlying story has been completely submerged. It is perhaps no longer possible to disentangle all the threads by analyzing it verse by verse, and we will not make this attempt. It does seem possible, however, to recognize the basic features in the oldest report and to compare them with the characteristic features known from other accounts.

We have first to eliminate large sections, which are written in the style of P, and thus break up the continuity of the story. To this belongs the whole of chapter 6 and the beginning of chapter 7, up to the commencement of the plagues (vv. 1-13). Further, the instruction about the offering of the Passover sacrifice and the celebration of the mazzoth festival (12:1-20), which are clearly intended for a later time (with a festival assembly on the first and seventh day! v. 16), and the Babylonian dating in verse 2, prove that all this section is a very late piece. Equally late is section 12:37b-42 with its impossible numbers and the conclusion of chapter 14:43-51, which gives special Passover regulations on the basis of post-exilic conditions. The same applies to the repeated exposition of the mazzoth injunctions, 13:3-10. It is curious that this section should separate the beginning of the chapter (vv. 1-2) from its continuation (vv. 11-16), showing that verses 3 to 10 were inserted even later and do not belong here at all; these verses, the regulation about the redemption of the firstborn, are added to the slaying of the firstborn by some scholars.

The plagues in several characteristic ways show that they grew gradually from a smaller number to ten. Popular imagination reveled in this victory over powerful Egypt, and the number of plagues was never too great. Amusing proof of this is the further development that the enumeration of the plagues received in the later Haggada: Rabbi Jose, the Galilean, proves that in addition to the ten plagues the Egyptians were smitten by fifty more at the Sea of Reeds; and Rabbi Akiba raises this number to 250! The artificial accumulation of the plagues results in several of them contradicting each other. With the first plague the Nile water turns to blood and all fish die; but the frogs apparently remain alive, for immediately afterwards they rise from the river as a second plague (7:28). The third plague (vermin) and the fourth (dogflies) are really repetitions of the same phenomenon. With the fifth plague, the cattle pest, all the cattle of the Egyptians die (9:6); with the seventh, the hail, the beasts are once more slain (9:25). In addition, the hail destroys everything green (9:25); then when the locusts arrive immediately afterwards they once more destroy everything green (10:12). Here a redactor noticed the contradiction and added ingenuously "all that the hail has left": but according to 9:25 nothing had indeed been left.

When we are looking in this confusion of plagues for traces of the oldest and simplest account, we have to recall its general characteristics. First, the account always relates events in an extraordinarily matter-of-fact and straightforward manner; inner contradictions scarcely occur in it. It further avoids, if possible, the reporting of miracles; the deity works through the powers of nature. This is most striking at the Sea of Reeds, which in the oldest report is dried up by an east wind and, when that ceases, the sea returns to its former bed. It likewise narrates the miracles of the quails and the manna as natural events. Furthermore, according to J, the Israelites dwell apart from the Egyptians in a special area of the land. The statement that the Israelites want to go out into the wilderness for only a three-day sacrificial feast, is characteristic of J. But permission for this has to be obtained by compulsion; the final exodus is then a flight, by which the pharaoh is deceived. It would thus be sufficient for J if the Egyptians were smitten by *one* plague, which they trace back to the God of the Hebrews, who is enraged by the refusal of the permission. Finally, with J the "elders" play a special part. Moses turns to them after the revelation to announce[37] the liberation by the God of Israel; with them he goes before the king; to them he gives directions for the exodus.

It is in fact probable that the oldest account told of one plague only. If our interpretation of the confused passage in Exodus 18:10-11 is right, this passage supplies the key (see 5:3). According to it Moses told his father-in-law that the exodus became possible by a pestilence sent by YHWH. In this connection it is interesting to see that, as in 18:11, *debher* has been wrongly written *dabhar* in 9:4, 5, and 6; the same mistake happened *three* times in the description of the plague itself. The first plague, described in the oldest account, is consequently now the fifth, the pestilence. This is at first a great slaughter of cattle. But it attacks the Egyptians also, among whom YHWH goes by night from house to house as a destroying angel. Thus the slaying of the firstborn is only a special consequence of the pestilence; and it leads immediately to the release of the Israelites.

In my opinion a more detailed analysis of the whole text confirms the assumption that the section dealing with the pestilence and the killing of the firstborn is the original account, on which everything else is built as a later expansion. But it would demand too much space and time here to develop this analysis in all its details. For now the text from Moses' first appearance before pharaoh until the catastrophe at the Sea of Reeds will be sufficient. By its simplicity and clear consistency it speaks for itself. 5:1a. "Afterwards they came [i.e., Moses and the elders] unto Pharaoh, 3. and said, The God of the Hebrews has met with us. Let us go, we pray you, three days' journey into the wilderness and sacrifice unto YHWH, our God; lest he fall upon us with pestilence or with the sword. 4. And the king of Egypt said unto them, Wherefore do you cause the people to break loose from their work? 9.5 And YHWH appointed a set time saying, To-morrow YHWH shall make the plague in this land. 6. And YHWH made this pestilence on the morrow and all the cattle of Egypt died, but of the cattle of the children of Israel there died not one.

12:21. "Then Moses called all the elders of Israel and said unto them, Draw out and take you lambs according to your families and kill the Passover lamb. 22. And you shall take a bunch of hyssop and dip it in the blood that is on the threshold and strike the lintel and the two sideposts with the blood that is on the threshold and not one of you shall go out of the door of his house until the morning. 23. When then YHWH will pass through to smite the Egyptians and when he sees the blood upon the lintel and on the two side-posts, then YHWH will leap across[38] the entrance and will not suffer the destroyer to come into your houses to smite you. 29. "And it came to pass at midnight that YHWH smote all the firstborn in the land of Egypt, from the firstborn of Pharaoh that sat on his throne unto the firstborn of the captive that was in the dungeon. 30. And Pharaoh rose up in the night, he and all his servants and all Mizraim; and there was a great wailing in Mizraim for there was not a house where there was not one dead. 31a. And he called for Moses by night and said, 31b. Go and serve YHWH, as you have said!

37. "And the children of Israel journeyed from Ramses to Succoth. 13:20. And they took their journey from Succoth and encamped in Etham at the edge of the wilderness. 21. And YHWH went before them by day in a pillar of cloud to lead them the way; and by night in a pillar of fire to give them light; that they might go by day and by night. 22. The pillar of cloud by day and the pillar of fire by night did not depart from before the people."

This account is so clear and simple that it is hardly necessary to explicate it. Only on two points not fundamentally important should something more be said, because they play a certain role in the discussion about this section. First, the injunction about the Passover sacrifice, 12:21-28, has been declared a later piece belonging to P. It is correct that the second part, verses 24-28, which contains the moral for the future, is a very late addition. But the first section is very old and part of the oldest account. That is evident when a comparison is made with the doublet in P, 12:1-20. The old short piece, verses 21-23, is indispensable for the context of the ancient account; it contains a primitive conception of God that later generations, it is true, have taken over but would never have formulated themselves. The injunction here refers only to the single case mentioned, and seeks to explain why the Israelites were not touched by the great plague. At the same time this section, in the undemonstrative manner peculiar to J, wants to give an explanation of the name *Pesaḥ* ("leaping across") without considering that this notion is introduced because it is well known and consequently old. The words in verse 22, *ha-dam asher ba-saph,* are changed by Kittel and others allegedly because they make no sense; they are rendered by Buber, Torczyner, and many other translators, following the old commentators, as "the blood in the basin." But *saph* wherever it occurs in the pre-exilic passages means "threshold" and that is its meaning here. Domestic sacrifice, presented to avert evil, is slaughtered *on the threshold* and the hyssop is dipped into the pool of blood, just as is done in the domestic sacrifices of the Arabs today.[39] The proof is that the only parts of the entrance smeared with blood are the lintel and doorposts. The threshold ought to be smeared first of all, because the demon crosses over it. It is not mentioned because, in any case, it is covered with blood.

    The second point concerns the famous exploitation of the Egyptians[40] by the Israelites who borrowed gold, silver, and clothes from them (Exod. 3:21-22; 11:2-3; 12:35-36). Eduard Meyer, who, it is well-known, was no friend of the Jews, deals with this episode with particular relish, devoting considerable space to it.[41] He takes pains to show that it belongs to J, but that is no doubt a misunderstanding by the great historian. The context in which it occurs for the first time, 3:19-22, certainly belongs to P. The typical idea, totally impossible in J, is that God will harden the king's mind, especially for the purpose of showing his wonderful might in Egypt. Meyer, who otherwise shows a fine understanding of the peculiarity of the J account, should have noticed that it would be impossible for J in particular, in such a single detail, to anticipate later events. J never relates events so clumsily that the suspense of the story is destroyed. Another strong reason to the contrary was seen by Meyer himself: according to J the Israelites live in Goshen entirely separated from the Egyptians, to whom "the shepherds are an abomination" (Gen. 46:34). How then can they borrow from the Egyptians? Meyer's explanation, hardly convincing, is that even then a sufficient number of Egyptians resided in Goshen from whom people could borrow. In that case, however, the characteristic of J, which enables us to distinguish between J and E, is no longer valid. The story of the malicious borrowing appears for the second time in the long-winded announcement of the killing of the firstborn (11:1-8), which would be quite impossible in J, and in which the late storyteller drops his role by going over into direct speech at the concluding announcement. The execution of this trick is then related in an impossible place in 12:35-36, namely, after the Egyptians are already pressing the Israelites to depart hastily, indeed while they are already departing, they lend them gold and silver vessels (every Egyptian has some of course!) and garments. The Egyptians would have to be still more foolish than the storyteller, if they handed them over. One can hardly credit J with a description of this kind. In all three passages we are confronted with an insertion of the latest stratum; just as in the accumulation of the plagues there is the same childish endeavor to invent and add yet another blow to the Egyptians.

It is generally admitted that the introduction to the march of the Israelites in 13:17-19 belongs to E. That applies both to the anachronism in verse 17, which mentions the Philistines, and to the notice about Joseph's bones with its literal quotation from Genesis 50:25 (certainly E). All that is necessary factually, on the other hand, is brought out by the brief account of J in 12:37a and in the sentences directly following, 13:20-22.

History or Legend

Does the story of the exodus of the Israelites belong to the realm of legend or of history? We have already seen that a sojourn of Israelite tribes in a border province of Egypt has every historical probability in its favor. From Egyptian sources we know analogous cases of the passage of Bedouin tribes from the Sinai district into Egypt. From a notice by E (Exod. 1:11), we know the names of two cities[42] in the district of Goshen where the Israelites are said to have constructed buildings in the service of the pharaoh. Historically the construction of these cities goes back to Ramses II. And finally, such an inglorious episode as the servitude of the tribes in Egypt would not have been retained by tradition, if it was not based on historical fact.

In the following section we will show that the experience at the Sea of Reeds must also go back to a historical recollection, and that we have here a biblical testimony which can claim historical validity. In that case, however, the exodus from Egypt must somehow be a historical occurrence too. All the details, it is true, are told in the form of legend. It would be a particularly fortunate accident for us to find the name of the leader in some historical testimony; that it was Moses we do not therefore have any need to doubt. But the revelation at the burning bush will be no more than a legendary account, and details like the death of the firstborn or the pillar of fire will not be considered historical events by anybody. (It is strange indeed that so shrewd an observer as Gressmann should try, page after page, to include the pillar of fire in the historical process by means of a rationalistic explanation!)

What really happened we do not know and we can only surmise. There must have been a special leader and a singular combination of favorable circumstances to enable the Israelites to effect the escape from powerful Egypt. The oldest account says simply that it was a pestilence. Even so, it still required a leader of genius who knew how to exploit the favorable hour in order to lead his people to freedom.

Passage through the Sea of Reeds and the Song of the Sea of Reeds

The Catastrophe at the Sea of Reeds[43]
In many passages of the Moses stories it can be shown that two or more sources exist, but in hardly any other place are the different sources as closely interwoven as in the account about the Sea of Reeds (Exod. 14). We can almost say that several parallel accounts have been combined. The best way to make that clear is to place the accounts side by side rather than to discuss them one after the other.

J.	E.	P.
		1. And YHWH spoke unto Moses saying: 2. Speak unto

J.	E.	P.

P.

the children of Israel, that they turn back and encamp before Pi-haḥiroth, between Migdal and the sea, before Baal-zephon, over against it shall you encamp by the sea. 3. Then Pharaoh will say of the children of Israel: They are entangled in the land, the wilderness has shut them in. 4. And I will harden Pharaoh's heart, and he shall follow after them; and I will get me honor upon Pharaoh and upon all his host; and the Egyptians shall know that I am YHWH. And they did so.

5a. And it was told the king of Egypt that the people were fled.

5b. Then the heart of Pharaoh and of his servants was turned against the people and they said: What is this we have done, that we have let Israel go from serving us?

6. And he made ready his chariots and took his people with him.

7. And he took 600 chosen chariots and three men upon all of them.

8b. and he pursued after the children of Israel

8a. And YHWH hardened the heart of Pharaoh, king of Egypt. 8c. whilst the children of Israel went out with a high hand. 9. And the Egyptians pursued after them, all the horses and chariots of Pharaoh and his charioteers

J.	E.	P.

P.

and his army and overtook them encamping by the sea, beside Pi-hahiroth, in front of Baal-Zephon. 10. Pharaoh drew near; then the children of Israel lifted up their eyes, and behold, the Egyptians were marching after them; and they were sore afraid, and the children of Israel cried out unto YHWH. 11. And they said unto Moses; Because there were no graves in Egypt, have you taken us away to die in the wilderness? Wherefore have you dealt thus with us to bring us forth out of Egypt? 12. Is not this the word that we spoke to you in Egypt saying: Let us alone, and we will serve the Egyptians; for it is better for us to serve the Egyptians than that we should die in the wilderness. 13. Then Moses said to the people: Fear not! stand firm, and see the salvation of YHWH, which he will work for you today. For as you see the Egyptians today, you will see them no more for ever. 14. YHWH will fight for you, and you have only to be still! And YHWH said to Moses: Wherefore do you cry unto me? Speak unto the children of Israel that they go forward. 16. And you, lift up your rod and stretch out your hand over the sea and divide it; and the children of Israel shall go

J.   E.   P.

into the midst of the sea on dry ground. 17. And I, behold I will harden the heart of Pharaoh that they come behind them, and I will get me honor over Pharaoh and all his army, upon his chariots and his charioteers.[44] 18. And the Egyptians shall know that I am YHWH, when I have gotten glory over Pharaoh, over his chariots and his charioteers.

19a. And the angel of God who went before the camp of Israel moved and went behind them,

19b. Then the pillar of cloud moved from before them and stood behind them.

20a. and came between the camp of Egypt and the camp of Israel.

20b. And when the darkness came, the pillar of cloud became a pillar of fire and it gave light by night.[45]

20c. And the one did not come near the other the whole night.

21a. And Moses stretched out his hand over the sea.

21b. And YHWH caused the sea to go back by a strong east wind all the night and made the sea dry land.

J.   E.   P.

21c. And the waters were divided. 22. And the children of
Israel went into the midst of
the sea upon dry ground; and
the waters were a wall unto
them on their right hand and
on their left. 23. But the Egyptians pursued and went in
after them into the midst of
the sea, all Pharaoh's horses,
his   chariots   and   his
charioteers.

24. And it came to pass
in the morning watch
that YHWH looked
forth upon the host of
the Egyptians through
the pillar of fire and
cloud and discomfited
the host of the Egyp-
tians. 25. And he
loosened the wheels of
their chariots and made
them to drive heavily;
so that the Egyptians
said I will flee from be-
fore Israel, for YHWH
fights for them against
the Egyptians.

26. And YHWH said to
Moses, Stretch out your hand
over the sea, that the waters
may come back upon the
Egyptians, upon their chariots
and upon their charioteers.
27a. So Moses stretched forth
his hand over the sea.

27b. And the sea re-
turned to its former bed
when morning appeared
and the Egyptians fled

J.	E.	P.
against it, and YHWH overthrew the Egyptians in the midst of the sea.		
		28. And the waters returned and covered the chariots and the charioteers, even all the host of Pharaoh that went in after them into the sea; there remained not so much as one of them. 29. But the children of Israel walked upon the dry ground in the midst of the sea, and the waters were a wall to them on their right hand and on their left.
30. Thus YHWH saved Israel that day out of the hand of the Egyptians; and Israel saw the Egyptians dead upon the seashore.		–
		31. And Israel saw the great work which YHWH had done upon the Egyptians, and the people feared YHWH; and they believed in YHWH and his servant Moses.

The division of the narrative into these different strata is not simple, but once carried through it is clear and convincing. The oldest account (J) starts with the fact that the king of Egypt has given the Israelites permission to go into the wilderness in order to celebrate a YHWH festival for three days. When the frontier guards report to him that the Israelites are turning south, he knows "that the people have fled" with the intention not to return and so he hurries after them. The second account (E), however, has previously related that the pharaoh allowed the people of Israel to go for good. It therefore motivates the pursuit with a change of mind on the part of the pharaoh. The third and latest account, which has an entirely theological bias (P), makes God "harden" the pharaoh's heart, that is, the king makes precisely those decisions which are to lead to his destruction in order to "glorify YHWH—in Egypt." Only the oldest and the latest accounts are well preserved and are completely parallel with one another; the middle one (E) is preserved in fragments only.

The picture which we usually have of "the passage through the Red Sea" is determined entirely by the latest account, which is the most detailed. A comparison of the two accounts, however, leads to the surprising discovery that the oldest account relates the events quite differently: the Israelites have "fled"; they have crossed the border of Egypt. When they go south they consequently are already on the east bank of the Gulf of Suez.[46] The course of events as related by this account is simple and almost without a miracle; the king of Egypt is pursuing the Israelites also on the east bank of the Gulf of Suez. YHWH prevents an encounter by stepping behind the Israelites and appearing as a pillar of fire, which blinds the Egyptians. During the night a violent east wind drives back the water and dries up the shallow inlet of the sea. Toward morning "YHWH looks upon the Egyptians from the pillar of fire" which is causing confusion and terror; at the same time, the storm from the east is abating and the waters return. Panic-stricken, the Egyptians flee toward Egypt, that is, toward the west, and rush into the returning waters, which destroy them.

According to the oldest account a passage of the Israelites through the sea does not take place at all. YHWH, who again appears as a terror of the night, assists his people by confusing the mind of the enemies and working through the forces of nature. Nor does the second account, which is preserved in fragments only, seem to relate anything about a passage through the sea.

Only the latest stratum of the sources, in which a clear idea about the geographical facts has been lost, brings a complete transformation of the account. The Israelites depart from the western shore, straight into the sea, which divides in front of them (the waters are "like a wall unto them on their right hand and on their left"), with the Egyptians following them. When the Israelites arrive at the eastern shore, the waters come rushing down over the pursuing Egyptians. These events, which have been used to paint over the unadorned picture of the ancient account, have remained the only visible ones for later tradition.

In this latest account Moses divides the sea and then leads the waters back by stretching his hand with the rod out over the sea. By divine command he carries out a magic act. In the oldest account, on the other hand, it is basically the forces of nature that are at work, guided, of course, by the deity: the storm from the east dries up the bed of the sea; when the storm is over, the waters return. *Moses is not mentioned at all.* The deity acts in a direct way in the form of the pillar of fire and through the forces of nature.

The Song of the Sea of Reeds[47]

After the salvation of the Israelites a song of victory and thanksgiving for those liberated is handed down. Or, more correctly, there are two songs which are handed down. The first song (Exod. 15:1-18) is introduced by the words: "Then sang Moses and the children of Israel this song unto YHWH." The second song (Exod. 15:21) is introduced by the words: "Miriam intoned before them." While the first song is rather extensive (eighteen verses), the second song has only a single verse, namely, the first verse of the first song: it, so to say, merely gives the "theme."

Two possibilities are open to us here: either the first song is an enlargement of the second and consequently a secondary elaboration or the second is merely a short extract from the first. A guide for a decision between these possibilities is found in the singer's name. At first sight it seems natural to find Moses' name in the first song. Miriam ("the prophetess, Aaron's sister"), hitherto unknown to us, is named as the songstress of the second song. Such a statement can hardly be invented, whereas it is quite possible and understandable to find a song, which was originally attributed to somebody else, ascribed later to Moses, the great hero. An analogous case exists in the killing of the Philistine Goliath, which in 2 Samuel 21:19 is ascribed to Elhanan of Bethlehem. But, as is well-known, in 1 Samuel 17, it is transferred to David, the popular hero. Here too the naming of a person who is otherwise entirely unknown would be impossible, unless it were implemented by a more primitive tradition.

The same result is obtained by examining the text of the songs. The representation given of the catastrophe at the Sea of Reeds by the Song of Moses corresponds not to the oldest but to the latest account. Therefore, it cannot date from a time close to Moses. The waters are standing like walls; the children of Israel pass between them, evidently contrary to the oldest account. Here for once it can plainly be shown how great is the significance of source analysis and how difficult it is to disentangle the oldest stratum. Later (v. 14), the land of the Philistines is mentioned; since the Philistines at the earliest invaded Palestine fifty years after Moses' death, this verse with its patent anachronism cannot date from Moses' time. In the Song of Moses there is again mention of the immigration of the Israelites into Canaan (v. 16), indeed, of the "mountain of your inheritance" and the "establishing of your (God's) dwelling" (v. 17). There can therefore be no doubt that we are here confronted with a late product of psalm literature which is certainly later than Solomon's building of the temple.[48] In this song only the first verse is old and is the one quoted from the Song of Miriam.

The Song of Miriam does in fact show features which give it a much older appearance than the psalm in 15:1-18. The text follows: 20. "And Miriam the enthused, the sister of Aaron, took a timbrel in her hand; and all the women went out after her with timbrels and with round dances. 21. And Miriam intoned before them, Sing to YHWH, for He is highly exalted; Horse and chariot has He thrown into the sea."

We first notice that the reading *rikhbo* is better than *rokhebho*. For, at that time, there was no cavalry in Egypt; horses were used for chariots only and only these are spoken of in the accounts. Furthermore, a small deviation from the Song of Moses is to be noted: the Song of Miriam begins with a call to the choir, "Sing". The Song of Moses, corresponding to the character of a psalm, begins, "I will sing." It is clear that here too the Song of Miriam represents the older form.

Those few words of the text have great interest. Miriam is described as the songstress. It is pure assumption to think that she is the same as the sister of Moses mentioned in 2:4 and 7 (a later addition). If that were right, then she ought to be called *Moses'* sister here as well as in Numbers 12:1. Both times, however, she is mentioned only in connection with Aaron. Here she is called Aaron's sister, a curious designation. It eliminates not only the possibility that she was Moses' sister but also that Aaron was Moses' brother. Here she is called *nebhi'ah,* the "prophetess." In this passage the word has been thought secondary but without justification, it seems to me. For in this ancient period *nebhi'ah* does not mean the prophetess but the ecstatic, the enthused. She appears as a leader of song and dance (like David in 2 Sam. 6:14) in a round dance by the women, whom she is leading with a musical instrument. She intones the first distich of the song with the dance, calling upon them: "Sing unto YHWH for He is highly exalted!" The choir responds with the second distich: "The horse and its chariot has He thrown into the sea." This is not the beginning of a song, but the whole song which is continually being repeated with the two voices alternating. Such a round dance and song, accompanied by continuous repetition of a one-line verse, can be found at Arab feasts today.

The short, precise form of this account, the sharply depicted situation it presents combined with the peculiar personal statement, which cannot be invented, make it most likely that, in the short section 15:20-21, we are confronted with a genuine historical piece of news from Mosaic days. By this, the event itself, the catastrophe of an Egyptian division at the Sea of Reeds, is proved to be a confirmed historical fact. It would be of great value to find Moses' name mentioned in this short but important testimony. But such identification is lacking.

4

The Kadesh Stories

The Goal of the Exodus[49]

It is always hard to dispose of old and familiar ideas. The exodus of the Israelites from Egypt eventually led them into Canaan. It has thus become quite natural for us to assume that from the start the goal of their exodus was Canaan. And not only to us born in a later age; after a few generations the tradition of the people of Israel also related events in this way. The problem then was: Why did the people stay forty years in the wilderness of the Sinai peninsula? Why did they not immediately take the shortest route to Canaan, which in about ten to eleven days along the coast of the Mediterranean would have brought them to the borders of the thoroughly settled land of Canaan?

To the latter question tradition later gives the well-known answer (Exod. 13:17) that this shortest route was too dangerous because of the warlike Philistines who inhabited the south of the coastal plain. This argument is wrong because it contains a gross anachronism: at the time when the Israelite tribes left Egypt, the Philistines were not yet in Canaan. This shows that the true reason why the Israelites chose another route was no longer known nor was the reason why the Israelites stayed for one generation in the wilderness before undertaking the conquest of Canaan. Searching for a reason, tradition fell back on the argument that because of some guilt (despondency following the report of the spies) the people as a punishment had to stay in the wilderness another forty years. During this long time tradition has the people roving around the wilderness, in reality an impossible situation.

The answer to the two questions is in effect quite different. At the exodus the goal of the Israelites was not Canaan at all. They stayed for decades in the wilderness, because their goal — even though a temporary one — was to settle down for a long time. This goal, which emerges from all the old accounts, was the oasis of Kadesh, which we will examine in the following chapters. This is why the Israelites did not go north along the coast but east into the wilderness.

The story of the exodus indicates that. According to the oldest account, Moses requests permission from the king of Egypt to make a three days' journey into the wilderness with the people in order to celebrate a sacrificial feast for their God, YHWH. But a sacrifice is not made somewhere "in the wilderness"; on the contrary the people go to the seat of the deity (as later to Shiloh or Jerusalem).

Where is YHWH's seat? We are again referred to Kadesh. Here is the burning bush, at which Moses receives the revelation of his mission. In its vicinity he was previously attacked by the deity. In fact, it is here that the first sacrifice to YHWH is offered up, about which we are told in the Moses stories (Exod. 18:12). When it is said in the revelation to Moses (3:8), "I shall come down to deliver them [the people] out of the hand of the Egyptians," it is the deity in the fiery flame in the shape of the pillar of fire which is leading the people out of Egypt to Kadesh and thereby returns to its seat.

This conception has been obscured for later generations and for us because the stories about the Sinai were inserted in between. According to these (Deut. 33:2), "YHWH came from Sinai and appeared from Seir upon them; and he shone forth from Mount Paran, and he came to Meribhath-Kadesh." But the oldest account mentions Kadesh only. Here begins and ends the people's liberation from Egypt. Only when this significance of Kadesh is correctly grasped can the accounts about Moses be truly understood.

The significance of Kadesh for the personality of Moses becomes evident because in the Moses stories Kadesh occupies by far the greatest space. Of seventeen stories about Moses, which are placed between the exodus from Egypt and the beginning of the battles in Transjordan, thirteen are assigned to Kadesh.

Kadesh is the largest oasis of the Sinai peninsula irrigated by several powerful springs. It stretches out several miles in breadth and about fifteen miles in length, covering an area of some sixty square miles and thereby offering space and sustenance to a population of several thousand people. The scanty reports we have from travelers agree that in the burning wilderness the oasis appears like a paradise. Murmuring brooks, rich vegetation of grass, trees and shrubs and flowers, birds and insects conjure up a truly fairylike picture to the traveler who is arriving from the desert. For the poor Bedouin who knows hardly anything except severe privations, this too is "a land flowing with milk and honey."

If Kadesh is considered to be the seat of the Israelites for any length of time, we must have some idea of the approximate population figure of the Israelites. We do not, of course, possess any direct indications of that. It is hardly necessary to discuss here the fantastic number given in Exodus 12:37 for the exodus: 600,000 men capable of bearing arms, which would indicate a population of about two and a half millions. With such a figure the Israelites would not have been obliged to emigrate from Egypt. They could have conquered it without much trouble and subjected their oppressors. With a column marching in fours, when the last were crossing the Egyptian border, the head of the column would reach to Hamath on the river Orontes in North Syria. The only useful figure from the historical point of view is the one from the Song of Deborah, which about a hundred years after the entry into Canaan estimates the number of men in Israel capable of bearing arms to be about 40,000, giving a population figure of about 150,000. Some conclusions can be drawn from this figure.

In the century between the invasion of Canaan and the battle of Deborah, the population made up of strong peasant stock is likely to have at least trebled, so that at the time of the invasion probably about 13,000 men were bearing arms. From this figure one quarter has to be deducted, because at the time of the immigration into Canaan the tribes of Reuben, Gad and Asher were already settled in the country.[50] For the southern tribes, on the other hand, about a quarter has to be added, which, we know, the Song of Deborah does not include among the Israelites.

But the figure of 13,000 is still too high. Not all these tribes were in Egypt. Part of them kept to their nomadic way of life and only later joined the growing nation in Kadesh (Kayin, Rechab, Jerachmeel, and probably also Caleb); for them a further third has to be deducted, reducing the total number to between 8,000 and 9,000. During those forty years in Kadesh the population likely doubled. Thus for the invasion of Kadesh we estimate from 4,000 to 4,500 warriors, that is, a population of 12,000 to 13,000 souls, and for this number the oasis had sufficient space.

A paradise in the wilderness,[51] which the oasis of Kadesh was, can never have been uninhabited. Even though we hear nothing directly about it, we must take it for granted that when the Israelites settled in Kadesh, they drove some inhabitants out from the oasis. Who were those previous inhabitants? Where did they go? We shall return to this problem in the course of our inquiry.

For this investigation the Kadesh stories can be divided into two groups: (1) the place and spring legends of Kadesh; (2) the legends about Moses. Outwardly these two groups cannot always be completely separated from each other, for it occurs repeatedly that elements of the place legends are linked with accounts about Moses, and it is almost a rule that the place legends about which we are told describe Moses as an acting person. But essentially these two groups have to be separated throughout, and each evaluated in its own context. The place and spring legends do not date from the thirty or forty years the Israelite tribes stayed in Kadesh. According to their nature they are dependent neither on these tribes nor on Moses. Rather, they are a legacy of the previous inhabitants or a witness to an even earlier connection which the Israelite tribes had to that oasis. The legends about Moses' achievements, however, bear an individual character. Their local coloring, the coloring of Kadesh, is indeed important and informative, but is not essential for the legend. Without being able to make a sharp division between these two groups, we shall still have to use them as elements of the description and refer to their differences again and again.

Place and Spring Legends of Kadesh

Marah (Exod. 15:22-26)
22. "And Moses led Israel onward from the Sea of Reeds and they went out into the wilderness of Shur; and they went three days in the wilderness (and found no water). 23. And when they came to Marah they could not drink of the waters of Marah, for they were bitter (therefore the name of it was called Marah). 24. And the people murmured against Moses saying, What shall we drink? 25. And he (Moses) cried unto YHWH, and YHWH showed him some wood,

and he cast it into the waters and the waters were made sweet. There he made for him a statute and an ordinance and there he proved him."[52]

This account, although short, is difficult, complicated, and important. The introduction joins this account directly with the catastrophe at the Sea of Reeds. In agreement with the oldest account of the exodus it speaks of three days during which the Israelites marched into the wilderness. When three days were requested for the journey to take them to the sacrificial feast, we have to assume that Marah is situated where the Israelites want to go. We have no indication, however, where the spring of Marah lay. The notice, placed entirely out of context with the story proper, states that this is the place of the giving of the law. That in any event indicates that Marah was thought of as one of the springs of Kadesh.

What apparently conflicts with this assumption is the reference to the distance. For, from the eastern border of Egypt to Kadesh is a distance of some 105 miles, consequently not a three days' journey but of six to seven. But this objection applies to the place of the sacrificial feast too. The Israelites do not want to sacrifice just anywhere in the wilderness but at YHWH's residence, and in fact the sacrifice concluding the march through the wilderness takes place at Kadesh (18:12). Moreover, those "three days" are merely a ruse intended to induce the Pharaoh to release the Israelites. It can be assumed without much difficulty that an exact statement of time corresponding to the real conditions was not meant here at all.

Let us first consider the spring legend itself. It explains the name of the spring, Marah, describing it as "bitter spring." Here, it is said, was once a bitter spring, the water of which was undrinkable. By a magic act on the part of Moses, shown him by YHWH, this bitter water becomes sweet. Bitter or salt water is a frequent phenomenon in the wilderness; what excites the astonishment of the desert pilgrim and stimulates his imagination is when he finds a good, *sweet* spring. We have to assume, of course, that the spring mentioned here was always sweet. What has to be explained is the name of the spring; and if it was sweet, then in fact the name Marah, "the bitter one," is unintelligible. Because of this name, which is curious for a sweet spring, the legend sought an explanation and found it in the transformation through Moses. This transformation is a deed which need not be bound up with Moses at all; other inhabitants of the oasis likely ascribed it to someone else. "Somebody" once upon a time made the spring sweet, yet nevertheless it retains its name Marah.

The solution of this difficulty is that the name Marah need not mean the "bitter one." The word is not derived from *mar,* "bitter," but from *marah,* "to be rebellious," "to be hostile." Consequently it is the spring of the rebellious; the explanation of why it was called a bitter spring is, as so often, popular etymology. (Originally in the text of 15:24, instead of *wa-yillonu* there was perhaps *wa-yamru,* alluding to the name of the spring.) How it obtained its name "spring of the rebellious" will be discussed in connection with the names of the other springs of Kadesh. Another later explanation is instead of *marah* to read *morah* "the spring of instruction" or "the oracle." The striking phrase *wa-yorehu,* "he instructed him," in verse 25 is to be considered an allusion to it. In any case, when the Israelites came to Kadesh they found the spring already named Marah. We can therefore assume that the legend, a genuine place legend, was also taken over and only then transferred to Moses.

We now come to the curious sentence in verse 25b: "There he made for him a statute and an ordinance, and there he proved him." This sentence, now entirely out of context, is quite evidently the remnant of a more detailed account. It is an unnecessary assumption to think, as some investigators do, that this sentence has come to be isolated from another context. It fits here very well, if the word "there" refers to Kadesh (which no doubt is right) and Marah is considered to be one of the springs of Kadesh.

"There he made for him a statute and an ordinance." Who is "he"; who is "him"? There are two possibilities: YHWH gave the law to Moses; or Moses gave the law to the people. The decision follows from the continuation, "and there he proved [or tested] him [or it]." This can only mean that YHWH proved Moses, for there would be no sense in saying that Moses proved the people. The possibility (considered by Eduard Meyer) that the subject changes within the sentence must be rejected altogether.

From this sentence we learn two very important facts. The first is that to Moses, and thereby to the people, "statute and ordinance" are given in Kadesh. In the narrative tradition later, when it became established in its final form, we are told nothing about the Kadesh event. It is well-known, according to the second conception, that the law was given on Mt. Sinai. In the Kadesh tradition there is no legislation which could exist *beside* the Sinaitic one, but there is a parallel tradition according to which this legislation takes the place of the Sinaitic one. On comparing these two traditions there can be no doubt at all that the Kadesh tradition is the older and original one. We come across it in the old legends which were fixed in writing at a very early time. It exists, as we shall see, in several traditions entirely independent of each other; the contrast to the conception generally accepted later makes the Kadesh tradition appear trustworthy. For that tradition too the law is YHWH's gift to Moses.

The second important statement of this verse is that in Kadesh the deity is "proving" Moses, that is, putting him to the test. It may be that the word *nissah* contains here an allusion to the name of the second spring of Kadesh, *massah*. That need not mean that the notice does not belong here but to another account about the spring Massah; it merely shows that the two springs are closely related to one another.

But to the point! What does "he proved him" mean? In the later revisions of these legends the word *nissah* is given a double sense: either the people by their disobedience are "proving" God in putting his patience to the test; this is out of the question here, since without doubt it is the deity who is "proving" someone. Or else God is proving man by putting his obedience to the test, as is the case in the well-known story of the sacrifice of Isaac. That too is out of the question here, since no other story is known in which Moses' obedience is doubted (concerning the correct interpretation of the story of Num. 20, see below). That is out of the question also because in this passage such a "test", whether Moses did or did not stand up to it, would not be so remarkable as to have it mentioned beside the fundamental fact of the legislation.

In this "test" which Moses had to stand in Kadesh — and he did stand it, for verse 15:26 is meant to proclaim his fame — there is, rather, quite a different meaning. In the Song of Praise for Moses in Deuteronomy 33:8, Moses is called "your [YHWH's] faithful one, whom you did prove at the spring of proving (*massah*), with whom you did strive at the waters of striving (*mē meribhah*)." Here we find the same atmosphere as in verse 15:25. The test is a contest with the deity in which Moses' shrewdness and dexterity are proved. Here the prize which Moses gained is also named: the Urim and Thummim, the oracular vessel, which enabled Moses and his successors to learn the will of the deity. That is also what is meant in our passage. Unfortunately the story reporting details about this contest of Moses with the deity is lost. It was probably lost because to later generations this representation, implying that a man might undertake a contest with the deity and win, appeared too presumptuous, nay, blasphemous. It was perhaps a story of the kind describing Jacob's fight with the deity (Gen. 32:25-32), in which the hero also comes out victorious (later toned down).

When we review the two parts of the Marah story, we find in them an excellent example of the two kinds of traditions. The former half is a typical place and spring legend, which in itself is impersonal. As far as a man has a part to play in it, Moses' part might just as well be taken by any person. The conclusion, however, is a typical Moses story, in which Moses, and he alone, plays the principal part. It is here in Kadesh that Moses made known to the people the legislation revealed to him; and in a contest with the deity he gained the prize, about which we can only guess: the Urim and the Thummim. The spring legend is timeless; the Israelites took it over from remote antiquity. The Moses legend, however, gives us in legendary form the echo of historical events concerning Moses: the legislation of Kadesh and the introduction of the oracle.

The Fight with Amalek[53] (Exod. 17:8-16)

8. "Then came Amalek and fought with Israel in Rephidim. 9. And Moses said unto Joshua: choose for yourself[54] men and go out for the fight with Amalek; tomorrow I will stand on the top of the hill with the rod of God in my hand. 10. So Joshua did as Moses had said to him and went out to fight with Amalek; but Moses, Aaron, and Hur went up to the top of the hill. 11. And it came to pass when Moses held up his hand, that Israel prevailed; and when he let down his hand, Amalek prevailed. 12. But Moses' hands became heavy; and they took a stone, and put it under him, and he sat on it, and Aaron and Hur supported his hands, the one on one side and the other on the other side; and his hands were steady until the going down of the sun. 13. And Joshua discomfited Amalek[55] with the edge of the sword. 14. And YHWH said to Moses: Write this as a memorial in the book and read it aloud to Joshua: For I will utterly blot out the remembrance of Amalek under heaven! 15. And Moses built an altar and called its name: YHWH is my banner. 16. And he said: Hand upon

the banner of YHWH! War has YHWH with Amalek from generation
to generation!''

At first it seems hardly possible to localize the fight with
Amalek at a particular place, for we know nothing about the situation
of Rephidim, the place named here. Nevertheless, indirect clues
make possible a more accurate conjecture. First of all this account is
found in the midst of the Kadesh stories: preceding it is the story of
Marah, the legend of the manna and the quails, which belong to
Kadesh, the legend of the springs Massah and Meribhah (in 17:1
Rephidim is directly named, though in a later revision); and after it
comes the story about Jethro, which also takes place in Kadesh. We
are entitled, therefore, to assume also the existence of Rephidim in
the vicinity of Kadesh.

The same result is obtained when we consider the geographical situation. Later, in reliable historical reports, we find the
tribe of Amalek in the Negev, north of Kadesh as far as the district of
Beersheba (Judg. 1:16) according to the correct reading of the LXX (1
Sam. 15:6). When the Israelites coming from the southwest engaged
in a fight with Amalek, it must have taken place in the district of
Kadesh.

This fight, however, has a rather peculiar character. The
Israelites were engaged in many other fights later and some were with
far more dangerous opponents, such as the Philistines. Never, however, do we find such an atmosphere of hatred and lasting enmity as
with Amalek. The solemn statements ''For I will utterly blot out the
remembrance of Amalek under heaven!'' and ''War has YHWH with
Amalek from generation to generation!'' are something unique. What
is the reason for this implacable hatred which continues to reecho two
hundred fifty years later in the days of Saul (1 Sam. 15:2-3)? Tradition
adduces the reason (Deut: 25:17-19) that in the wilderness Amalek
had put the tired camp followers to death — a common practice in
desert warfare, however — and that no doubt happened frequently
elsewhere.

But the true explanation of that hatred, which has slipped
from the people's minds, is in reality a different one. Amalek is the
previous owner of the oasis of Kadesh. When the Israelites were
turning to Kadesh, they had first to expel Amalek. An ancient notice
in the curious account in Genesis 14, from pre-Mosaic time, still gives
us some information, an account which also contains very good

geographical information about other places. Here it is said (v.7): "They came to *'en mishpaṭ*, the same is Kadesh, and smote all the country [LXX and Syriac: all the princes] of the Amalekites." Here Amalek is definitely named as the owner of the oasis of Kadesh at the time before the exodus of the Israelites.

But still that is not all. It explains sufficiently Amalek's burning hatred of Israel but not Israel's lasting hatred of Amalek. The latter is bound to be based in the fact that at an even earlier period, which is no longer historically identifiable for us, the Israelites had special connections with this oasis. How otherwise could the Israelites hit on the idea of choosing Kadesh as the goal of the exodus? What else can have induced Moses to lead his people there? How else was it possible for them to preserve such an abundance of place and spring legends? We shall be able to consider these questions more precisely only when we have gained a better view of all the Kadesh legends by examining the spring names in their context; we thereby will acquire a deeper insight into the role played by the Levites. For the present it can only be said that the hatred of Amalek must have other and older roots than the events of the Mosaic period.

We will now examine in more detail the account of the fight with Amalek. This account as it exists today seems to belong to the literary stratum which is usually called the Elohist. The use of the divine name Elohim, at least in the account proper of the fight, the appearance of Joshua by the side of Moses and in a leading position, as well as the occurrence of the rod of God point in that direction. It may be more correct to say that here the ancient account has undergone a slight revision in the style of E, whereas in some typical features at the conclusion there reemerges the original account.

Moses appears here only in a priestly function. He does not take part in the battle but, by holding high the rod of God, he influences its course through a magic action. Quite apart from its magic effect this rod has the function of a banner; thus it is called at the conclusion of the account "YHWH's banner." Here a concept is developed which has remained alive to the present time. As long as the banner, the flag, the eagle's staff is held high and remains visible, it is the symbol for the army that raises its courage. When the symbol falls, the courage will fail also.

Two more men appear beside Moses; only their names are mentioned. They support Moses' hands, enabling him to hold the banner high until the moment of victory. Of those two men one, Hur, is otherwise unknown to us (he is mentioned as a nobleman only once more in a short notice, Exod. 24:14, again beside Aaron). The other one, however, the well-known Aaron, for later generations Moses' brother, here is nothing more than one of two noblemen among the people assisting Moses.[56] Not by a single word is he characterized as Moses' brother or even as a man who has a closer relationship to him than Hur.

The account contains some play on words and allusions to the name of the locality. In this connection the name Rephidim is apparently understood as "weak hands" or else derived from rephidah, "support." In either case we have to assume that the name is original and that the story has been spun out of it. The allusions, however, are scarcely recognizable any longer, because the rare word supporting them has been replaced by a current one; only small peculiarities still indicate their place. In verse 12 it is said wide mosheh kebhedim, showing a grammatical blunder, since yad is feminine. Originally perhaps it was said raphu yadayim or raphim, an allusion to the name Rephidim. And the strange word wa-yahalosh, "he discomfited," in verse 13 is perhaps a subsitute for wa-yerappeh, again an allusion to the name.

At the conclusion of the account and without any direct connection with it are found the two above-mentioned formulas of curses. At the same time it is reported that Moses put up an altar, which he named "YHWH is my banner." Since an altar is only put up in a locality where it will be devoted to the permanent worship of the deity, this too supports the fact that in this account we are in Kadesh. To set up the altar at any place during the migration in the wilderness would not make sense.

The second curse formula is likewise interesting. The introduction "hand upon the banner [or as it is said in our text: the throne] of YAH"[57] betrays its great age by the original short form YAH for YHWH. "War has YHWH with Amalek from generation to generation." In the context in which it is found this announcement makes no sense at all. Why this assurance after the battle and, especially, after a victorious battle? This challenge makes sense before a battle only, or more likely after a battle lost, as an oath of vengeance or an expression of hatred. Moreover, this formula points to the past; it did not originate with the present case, but was taken

over from the past. It proves our suggestion above that in the past
there must have been warlike encounters between Israel and Amalek,
in which Israel suffered a defeat and swore vengeance.

The conclusions drawn here completely confirm the suppositions we previously made in another connection. We shall learn
of further allusions later. We cannot possibly expect more than allusions, with perhaps some degree of historical certainty, about events
which belong to a prehistoric period.

Massah and Meribhah[58] (Exod. 17:1-7)

The oldest account reads:

1b. "There was no water for the people to drink. 2. Wherefore the
people strove with Moses and said, Give us water that we drink!
And Moses said unto them, Why do you strive with me, and why do
you try YHWH? 4. Then Moses cried unto YHWH and said, What
shall I do with this people? They are almost ready to stone me! 5.
And YHWH said to Moses, Pass on before the people and take with
you the elders of Israel, and your rod take in your hand. Go 6b. and
smite the rock, and there shall come water out of it that the people
may drink. And Moses did so in the sight of the elders of Israel. 7.
And the name of the place was called Massah and Meribhah because
of the 'contention' of the children of Israel, and because they 'tried'
YHWH."

The analysis of the text is comparatively simple. The introduction of verse 1 belongs to the later revision of P; that is proved
by the expression 'edah,' "congregation," which occurs in P only,
and by the apparently exact indications of places that in reality are
wrong. It is hardly possible to decide whether the mention of the
place Rephidim, which subsequently is the locality of the fight with
Amalek, has any justification. In verses 2 and 3 are two manifestly
parallel beginnings of the account; the first belongs to J and the second to E. To this second stratum, verse 6a belongs in the continuation. Here suddenly appears the name Horeb used in E for Sinai.
Here too the ancient observation can be traced, as in 3:1, which
transfers the mountain of God to the area of Kadesh. Two additions
in verses 5 (middle) and 7 (end), which can readily be recognized,
have been eliminated.

The story is a typical spring legend of Kadesh. It reports
about the origin of the great main spring of Kadesh that here has the

double name Massah and Meribhah; perhaps indeed we have two
sources. But are we not also dealing with a Moses legend? Is it not
Moses who strikes the spring out of the rock? One has to be absolutely clear about this difference. The springs were already flowing
when the Israelites came to Kadesh; they have flowed ever since
men inhabited the oasis, for the existence of the oasis is bound up
with the springs. But the people who are coming here marvel at the
springs which have created this paradise-like oasis. Legends and
fairy tales describe it, how once upon a time in primeval days these
springs may have arisen. That has nothing to do with Moses and his
time. The legends are rooted to that place and are timeless; and it is
immaterial with which personality they are linked. But there are
other things which can be related only to Moses or some other definite figure, such as the giving of the law or the origin of the Urim and
Thummim. The same consideration applies for the names of the
springs. The springs did not arise through Moses' magic wand.
Therefore, the explanation of the names also cannot be the right
one, bound up as it is with this particular occurrence, the grumbling
of the people, and their refutation by the miracle of the spring. We
find here the same situation as at the spring of Marah. Meribhah
means "spring of contention," but not because the Israelites were
contending with God or with Moses. The name is older, and the Israelites found it already attached to the locality; they have only reinterpreted it to fit their own hero and his experiences. In reality
"spring of contention" signifies the spring at which the contending
parties bring before the deity their disputes for decision. Also Massah, "spring of trial," is so named not because the Israelites tempt-
ed God, but because that was already its name. The spring was
given this name because that is where the evidence of contending
parties is examined. It is a remarkable phenomenon that the three
springs which we have come to know in Kadesh make probable a
common relationship to legal disputes by their names. In this connection, which the authors of our accounts were apparently no
longer aware of, we are now reminded of the name that the spring of
Kadesh had in pre-Mosaic times: 'en mishpaṭ, "spring of judgment." Even if this name should be later than the events narrated in
this chapter, it supplies the direct and desired confirmation that
somehow Kadesh plays a special role in the jurisdiction.

Meribhath-Kadesh (Num. 20:1-13)

This account, a variant of the preceding from the point of view of contents only, is textually so important that we have to analyze more exactly its structure in which two sources have shared; these sources can be recognized with great certainty as J and P. The characteristics of P are the exact date of verse 1,[59] the use of the words 'edah and ḳahal, and the introduction of Aaron by the side of Moses. In order to simplify the interpretation the two literary sources are placed side by side.

J.	P.
	1a. When the children of Israel, even the whole congregation, came into the wilderness of Zin, in the first month,
1b. When the people abode in Kadesh, Miriam died there and was buried there.	
	2. there was no water for the congregation: and they assembled themselves together against Moses and Aaron,
3a. The people strove with Moses and spoke, saying:	3b. saying: Would that we had perished when our brethren perished before YHWH! 4. Why have you brought the assembly of YHWH into this wilderness to die there, we and our cattle?
5. Wherefore have you made us to come up out of Egypt, to bring us unto this evil place? It is no place of seed or of figs or of vines or of pomegranates; neither is there any water to drink.	
	6. And Moses and Aaron went from the presence of the assembly unto the door of the tent of meeting and fell upon their faces; and the glory of YHWH appeared unto them.
7. And YHWH spoke to Moses saying, 8a. Take the rod	8b. [YHWH spoke to Moses], Assemble the congregation, you and Aaron your brother, and speak unto

J.

P.

8c. And you shall bring forth to them water out of the rock.
9a. Then Moses took the rod.

the rock before their eyes that it give forth its water,
8d. and you shall give the congregation and their cattle drink.

10. And Moses and Aaron gathered the assembly together before the rock, and he said to them, Hear now, you rebels! Are we to bring you forth water out of this rock?

11a. And Moses lifted up his hand and smote the rock with his rod twice; and water came forth abundantly.

11b. . . . and the congregation drank and their cattle. 12. And YHWH said to Moses and Aaron: Because you did not believe in me to sanctify me in the eyes of the children of Israel, therefore you shall not bring this assembly into the land which I have given them.

13. These are the waters of Meribhath-Kadesh[60] because the children of Israel "contended" with YHWH and he was sanctified in them.

This section challenges us with one of the most interesting examples of a conflation of two accounts. When we eliminate what belongs to P by following the characteristics given above, there remains an old J account, which is preserved in its entirety and can be read by itself without a break. At first sight it might appear that the same applies to P; that is, that P is a consistent and independent account and that subsequently both accounts were intertwined. But in one passage it becomes clear that P presupposes the J account and is merely a revision: 11b (P) does not follow 10 (P), but presupposes 11a (J). We shall presently see that this is of great significance. For in their whole conception and approach these two accounts are totally different from one another.

The older account is a typical spring legend, as we have come to know it above. Its purpose is to tell the origin of the spring

Meribhath-Kadesh and, particularly, to serve as a glorification of Moses. The people are thirsty and grumbling against Moses. By striking the rock at the order of the deity, Moses makes the spring emerge. He strikes twice and the spring becomes very strong. At the conclusion, as is often the case, there follows the interpretation of the name given to the spring.

The second account begins by relating events in a similar way. But it relates the story for quite a different purpose, which is entirely alien to the older account. Moses (and Aaron) receives the command to *speak* to the rock. Instead he *smites* it. (Here the verse is connected with the first account.) Because of this disobedience Moses is not going to enter the Promised Land. The account is intended not to glorify Moses but to condemn him.

It is a strange thought which P is following here. The historical fact that Moses did not enter the Promised Land seems to a later storyteller to warrant an explanation. Such a special explanation is not warranted by the subject matter itself. Moses, old and weary of life, died a natural death before he had reached his final goal. So it has happened to many great men. But in order to account for it this storyteller is looking for a sin on the part of Moses; and in the blameless life of this hero he could find no sin other than this slight disobedience. And this disobedience was created by the storyteller himself, for the ancient account knows nothing of it! And how illogical is the story after all!

If God wanted the rock to give its water after the spoken word, then when Moses struck it, it merely needed to remain dry. That would have shown his disobedience to the entire people and would give a reason for the threat of punishment. But the miracle is performed mechanically, against the will of the deity. For in this point the later storyteller was bound by the older account, since the spring was in existence! There is a flaw throughout the account. This revision has turned the meaning of the original account into a completely contrary story. And this superimposition by the later story has effaced the older one to such an extent that our picture of Moses' fate is really determined by the later account. Only a critical analysis can restore the original. P undertook to transform a typical spring legend into a real Moses legend which cannot be separated from the personality of Moses. That is why the account is a bastard: for the spring did exist before Moses.

Now that we have studied the later account in more detail, we will consider some special features of the older account.

The story is preceded by a short notice about Miriam that has no connection with the account and, it seems, happened to be placed there accidentally. "Miriam died there (in Kadesh) and was buried there." That is a genuine place legend. In Kadesh a tomb of Miriam was shown and about this Miriam two stories have been handed down: it is she who sang the song at the Sea of Reeds; and it is she, along with her brother Aaron, who rebelled against the leadership of Moses (Num. 12). It is remarkable that the name Miriam, like that of Moses, is purely an Egyptian one. It is derived from the Egyptian word *mrij,* "beloved" (of the deity). We will not discuss here what conclusions may be drawn from that.

The story itself evolved from the usual motif. The Israelites are thirsty and are grumbling at Moses. In the wilderness, water is the first requirement, even more than food. In a negative form their complaint contains a good description of Kadesh: Why have you brought us into a country where there is *no* corn, *no* fig trees, *no* vines, *no* pomegranates? We are meant to understand that all those things existed in Kadesh only after the blessed spring had emerged from the rock. They all existed, of course, when the Israelites entered the oasis, for the spring was already there. The legend wants to explain why there was in the midst of the wilderness that extraordinary phenomenon. It is a very picturesque image of reality that is painted here, giving genuine color to the place legend: water in abundance, waving corn, trees, and wine. The naive feature of the legend — that Moses struck twice — is delightful. To conjure water from the rock, the beloved of God need only strike the rock; to conjure up *this* abundance of the spring Meribhath-Kadesh, he had to strike twice. There is nothing here of any disobedience or guilt by Moses, no mention of another land of promise. For the Kadesh legend knows nothing of such a land. Kadesh is the promise and its fulfillment.

Basically the attachment of the legend to Moses is quite flexible. For the Israelites of post-Mosaic times, it is true, all that existed in Kadesh was the great hero's work. The legend itself, however, contains nothing that could not be related about anyone before him. It is a place legend, not a Moses legend. That is why at the conclusion the explanation of the spring name Meribhath-Kadesh is as right and as wrong as in the other stories. The spring is thus called, not because the Israelites were there and quarreled with Moses, not because God proved his holiness in them (here this is little more than a phrase), but because it had always been called thus, even much earlier; it is the sacred spring of the legal dispute, the *en mishpaṭ*.

The Manna[61] and the Quails[62] (Exod. 16)

The structure of this account as we have it today is so extraordinarily complicated that none of the existing analyses are really satisfactory. We confidently hope to penetrate a step deeper because it is not our task to follow the changes of the account through all its stages, but to go back to its oldest form. The analyses existing so far have not been successful because they proceeded from false assumptions. The most careful investigator of these legends, Gressmann,[63] like many others, assumes that two unconnected stories, that of the manna and that of the quails, were later combined. He employs great acumen to separate them again. But this assumption is wrong. Precisely in the most ancient account the two stories belong together. Other legends of this cycle, the spring legends, report how the Israelites were supplied in a special way with the most urgent need of the desert wanderer, namely water. After a man's thirst has been quenched, hunger makes itself felt. The Bedouin lives sparingly on what his camel supplies him: milk, cheese, and occasionally meat. But normally he has no bread. Our legend intends to relate more than the supplying of the most urgent need, for it relates something about Kadesh. The Israelites had not only water and not only the most needed food of the Bedouin, but luxury food: bread and meat. When the Bedouin wants to speak about good and plentiful food, he speaks of bread and meat. When at God's command the prophet Elijah is wandering into the wilderness, God sustains him on his way and feeds him abundantly: the raven brings him meat in the evening and bread in the morning (1 Kings 16:7, according to the correct reading of the LXX).[64] These two things belong together in reality, and they also belong together in our account.

The second error made by most investigators is that they proceed from the customary view created by the later accounts, namely, that manna was the regular food of the Israelites during the entire forty years of their migration through the wilderness. There is no doubt that the legend in its later form related events in this way.

But even Gressmann, who correctly recognized that the legend is located in Kadesh, does not recognize that in this form it cannot be the original place legend, since then the whole wilderness of Sinai would be its scene. *Originally the miracle of the manna,* exactly like that of the quails, *happened only once.*

The thoroughgoing revision of the legend, the local and temporal expansion of the miracle of the manna, the insertion of the Sabbath motif, the description of the collecting of the manna, all have strongly obscured the original account and interfered with its order. The introduction of the ancient account has been replaced entirely by the later one. It would occupy too much space and labor to try and describe in detail the entire critical work. The result, however, is so plausible that it is convincing in itself and we are satisfied to quote it.

The Israelites are grumbling at Moses, presumably with the words of 16:3: "Would that we had died by the hand of YHWH in the land of Egypt, when we sat by the flesh-pots, and when we did eat bread to the full! 11. And YHWH spoke unto Moses saying: 12. I have heard the murmurings of the children of Israel. Speak unto them saying: At dusk you shall eat flesh, and in the morning you shall be filled with bread; and you shall know that I am YHWH, your God. 6. And Moses said unto the children of Israel: At even, then you shall know that YHWH has brought you out of the land of Egypt; 7a. and in the morning, then you shall see the glory of YHWH, 8a. when YHWH shall give you in the evening flesh to eat and in the morning bread to the full. 13. And it came to pass at even that the quails came up and covered the camp; and in the morning there was a layer of dew round about the camp. 14. And when the layer of dew was gone up, behold upon the face of the wilderness a fine scale-like thing, fine as the hoar-frost on the ground. 15a. And when the children of Israel saw it, they said one to another: What is it? [*mān hu'*], for they did not know what it was. 31. And the children of Israel called its name *mān* "manna"; and it was like coriander seed, white; and the taste of it was like wafers made with honey."

In this, its most ancient form, the account is simple and clear. The Israelites obtain not the necessary food (bread) and delicacies (meat) but the two things which are delicacies for the Bedouin: bread and meat. The miracle occurs *once* like the miracle

of the water, for it is intended to prove YHWH's might. Even if it is
a mistake to explain miracles in a rationalistic way, here an interpretation is suggested that points to Kadesh as the place of the legend.
It is no rare occurrence and is repeatedly reported by travelers that
migratory birds, tired of flying across the hot desert, suddenly appear in large numbers; worn out they descend upon the oasis to
quench their thirst and thus supply the inhabitants of the oasis with a
rare and desired meat dish. But the manna too is bound up with the
oasis; it is likely to be the sweet, resin-like product of certain kinds
of tamarisks, which drops down from the trees.

The guiding motif which conntects the two miracles in
the most ancient account is "evening and morning." It occurs three
times, teaching us that the two miracles belong together and are a
one time occurrence (cf. also "the evening and morning" in the Elijah story above). This "evening and morning" is a characteristic of
the ancient J account and contradicts every other interpretation of
the stories. Only when we conceive them as we are, do we find, too
(as at the Sea of Reeds), the characteristic quality of J, which describes whenever possible natural forces at work as though they
were "miracles." In the case of the miracle of the quails that is
clear; but the miracle of the manna also is "understandable" only as
occurring once, as a one time offer of food, which may be taken as a
subsitute for sweet bread or cake. To consider the manna as a
habitual food of the people for forty years is a grotesque exaggera-
tion of the miracle, which belongs to a later stratum of the story
only. From it comes the addition and present-day conclusion of the
story (v.35), which (again in two parallel versions) says: they ate
manna until they reached the border of the land of Canaan. After
this expansion of the original account had once been made, an account about the miracles on collecting and storing the manna was
added. The next stage is the "discovery of the Sabbath," which is
taken by Gressmann, strangely enough, to be the oldest component
of the story. The latest stage (P) then brings the preservation of a
"manna-sample" for an everlasting memorial of the miracle, the
typical attempt of a late storyteller to supply "proofs" for the miracle. Thus an unusually complicated and involved story gradually
arose from the simple place legend of Kadesh. Its most ancient kernel, as we have seen, is the place legend. It is bound up with the
place, but timeless. Basically it is not bound up with the presence of

the Israelites, for quails and manna have always existed in Kadesh. It is not bound up with the personality of Moses either, who in it merely plays the part of an announcer of the miracle, which could just as well be assigned to anyone.

Moses Legends from Kadesh

In distinct contrast to the place and spring legends of Kadesh there are a number of other stories in which the shading, it is true, points to Kadesh, but which cannot be dissociated from the personality of Moses, since they presuppose him as the actor. The distinction between the two groups is not always sharp; for example, the fight with Amalek may be considered with full justification to belong in the second group. Only because of its important general retrospects into the past of Kadesh have we dealt with it earlier.

For anyone who wants to recheck our analysis of the text, the distribution of the individual passages to the different strata of the documents may be given in short catchwords: verses 1-3: P (Babylonian date in v. 1; *'edah,* v. 1 and 2; Aaron, v. 2; *kahal,* v. 3). Verses 4 and 5 are later strata of J (J2): verses 4 and 5: anticipation of the Sabbath motif, announcement of the miracle of the manna, which is made once more in verse 6. In verse 6 Aaron is an addition, evident from the singular of the verb. Verses 7b and 8b: J2 (that God has heard the complaints comes only in verse 12; the two sentences are joined in a clumsy way). Verses 11 and 12 before 6 and 7, because the command of the deity to Moses is bound to come first, and then Moses' communication to the people. Verse 31 follows immediately on verse 15a. Therefore 15b belongs to J2. Verses 16-20 and 22-26 belong to P: discovery of the Sabbath by Moses; use of the late word *'omer.* Continuation of verses 27-30 where verse 27 must come after verse 30. Verses 32-34: quite a late stratum of P, use of the word *'omer;* the concluding sentence being quite late is the explanation of the measure *'omer.* Verses 35 and 36 are two recensions of J2: the manna as a continuous miracle.

To the stratum, which we have designated as J2 (the manna as continuous food), belongs a variant of the story of the quails, which is found in Numbers 11 (vv. 4-6, 13, 23, 31-32). The people greedily long for meat, thinking sadly of the variety of the diet available in Egypt. "But now our soul is dried away; there is nothing at all; we have nought save this manna to look to." Moses is almost in despair, but YHWH comforts him with a reference to his omnipotence. A wind brings an enormous quantity of quails from the sea into the camp, and the people eat more than their fill of meat. In all its features the story is clearly later than the variant discussed above and therefore of no significance for our purposes.

The second group comprises historical legends in the narrower sense. While historical conclusions can be drawn from the first group only in a general way, the stories of the second group are a reflection of real historical events. One can say that in a period so early that history was not yet written, the legend is the only legitimate form of historical tradition. The events related by the legend have a historical kernel; but they are related in a legendary form with the intervention of the deity, with miracles and the making of heroes of the persons participating. As typical of such stories we may take the account about the Sea of Reeds or Moses in Midian. Precisely here it is essential to go back to the most ancient form of the account which, because it is closest to the actual events, more readily preserves historical features. Considering the manifest literary unity of the oldest account, the possibility of testing in small details whether the reporting source in its assumptions agrees with the most ancient stratum or not will arise repeatedly.

Jethro's Visit (Exod. 18:1-12)

The story is clearly composed of two sources, which we may designate as J and E. The basic thread of the story belongs to the J account. The second account is entirely dependent on the first with small additions, which, however, do not substantially change the total picture. E is recognizable by the use of the divine name Elohim, by the mention of personal names missing in J, by the change in the locality, and by contradictions to the presuppositions of J. While J, as is well-known, relates (4:20) that Moses took his wife and child with him when he returned to Egypt from Midian, E leaves the family in Midian; only in this account is the family again taken to him by his father-in-law. In what follows we are quoting the text of the ancient account adding to it in parentheses the additions of E in order to facilitate the survey.

18:1. "Now (Jethro), the priest of Midian, Moses'

father-in-law, heard (of all that God had done for Moses and for Israel, his people) that YHWH had brought Israel out of Egypt, (2.
and Jethro, Moses' father-in-law, took Zipporah, Moses' wife,[65] 3.
and her two sons;[66] 5. then came he (Jethro, Moses' father-in-law,
with his sons and his wife) unto Moses (into the wilderness where he
was encamped at the mount of God) 6. and he said unto Moses: I,
your father-in-law (Jethro), am coming unto you (and your wife and
her two sons with her). 7. And Moses went out to meet his father-in-
law, and bowed down and kissed him and they asked each other of
their welfare; and they came into the tent. 8. And Moses told his
father-in-law (all that YHWH had done unto Pharaoh and the Egyptians for Israel's sake) all the travail that had come upon them by the
way and how YHWH delivered them. 9. And he (Jethro) rejoiced for
all the goodness which YHWH had done to Israel (in that he had delivered them out of the hand of the Egyptians). 10. And he (Jethro)
said: Blessed be YHWH who has delivered you out of the hand of
the Egyptians (and out of the hands of Pharaoh).[67] 11. Now I know
that YHWH is greater than all gods, for by the plague he has saved
the people from the hand of the Egyptians who dealt wickedly towards them. 12. (JE) and Jethro, Moses' father-in-law, brought a
burnt-offering and sacrifices[68] for God; and Aaron came and all the
elders of Israel to eat bread with Moses' father-in-law before God.''

When we read this account as we have it today, with the
additions by E, we visualize an idyllic family scene. The general atmosphere which lies over it is remarkable. The dangerous adventure
of the exodus from Egypt and the migration through the wilderness
are at an end; the participants and the guest look upon them as
something in the past, of which the people tell because they are glad
to have overcome the dangers. Now Moses and his people are at rest
and secure. As a thoughtful husband and father Moses has left his
wife and child (or children) in Midian or sent them there before the
exodus, leaving them in his father's-in-law care. Now his father-in-
law is bringing his family back to him. All are thanking God. To express this gratitude the Midianite priest is offering up a sacrifice to
YHWH.

The whole atmosphere uniformly points to a definite
place, Kadesh, particularly in the sense of the most ancient account.
Kadesh is the goal and the end of the march through the wilderness.
The people have arrived ''at their place''; nobody thinks of leaving

again. The notion of roaming about in the wilderness for forty years is simply incompatible with this atmosphere of the story. If that were to happen, Moses would not have made his wife and child come with him.

But this family idyll contains some contradictions. The most important one is that according to the most ancient account Moses took his family with him to Egypt. There is no question about sending them away; such a plan would not agree with Moses' trust in God. If the family did not leave, there was no need to bring it back to him. Jethro's visit, therefore, has no purpose.

What, however, did J relate? Following J it looks as if Jethro made the journey through the wilderness only to welcome Moses and listen to the story of his adventure. A meager motive! Above all, there was no need to hand down an account for that reason. Elsewhere we notice that each of the stories is full of meaning. A special meaning has to be sought in this story too.

The solution lies in verse 12, the last sentence of the story. In the form in which we have it today, it bears the external characteristics of belonging to E (the divine name Elohim, the mention of the name of Jethro). But there can be no doubt that in a similar form the verse was included in the most ancient account. Although it is true that in the beginning Jethro's name is given, at the end it only says, "Moses' father-in-law"; E never writes like this but J always does. In fact, this verse contains the point of the J account, which otherwise would be missed.

Let us consider this verse in more detail: "And Jethro, Moses' father-in-law, took a burnt-offering and sacrifices for God; and Aaron came and all the elders of Israel to eat bread with Moses' father-in-law before God." One thing strikes us immediately: Why does the foreign Midianite priest offer up the sacrifice? Why not Moses? Yet even among the guests at the sacrifice Moses is not named; his absence here is even more remarkable. Aaron who is named does not appear as a priest but, together with the elders, as *primus inter pares,* just as happens in the account about Amalek, which also indicates the antiquity of the notice. But Moses cannot possibly have been absent from this sacrifice; if in our text he is missing, this text is bound to have undergone a revision. There must have been something here about Moses which was so objectionable to the later redactor E that he deleted it. What he left, however, is transparent enough to let us recognize what may have been related. If it was Jethro, the priest of Midian, who offered up the sacrifice, it can only have been related that on this occasion he either consecrated Moses a priest or instructed Moses in the offering up of the sacrifice. Such a fact, that the sacrificial rite should go back to a Midianite, which the most ancient account probably related with ingenuous truthfulness, would appear so incredible and shocking to a later writer that he would delete it.

If this was so, then along with it the motive for Jethro's journey, missing in J, is also given. Moses called his father-in-law to Kadesh not to bring him his wife and child (for they were in Kadesh), but to let him introduce an ordered sacrificial service. That is subsequently confirmed by the story of Moses' stay in Midian and his relationship by marriage with the priest. To say that this Midianite priest was a servant of YHWH, indeed the true founder of the YHWH religion in Israel, is an entirely erroneous assertion, an assertion which has been made by some scholars and by Gressmann with slight reservations. Rather, Jethro's part is likely to have been quite similar to that in the story immediately following about the ordering of the jurisdiction: here he has definite merits in setting on foot the jurisdiction, and, there, the sacrificial rite. But the real contents of both the religion and the law are an Israelite heritage, bearing as they do the stamp of the highly gifted personality of Moses. Neither before nor after do we ever find the slightest trace of a spiritual revolution going back to Midian for its starting point.[69] The sacrificial rite mentioned here remained basic for Israel, at least in the older period of its history. Those offering up a sacrifice are united at a solemn meal "before God"; the deity is conceived as a participant of this meal, or rather as the host, and this common meal "at the table of the deity" forms the connection between God and man.

Moses as Judge[70] (Exod. 18:13-27)

Closely connected with the preceding story is a second one which has for its subject Moses' activity as a judge. It too is handed down in two versions, which can be recognized as J and E. They are entirely parallel and closely interwoven with one another. It will again be most useful to place the text of the two versions side by side.

J.

E.

13. And it came to pass on the morrow that Moses sat to judge the people; and the people stood about Moses from the morning unto the evening. 14. And when Moses' father-in-law saw that (he said):

(When Jethro saw) all that he did to the people, he said: What is this thing that you are doing with this people?

Why are you sitting alone and all the people stand about you from morning until evening? 15. And Moses said unto his father-in-law:

16. When they have a matter of dispute, they come unto me and I judge between a man and his neighbor.

(then Moses said): because the people come unto me to enquire of God;

17. And Moses' father-in-law said unto him:

and I make them know the statutes of God and his laws.

18. You will surely exhaust yourself, both you and this people that is with you.

(Then Jethro said to Moses) the thing that you are doing is not good.

for the thing is too heavy for you; you are not able to perform it yourself alone.

19. Hearken now unto my voice:

I will give you counsel and God will be with you: be you for the people before God, and bring you their causes unto God. 20. And you shall teach them the statutes and the laws and shall show them the way in which they must walk and the work they must do. 21. Moreover you shall provide out of all the people able men, such as fear God, men of truth, hating unjust gain;

21b. Place over them rulers of thousands, rulers of hundreds, rulers of fifties, rulers of tens. 22. And let them judge the people at all seasons; and it shall be that every great matter they shall bring unto you, but every

J.   E.

small matter they shall judge themselves.
                                                        so they shall make it easier for you
                                                        and bear the burden with you. 23. If
                                                        you do this thing and God command,
                                                        you so, then you shall be able to en-
                                                        dure and all this people also shall go
24. So Moses hearkened to the voice   to its place.
of his father-in-law and did all that he
had said. 25a. And Moses chose   (Moses chose) able men out of all
                                           Israel and made them heads over the
25b. rulers of thousands, rulers of   people.
hundreds, rulers of fifties, and rulers
of tens. 26. And they judged the people at all seasons: the hard cases they
brought unto Moses, but every small
matter they judged themselves. 27.
And Moses let his father-in-law depart; and he went his way into his
own land.

The two versions differ from one another very little. J
stresses more the judging, E the consultation of God for the purpose
of a judicial decision. But both agree that the introduction of a sound
organization of the judiciary goes back to the counsel of Jethro, the
Midianite. Until then, it is said, Moses did all the work on his own; the
story is meant to give at the same time a picture of the enormous
capacity for work of this man who single-handed could act as judge of
an entire people. But here too, as in the preceding story, the question
is only that of creating the external form of the organization. Moses
remains the only source for the contents of the law, or rather it is the
deity with which Moses remains in permanent contact, the deity
which gives him his "laws and statutes."

The character of the two connected stories is clear. Although both take place in Kadesh,[71] they have none of the characteristics of a place legend. They report events which are inextricably
connected with the personality of Moses. Both stories must somehow
be based on historical recollections. Certainly the surprising point in
both, that Israelite institutions are traced back to a Midianite priest, is
something that cannot be invented; it is something that would not

have been related unless a firm tradition had compelled people to do so. Connections with Midian and its civilization are undoubtedly given here and we shall soon see a further element pointing in this direction.

Miriam and Aaron as Opponents of Moses
(Num. 12:1-10)

The story of Miriam's and Aaron's rebellion against Moses is certainly most ancient. In the form in which we have it, however, it is almost incomprehensible in many sections because of a faulty tradition of the text, and omissions, revisions, and additions. The place of the story is clearly Kadesh. The tradition, which, it is true, is a later one and adapted to the pattern of a forty-year march through the wilderness, names Ḥaṣeroth (farmsteads), otherwise unknown, as the place in question, but it is located in the vicinity of Kibhroth ha-ta'abhah, the site of the second story about the quails, which we have already placed in Kadesh. Moreover, we know from the entirely isolated and therefore credible notice in Numbers 20:1 that Miriam is said to have died in Kadesh; consequently our story, which reports the punishment and severe illness of Miriam, perhaps in conjunction with her death, is likely to be located in Kadesh. Two persons rise up against Moses: Miriam and Aaron. Not one word is said about the relationship in which they stand to one another. But we remember from Exodus 15:20 that Miriam was described as Aaron's sister, and that would provide a good explanation of why they appear here together. Above all, there is not the slightest hint that Miriam may be Moses' sister or Aaron his brother. In this passage such a close relationship could hardly have remained unrecorded if it had been known to the ancient storyteller. The fact that it is not mentioned at all strongly suggests that this relationship is only a product of a later development of tradition.

When the text is considered in more detail, it is found that two entirely different reproaches are leveled at Moses: one, that he married a Cushite wife; the other, that he claims without justification the proclamation of the divine word as his monopoly, whereas Miriam and Aaron have a right to it also. It may thereby be guessed that in this story two threads are interwoven. In fact, in the course of the account, further parallel phrases are found: verse 9 parallels 10a; 10b parallels 10c. We are thus entitled to try to disentangle the two threads. As always in such cases, in those passages of the extant text in which the two formerly separate stories were joined, some single words were changed or dropped out.

(1) 12:1. "When they were in Haseroth Miriam spoke against Moses because of the Cushite woman whom he had married.[72] 2b. When YHWH heard it, 9. the anger of YHWH was kindled against her and He departed. 10a. And behold, Miriam was leprous as snow.

(2) 12:2. And they [Miriam and Aaron] said: Has YHWH indeed spoken only through Moses? Has He not spoken also through us?[73] 4. And YHWH spoke suddenly unto Moses, Aaron, and Miriam: Come out you three to the tent of meeting. And the three came out. 5. And YHWH came down in a pillar of cloud and stood at the door of the tent and called Aaron and Miriam, and they both came forth. 6. And He spoke to them: Hear now My words: if there be a prophet of YHWH among you,[74] I do make myself known unto him in a vision; I do speak with him in a dream. 7. My servant Moses is not so; he is trusted in all my house; 8. with him do I speak mouth to mouth[75] and the similitude of YHWH does he behold; wherefore then were you not afraid to speak against Moses my servant? 10a. And the cloud removed from the tent, 10b. and Aaron turned round to Miriam and, behold, she was leprous."

The remainder of the story (vv. 11-16) is not only for the most part unintelligible but also has apparently been padded. It is, however, not important to decide this question, since the essentials are given without this addition

The two threads, which we have now separated, cannot be independent stories existing side by side but are variants of the same motif: Miriam and Aaron rebel against Moses and are punished. For Miriam cannot very well become leprous twice because of two revolts. That may have been felt by the supplementing redactor too, who then reports a healing of Miriam. Assuming that we are confronted by two variants of the same story, the first is sure to be the older one. It speaks of a personal reproach against Moses, whereas the second one is based on a spiritual conflict about the leading position of the prophet. The conception of the tent of meeting outside the camp and of the descent of the pillar of cloud also points to a later time. Further, the lesson which the deity gives the rebels bears the spiritual character of a later time. After this lesson from the deity, a fight with spiritual weapons, the punishment of leprosy is almost too harsh and no longer in keeping with the times.

What is common to the two versions is that Miriam and Aaron (perhaps conceived here as her brother) appear as Moses' opponents. Miriam's leprosy is found in both versions as a punishment for her rebellion. The very peculiar and striking phenomenon that Aaron remains free from punishment is common to the two versions also, although his transgression is to be judged rather more severely than Miriam's. In fact, it is so striking that we are forced to assume an alteration of the original account. Originally it *must* have been part of the story that Aaron was also severely punished, perhaps even by death. But this strange leniency toward Aaron is likewise found in the story of the Golden Calf, and again without sufficient grounds. That can be explained only by assuming that a later hand eliminated this punishment because, for that redactor, Aaron was the pious high priest. Still, we must be grateful to him for not entirely eliminating all these stories, which cast such an ugly shadow upon Aaron. That the redactor should not have done so shows how firmly the fact itself, Aaron's rebellion, was embodied in the tradition.

Considering the peculiar form in which this tradition has been handed down to us, namely, as a historical legend, it will hardly be possible to determine in detail which historical events are the bases for these stories. But it may be considered certain that the great leader was not spared severe opposition from the leading representatives of the people. Precisely this subject is treated repeatedly in the Moses stories. In view of the later shaping of the tradition, there is special significance in that almost everywhere in the most ancient accounts where Aaron appears, he appears as Moses' opponent. The peculiar problem of this figure, Aaron, will therefore occupy us again in a later chapter.

The Rebellion of Dathan and Abiram[76] (Num. 16)

The accounts of two rebellions against Moses, which in themselves are entirely different, have a similarity which has brought them together and intertwined them (Num. 16). One is the story of Dathan and Abiram's rebellion, the other the story of Korah's rebellion. The separation of the two accounts in our present text is not easy to follow, but it can be achieved by careful observation of the parallel repetitions and small differences between them.

We have to assume that Kadesh is the locality of the Dathan and Abiram stories, although they are inserted into another context. The two rebels are complaining that in spite of his promise Moses has not led the people into a land of milk and honey but into an inhospitable place; they are dissatisfied with it, since not everybody can obtain here his "inheritance of fields and vineyards." Nevertheless, the people are staying at a place which they think is their final goal, and that can only be Kadesh.

As is always the case, through the intertwining of the two accounts, the seams are somewhat effaced.

16:1. "Dathan and Abiram, the sons of Eliab,[77] 2. rose up in the face of Moses. 12. And Moses sent to call Dathan and Abiram, the sons of Eliab; and they said, We will not come up! 13. Is it a small thing that you have brought us up out of a land flowing with milk and honey to kill us in the wilderness, but you must needs make yourself also a prince over us? 14. Moreover, you have not brought us into a land flowing with milk and honey nor given us an inheritance of fields and vineyards; will you put out the eyes of these men? 15. And Moses was very wroth and said, 15c. I have not taken one ass from them neither have I hurt one of them! 25. And Moses rose up and went unto Dathan and Abiram; and the elders of Israel followed him. 27b. And Dathan and Abiram came out and stood at the door of their tents with their wives and their sons and their little ones. 32a. And the earth opened her mouth and swallowed them up and their households, 33a. and so they and all that appertained to them went down alive into Sheol."

The account is not fully preserved. At the beginning particularly the more detailed complaints which induced Dathan and Abiram to rebel are missing. From the passage following it may be concluded that they are making several reproaches against Moses: selfish enrichment, ill-treatment of the people, lack of capability as a leader, and broken promises. The whole conflict lies in the secular field; and this observation is useful when we judge the Dathan-Abiram stories against the Korah story. Moses rejects with indignation these reproaches so far as they are of a personal kind: never did he appropriate anybody else's property for himself and never did he ill-treat anybody (v. 15). He does not mention reproaches concerning his leadership; that is for God to decide, since he has been acting under God's mandate. At first Moses tries to call the rebels to account as though he were a judge, summoning them to appear before him. But they openly defy him, refusing to appear before him. He then goes out to meet them and YHWH decides the dispute: the earth opens its mouth, swallowing up the rebels and their families.

It is not certain that the rebels belonged only to the tribe of Reuben. The conclusion of verse 1 is no doubt a later addition; the On ben Peleth ben Reuben named here is not mentioned again in the entire account. Perhaps this supplementing redactor has chosen the tribe of Reuben only because, according to the imperfectly preserved legend of Genesis 35:22, their ancestor, Reuben, behaved disrespectfully towards his father Jacob.

Without any doubt the account appears in the manner of legend; that is shown in particular by the conclusion. But just as surely it is the echo of real events. More than any other account it throws light on the unending difficulties that Moses had to overcome in his work. It is hardly ever mentioned directly, but the "grumbling of the people" is an ever-recurring motif of the stories. It was not easy to transform a gang of slaves into a people and, more difficult still, to direct their minds toward a great goal beyond the needs of the day. It could certainly not be achieved without some harshness and severity.

That the people were dissatisfied with the conditions under which they lived in Kadesh might cause surprise. Did we not say that Kadesh was a little paradise? Here, it seems to me, our account affords important insight into a somewhat later period. When the Israelites came from the wilderness to Kadesh, the oasis surely appeared a paradise to them. But within forty years the population doubled. At this period other related tribes certainly joined them, tribes which had never been in Egypt but had pitched their tents in the Sinai peninsula until, under Moses' leadership, the coalition of the twelve tribes was formed. Now the space in Kadesh became too small; the oasis could no longer feed the growing mass of people. It may well be that some of the tribes continued their Bedouin existence in the vicinity with only a distant attachment to the oasis. Among them, particularly, rebellious moods like those of Dathan and Abiram are readily understandable. They received no "inheritance of fields and vineyards" like the privileged ones who dwelt in the center of the oasis; they felt they had been tricked and reproached their leader with enriching himself at their expense. Thus this account apparently gives us a picture of the time before the departure from Kadesh. We can now understand too why Moses and his people should again migrate, which is totally unintelligible in our traditional account. It was bitter necessity which impelled them to move toward the cultivated land, typical of all Bedouin migrations.

Korah's Rebellion[78] (Num. 16)

The account of Korah's rebellion deals with a conflict very different from that of Dathan and Abiram, which was a fight for the secular leadership of the people. The story of Korah is a fight for the priesthood. It is preserved to us only in the version of the Priestly Code; that emerges clearly from the linguistic characteristics. We find here the characteristic words *'edah, ḳahal, mishkan,* which occur in P only. That does not of course exclude the possibility that P may have drawn on an older account; the way in which P has put the problem makes such a conclusion certain.

According to the description in our text Korah is a Levite and contests Moses' and Aaron's privileges. This is a flaw in the account; the original source could never have reported it in that way. For, what are the privileges of the leader which Korah rebels against? The priesthood? But, according to all the ancient sources, all the Levites are priests (see in particular the story of the Golden Calf, Exod. 32, and the Blessing of Moses, Deut. 33:9). This conflict regarding the priesthood is possible only in the late view of P, according to which only Aaron's descendants are destined for the priesthood; the rest of the Levites are to perform only menial, auxiliary services in the sanctuary. This view became possible only after the necessary historical conditions had been created by Josiah's reform in the year 622. It is logical to find that the most recent stratum of the account should explain that clearly (vv. 8-11). According to the presuppositions of P, what reasons could the two hundred and fifty noble Israelites (who are expressly designated as non-Levites) have had to take sides in the private disputes among the Levites and take the part of Korah?

In reality Korah *cannot* have been a Levite at all; the rebellion is, rather, an attempt of the non-Levites to assail the priesthood of the Levites to whom Moses (and Aaron) belong. Only in this way can the older account have related events; its description, which can still be easily and surely followed, must therefore be remembered through the obscurity of the later writers.

The present form of the text is rather complicated, as we shall see. Before quoting the text, therefore, we will make some brief remarks about it.

The first word of verse 1, *wa-yikkah*, must be wrong, for the object is missing. Probably *wa-yakom* was the word, which is used again in verse 2. Verses 2-7 then belong to the Korah story. The last words of verse 7, "enough with you, ye sons of Levi," make no sense at all in the passage in which they are found today; they cannot have belonged to the ancient account, since Korah was not a Levite. They belong in the middle of verse 3, where today only the words *rabh lakhem* are found in a mutilated form. The writer of the P account correctly observed that they must not remain here in his context, since it, of course, makes no sense when the Levite Korah addresses Moses and Aaron, ye sons of Levi. But their mutilated state is, nevertheless, the best proof that they were found here origi- nally and that, in the most ancient account, which was before P, Korah was *not* a Levite. In verses 5-7 Moses proposes an ordeal to decide who is to be called to the priesthood.

Verses 8-11 as mentioned above are later than 622, later even than Ezekiel 44 (573 B.C.; cf. Ezek. 40:1). In this late addition it is explained to the Levites that they have to be satisfied with doing menial services at the sanctuary *(mishkan)* and that they are not to strive after the priesthood. These polemics and this conception of the Korah problem would not have been intelligible to an ancient storytel- ler; for, in the old period, all Levites without any ceremony had the right to act as priests. Thus in a simple and relevant manner it is still expressly stated in Deuteronomy 18:7, where the priests officiating in Jerusalem also are designated as Levites.

Furthermore, to the Korah story belongs the second half of verse 15a, where the sacrificial gift is spoken of. At the conclusion of verses 16 and 17 the following words are to be de- leted as wrong additions: you and Aaron, etc., since the word "you" in the singular can refer to Moses only, which makes no sense in a speech by Moses. The continuation of verse 19 comes only in verse 35. All intervening words are later amplification. For, as the text is today, only the families of the Korah people are swallowed up by the earth, whereas Korah and his two hundred and fifty adherents are killed by the fire of God. This is certainly more likely to be the original account, since it corresponds to the preparations of the story and concludes in a short and dramatic way; since it immediately describes the ordeal demanded by Moses and only affects the sinners and in particular where they have sinned (see also the parallel, Lev. 10:1-2). The sinking into the earth has been inserted in analogy to the Dathan-Abiram story. The text follows:

16:1. "Now Korah rose 2. in the face of Moses and with him two hundred and fifty men of the children of Israel, princes of the congregation, the elect men of the assembly, men of renown. 3. They combined against Moses and against Aaron and said unto them: Enough with you, ye sons of Levi! For all the congregation are holy, everyone of them and YHWH is in their midst; wherefore then do you lift yourselves up above the assembly of YHWH? 4. And when Moses heard it, he fell upon his face. 16. And Moses said unto Korah: Be you and all your congregation before YHWH, 17. and take every man his fire-pan and put incense upon them and bring before YHWH every man his fire-pans, two hundred and fifty fire-pans. 18. And they took every man his fire-pan and put fire in them and laid incense thereon and stood at the door of the tent of meeting with Moses and Aaron. 19b. And the glory of YHWH appeared unto all the congregation. 35. And fire came forth from YHWH and devoured the two hundred and fifty men that offered the incense."

When we transpose this story from the language of the Priestly Code into that of the older account which can be traced through it, we learn the following: A movement is arising among the people directed against the priestly privileges of the Levites. These Levites, however, do not appear here as a priestly tribe of hundreds or even thousands of members, but as a small group represented by Moses and Aaron. Addressing them as "ye sons of Levi" sounds as if they are a small aristocratic circle of families. Here P has preserved a correct recollection even though he is not interpreting the situation accurately, as if the remaining Levites has rebelled against the priestly family of Aaron. What we know from the truly ancient sources about the Levitic priests agrees with this. From the oldest period only the members of the family of Moses and Aaron are known to us historically as Levites — or as priests, which means the same. In the Blessing of Moses (Deut. 33:8) the Levites are called "the men of my faithful one": that is, Moses; apart from a grandson of Moses (Judg. 18:30) and the family of Eli we know of no Levitical priests in the ancient period. Possibly Aaron and his sister Miriam should be counted as Levites too.

Such opposition to the priesthood may not have been entirely rare in ancient times. We find its echo in the strong malediction which the Blessing of Moses (Deut. 33:11) has ready for the opponents of the Levites. Here arises the question as to how the Levites attained their status of priests; but the reply will be possible only if we can survey the entire material of the cult legends.

Spring Names of Kadesh and the Prehistory of the Levites

The Spring Names

Kadesh means *sanctuary*. The whole oasis bears this name, even to the present day. A special sanctity has always clung to the locality; and undoubtedly the fact that it was bound up with the springs gave the oasis its life. It no longer needs to be proved in detail that this sanctity of Kadesh goes back only to the stay of the Israelites; it existed long before. Quite apart from the direct testimony of Genesis 14:7, which dates from the pre-Mosaic period, we have set out in the discussion of the spring legends the considerations decisive for this conclusion. The spring legends of Kadesh are bound up with the locality but not with the period of the Israelites or the person of Moses. They are always older, bearing witness to the fact that long before the Mosaic period the oasis and its springs were sacred.

A number of spring names have been handed down to us. We are not going to decide whether a particular spring corresponds to each name or whether the same spring may be given several names. The whole oasis or its principal locality, at least in the early Israelite period, bears the name Kadesh Barnea. But this does not lead us any further, since no one has yet been able to give a plausible explanation of the name Barnea (as a hypothesis I propose *bir noʻa,* "gushing spring").

One of the principal springs was called *ʻAin Ḳadis,*

"the sacred spring." In other passages this same spring seems to appear under the name Meribhath-Kadesh (Num. 27:14; Num. 20:13 and Deut. 33:2 in the same sense originally, it seems). One might think here of a double spring, therefore perhaps the twice repeated striking of the rock in Numbers 20:11. An additional name for the spring of Kadesh is preserved in Genesis 14:7: *'En Mishpaṭ*.

The name Meribhah occurs in another spring legend as the name of still another spring (Exod. 17); and, again, Massah is a fourth name. Both springs are closely associated here, which probably also indicates a local connection. Massah and Meribhah are also named together in Deuteronomy 33:8. We have found Marah is a fifth spring name (Exod. 15:23).

Three of these springs have been rediscovered and described by recent travelers. The accounts come from Rowland, Trumbull, and Musil. The modern names of the springs described so far are 'Ain Kdes, 'Ain-el-Ḳderat, and 'Ain Kusēme. Only one of them, 'Ain Kdes, has preserved the ancient name; the remaining ones have not yet been identified. However, even more springs exist.

When we review the ancient names, the special kind of sanctity attaching to them clearly emerges: they are springs at which justice is administered.[79] Whether they are sacred because judgment is passed at them, or whether judgment is passed at them because they are sacred cannot be decided offhand, and it is perhaps not particularly important.

Following the analogy of other nations, it is likely that what is primary is the sacredness of the spring. This is motivated by the veneration extended to the spring which produces, as if by magic, the paradise-like oasis out of the arid desert.

Wherever such an oasis is found in the wilderness, it is a junction for traffic. Markets are connected with it. At certain fixed times, the Bedouin tribes of the surrounding area meet here to exchange goods. Strict laws regulate the use of the springs by strangers; a truce, existing under divine sanction, for the duration of the gatherings secures the possibility of trade among the tribes. The custom developed quite naturally that at these springs and under the protection of the truce sanctioned by the deity, the tribes settled with one another their differences, which would otherwise lead to bloody feuds. It became natural too for single individuals to recognize and invoke the jurisdiction of the oasis for their legal disputes; for the owners of the springs to be recognized as judges; and in the course of long periods of time, for a firm legal tradition and practice of law to develop among them. Among all peoples of antiquity the law has the closest connection with religious conceptions and religious usages. In such a center of law there is consequently bound to grow up a religious center also; often complicated legal cases are settled by means of a divine decision, that is, by an oracle. These oracles too are the venerated property of the masters of the oasis.

This special sacred character of the Kadesh springs as places of jurisdiction emerges most clearly in the name of the principal spring *'En Mishpat. Mishpat* means the decision by judges. There can be no doubt here about the meaning and purpose of the name. When on this basis we review the rest of the spring names, each one that appears to us will have a meaning other than that given by the tradition of the stories. They all show some relationship to jurisdiction: *ribh* or *meribhah* is the "proceedings"; consequently *Mē-meribhah* is the "spring of proceedings"; Massah is then not "trial" but "examination," "investigation," and the spring bears the name "spring of examination," because perhaps, as suggested by Eduard Meyer,[80] the testimony of the witnesses was examined here. The last name, Marah, has been explained above as "spring of the rebellious," and as a place for settling lawsuits. Even more striking is another derivation, if it is agreed (and I see no difficulty in it) to read the name of the spring *Morah*; namely, from the root *yarah,* "to cast the lot," from which the word *torah,* "divine instruction," originally the "oracle lot," is also derived. Consequently, the name of the place where the lot is cast signifies "the oracular spring."

If there was only one such spring name in Kadesh, we might think it an accident or that there were special factors influencing this example of a particular name. If, however, *all* the springs of Kadesh manifestly bear some relationship to jurisdiction, it proves that the facts are as our theory suggests: Kadesh was the center of the jurisdiction and therefore sacred. There is a sufficient number of analogous cases in the ancient east. We would recall only the completely identical part which the oasis of

Mecca has played as a market, a place of jurisdiction, and a religious center in the hands of the Kuraish, and is still doing so today.

This characteristic of the oasis of Kadesh, however, must be far older than its occupation by the Israelites. The springs were already there and had been named. One can hardly avoid the impression that the biblical tradition is at pains to efface and obviate the recollection of this pre-Israelite function of Kadesh. Deliberately, so it seems, it does not interpret a single one of the spring names in its original sense; it deliberately endeavors to create a new tradition in place of these old recollections and to link in a novel way the springs and their function with the events of the Mosaic period. It proceeds here exactly as it does in the patriarchal legends, explaining their attitude toward the Canaanite sanctuaries, and for the same reasons. It will not admit that here elements of an old civilization had been taken over and adapted to Israelite life.

But who were the former bearers of this civilization of Kadesh? It can be assumed almost with the certainty of an axiom that the important oasis, the largest and most fertile of the Sinai peninsula, was not uninhabited when the Israelites invaded it. But only once on this march do we hear that the Israelites had a battle: the battle with Amalek. We have already suggested, on the analysis of this story, that Amalek was the tribe which was displaced from Kadesh by the Israelites. But was Amalek always there? Was Amalek the creator and bearer of the legal culture of Kadesh? Can we penetrate still further into the past of Kadesh?

Let us attempt an explanation from another angle, that of the Israelites. Above we have concluded from the abysmal, solemn, and religious hatred of the Israelites (and YHWH) against Amalek, that in times past Amalek must have dealt Israel a formidable blow. We have suggested that once before Israelite tribes were connected with Kadesh and were driven out by Amalek. Can this suggestion be made more plausible from any other point of view?

When tribes like the Israelites left the fertile land of Egypt and went into the wilderness, they must have had a definite goal for their migration. Without one they would be lost. From the analysis of the oldest accounts it has been clearly proved that this goal was the oasis of Kadesh. But how did they hit on Kadesh which after all was some 106 to 113 miles from the borders of Egypt? How above all did such a discerning and purposeful leader as Moses come to think of Kadesh? That can only be explained because the Israelites already knew about the oasis from earlier times, and because the tribe to which Moses belonged already had an older association with Kadesh.

The Tribe of Levi[81]

Since the immigration of the Israelites into Canaan, the tribe of Levi existed only in a very remarkable form: it owned no territory like the rest of the tribes; its members lived scattered among the Israelite tribes and carried out priestly functions among them. Levi, then, is a "priestly tribe." According to all the statements of the Moses stories this is the situation at the time of Moses. This status is so curious and without other examples that doubts have been raised if Levi should be reckoned among the "tribes" at all. The great historian Eduard Meyer[82] concluded that the priesthood represented only a fictitious family association, the members of which, properly speaking, formed a guild, but that, according to the pattern of the tribes, they gave themselves an ancestor (Levi or Moses). But in the face of the evidence we have, this view cannot be maintained. The Levites, we know, have a genealogical connection with each other; our information is much more detailed about them than about any other tribe. Just as landed property is inherited by the tribes, so do the Levites inherit priestly functions; family lists reach from the oldest biblical period right down to the most recent. One cannot, then, speak here of a "fictitious genealogical union."

What is right, however, is that historically we no longer have any information about a secular tribe of Levi. And yet, once such a secular tribe, possessing a fixed residence, must have existed, because several pieces of information refer to it. In fact, Eduard Meyer too concludes from the Kadesh legends that a secular tribe of Levi existed which, closely associated with Simeon, dwelt in the south with Kadesh as its center. But he believes that there is no connection between this tribe of Levi and the later Levitical priests — an untenable assumption, for the connection is given through Moses.

What do we know about the ancient secular tribe of
Levi that was later forgotten? The tribe is always mentioned in
close connection with the tribe of Simeon, which always, including the post-Mosaic period, had its seat in the extreme south of
Palestine, the Negev. Consequently we also have to look there for
Levi, and indeed still further south, so that accordingly its center
must lie somewhere in Kadesh. In the most ancient tradition Simeon and Levi are considered very closely related, as "brothers"
in the proper sense. Both tribes have the reputation of marked
ferocity. In a certain sense both also have a similar fate. For
when the other Israelite tribes step into the full light of history,
Simeon as well as Levi no longer existed as a unit which can be
localized geographically. The areas which are ascribed to these
two tribes in the oldest tradition were gradually absorbed into the
stronger, spreading tribe of Judah. What the cause of this process
was we do not know; we know only the result. The result was put
aa a prophecy in the mouth of the patriarch in the "Blessing of
Jacob," which dates from the first period of the kings (Gen.
49:5-7): 5. "Simeon and Levi are brothers, weapons of violence
their kingship.[83] 6. Let my soul not come unto their counsel, unto
their assembly let my glory not be united. For in their anger they
slew men, and in their self-will they houghed oxen. 7. Cursed be
their anger for it was fierce, and their wrath for it was cruel! I will
divide them in Jacob, and scatter them in Israel."

Here the present state of affairs is transposed into a
past prediction of the future. At least it certainly applies to Levi
in this period: he is "divided up in Jacob, scattered in Israel." By
what means this fate was brought to pass we do not know. The
simplest assumption is that the two tribes were scattered by a
warlike catastrophe. In this connection scholars have referred to
the story of Genesis 34, according to which Simeon and Levi attacked the town of Shechem and brutally murdered its inhabitants. But there is no mention at all of a defeat and catastrophe for
the attackers; it is altogether questionable whether we have the
right to translate into history this legend narrating a feat of the
ancestors of the tribes.

A trace of what happened to Simeon has perhaps been
preserved by the Chronicler in an obscure notice in the very latest
source of the Bible. This work, on the whole historically worth-

less, gives at times single antiquarian notices of significance, which are apparently drawn from the genuine old sources. The Chronicler reports (1 Chron. 4:38-43) that a part of the tribe of Simeon migrated and found new homes "east of the valley" (the Araba?). Another section settled in Mt. Seir and here blotted out "the remnant of Amalek" (this again might be combined with 1 Sam. 30:17). If the information is reliable, this occurrence points to a warlike dispersion of the tribe that agrees with our assumption.

There is a similar indication of a catastrophe that overcame the tribe of Levi and, indeed, from an extra-biblical source. In el-Ola in Northern Arabia the Mineans, some centuries later it is true, founded a colony from which numerous inscriptions have been preserved to us. In three of these inscriptions the word *lw'* occurs with the meaning "priest." As the root does not have this meaning in any Semitic language, several scholars have assumed that this is a form derived from the tribal name Levi and retained as a foreign word.[84] This would imply that at a dispersion of the tribe of Levi, Levite priests migrated south, as they had done in the north, towards Judah and Israel, also practicing their profession among Arab tribes.

Since the tribe of Levi dwelt in and around Kadesh from ancient times, its dispersion can be explained only by the oasis passing into foreign possession after a sudden assault on it. The enemy can only have been Amalek. We have thus arrived at the same conclusion as we did when we analyzed the Kadesh legends. Consequently, in ancient times before the Amalekites, Levites dwelt in Kadesh. These Levites have to be assumed to be the bearers of the legal traditions and the cult of Kadesh connected with them.

On this assumption all preserved traces converge to form a reasonably clear picture. We now understand how the numerous local traditions of Kadesh could from ancient times be preserved among the Israelites through Moses. We understand the deeply embedded hatred toward Amalek. We understand how Moses and the Israelites came to choose Kadesh as the goal of their exodus from Egypt. At last we can look through a rent in the curtain which has been concealing from us the prehistoric past of Israel and see in the ancient Levitic civilization of Kadesh one of the spiritual roots from which grew the innovation of Moses in world history, the religion of Israel.

Precisely this latter problem would naturally captivate our interest to the highest degree. Some further insights into the nature of this very ancient Levitic religion are attained by an investigation of the cult legends preserved to us.

5

The Cult Legends

The most important group of legends referring to cult and religion are the legends of Sinai. Because they are significant and, more, because their literary problems are particularly difficult and complicated, a special discussion must be reserved for these legends.

Besides these we find in the Moses stories a considerable number of other cult legends. What they have in common, with few exceptions, is that they are either handed down in a particularly fragmentary condition, almost unrecognizable and difficult to understand, or merely preserved in allusions. That is no accident. In a field in which people of the later period are especially sensitive, they reflect a stage of religion that was later felt to be downright objectionable. Often one succeeds only by a special effort to penetrate to the oldest core of these legends and to detect their particular meaning, which by deliberate revision has been completely obscured or even changed outright into an opposite meaning.

Some of the stories discussed later are located at Sinai. For the present we will not discuss the question as to where they are to be located, Mt. Sinai or any other place, but instead consider the subject matter only.

YHWH as a Guide in the Wilderness:[85]
His Theophany before Moses (Exod. 33:12 to 34:9)

Whoever wants to traverse the wilderness must have a guide familiar with the route. The better the guide, the more sec-

ure the march. What could be a better guide than the deity itself?
That is why Moses endeavors to prevail on YHWH to take over
the guidance. This is the gist of an account in Exodus 33:12 to
34:9, which in its present form is completely confused, and much
revised. A theophany before Moses is connected with that account and, as we shall see, belongs in fact to the story itself. The
inserted scene, however, with the tables of stone (34:1-4) is entirely foreign to it. The thread of the story is the leadership of
YHWH. Regarding the proposed separation of strata, we find that
33:13 is a later expansion of a general character, which does not
belong to the subject matter. Verses 14 and 15 cancel out each
other; neither originally belongs here. If in verse 14 YHWH a-
grees that his "presence" (literally, "face") shall go with the people, all that follows would be superfluous. Also verse 17, a second
agreement by YHWH, must be discarded for the same reason.
Because Moses does *not* receive an affirmative answer, he asks
for something else, namely, the theophany of YHWH. This is
granted to him. But at the decisive moment he uses the favorable
opportunity to repeat his original request. The decisive verses are
34:5 and 8: verse 5, "And YHWH descended in the cloud and
stood with him there; then he proclaimed the name of YHWH."
"He" is of course Moses. The beginning of verse 6 as a transition
to verse 8 belongs to this also: "And when YHWH passed by before him, Moses made haste and bowed his head towards the
earth," etc. With verse 9a the story breaks off abruptly. Besides
34:1-4, which does not fit into this context at all, verses 6 and 7
also have to be eliminated, since the enumeration of the divine attributes does not belong here at all, and is only meant to veil the
proper meaning of Moses' action. We now give the text:

      33:12. "And Moses said unto YHWH, See, you say
unto me: Bring up this people; and you have not let me know
whom you will send with me. Yet you have said, I know you by
name and you have also found grace in my sight. 16. For wherein
now shall it be known that I have found grace in your sight, I and
your people? Is it not in that you go with us? 18. And he said
further, Show me, I pray you, your glory. 21. And YHWH said,
Behold there is a place by me, when I stand upon the rock. 22.
And it shall come to pass, while my glory passes by, that I will
put you in a cleft of the rock and will cover you with my hand

until I have passed. 23. And I will take away my hand and you shall see my back; but my face[86] shall not be seen. 34:5. And YHWH descended in the cloud and stood with him there. And he proclaimed the name of YHWH. 6a. And when YHWH passed by before him, 8. Moses made haste and bowed his head toward the earth and prostrated himself, 9. and he said, If now I have found grace in your sight, O Lord, I pray you, go in the midst of us.''

It is very doubtful if this whole story belongs to the oldest account. Its phraseology is mostly that of a later time. What is reported in it, however, is so obviously mythological that a story belonging to the oldest stratum is bound to underlie it.

Moses entreats YHWH to journey with the people as their guide. It is consequently presupposed, as everywhere in the oldest view, that YHWH dwelt in a definite locality and was tied to it. This alone is a strongly anthropomorphic conception. As the deity did not at once agree (in the original text there was, to be sure, an outright refusal), Moses, apparently as a substitute for the rejected request, asked for a full revelation of the deity. This request is not conceived in a spiritual sense, but quite spectacularly: "Let me see your glory." The request is granted, if indeed with the limitation that the face of the deity cannot or may not be seen but only its back. There can hardly be any doubt that the deity was conceived in a markedly physical, human form. The deity has a face and a back, and it is visible, even if only for its favorite (for others it need not be invisible, but they would die at the sight of it). Now the ceremonial of the meeting is laid down in detail. YHWH is going to stand upon the rock and Moses will be nearby, in a niche of the rock, to avoid contact with the deity. While the deity passes by him, it will cover Moses' eyes with its hand, for he must not gaze on the deity's face. Then when YHWH withdraws his hand, Moses will see the deity's back. This too is markedly anthropomorphic.

Now comes a highly dramatic and intensely mythological scene. When the deity is standing beside Moses and is about to pass by him, Moses breaks through the agreed upon program! He calls YHWH by name, and thereby holds him by a spell. Moses throws himself into his path and repeats his original, rejected request once more, that YHWH should journey with them in the midst of his people.

It is a struggle of the human being with the deity, in which the man by his shrewdness overcomes the deity, compelling it to accept his will. It completely parallels the Jacob fight, only that in the case of Moses it is not brute strength but shrewdness which enforces his victory. This parallel shows quite clearly that the two stories belong to the same stratum of storytelling and to the same age-old ideas. Its core is the magic power of the divine name and its magical usage. But while Jacob does not learn the name, Moses possesses it and employs it as a weapon in order to make the deity tractable to his will.

Here the story suddenly breaks off. In the old account there was of course more; but what followed appeared so monstrous to later more refined sensibilities that it had to be deleted. For only one sequel is possible: the deity yields to the magic power and journeys on with the people. We also know from other accounts the form in which it does so; only there are two variants. One relates that God descended as a cloud upon the tent of meeting; the other relates that the deity, invisibly enthroned above the ark, was carried along. We have accounts about the first version from later strata only, and it is quite possible that this conception represents a later development which was believed to be less objectionable. About the ark, however, we have accounts from the oldest stratum.

We shall have to look for an account of how the ark came to the Israelites, and what the deity's relations to it were. In fact, we do find such an account.

Jethro and the Ark (Num. 10:29-36)

The account is again parallel to the previous one in that it is based on the motif that Moses is looking for a guide through the wilderness. But this time the course of events is entirely played out on the human plane. The text is so simple and well-preserved — as far as it is preserved! — that we can quote it without reservation.

Num. 10:29. ''And Moses said unto (Hobab ben Re'uel, the Midianite) Moses' father-in-law: We are journeying to the place of which YHWH said: I will give it you: Go with us and

we will do you good; for YHWH has spoken good concerning Israel. 30. But he said to him: I will not go; but I will depart into
mine own land and to my native place. 31. Then he [Moses] said:
Do not leave us in the lurch, for you know our camping places in
the wilderness and you shall be our guide (literally, "eyes"). 32.
If now you go with us, then the same bounty that YHWH grants
us, we will extend to you."

Here the story suddenly breaks off. What now follows
is very remarkable. 33. "They set forward from the mount of
YHWH three days' journey; and the ark of the covenant of
YHWH went before them[87] to seek out a resting place for them."
Verse 34 belongs to a later stratum: "And the cloud of YHWH
was over them by day, when they set forward from the camp."
Cloud and ark as guides are variants which exclude one another.
Then follow the two sayings about the ark, which are of such extraordinary significance that I shall devote a special section to
them, although they undoubtedly still belong to the story as its
conclusion.

When and where does this story take place? We know
of a visit of Jethro to Moses in Kadesh (Exod. 18), shortly after
the arrival of the Israelites at the oasis. This cannot be the same
visit since there it is expressly stated that Jethro returned again to
Midian (18:27). Moreover, the Israelites had come there to settle
and had no intention of journeying further. We then have to assume a second visit, at a later period but before the people again
departed from Kadesh.

Geographical considerations also point in this direction. When Moses presumes that the Midianite knows the way
through the wilderness particularly well, Midian or the adjoining
part of the wilderness must be meant. That fits the journey from
Kadesh to Canaan only. In fact, the Israelites later march round
Edom in the south and on that occasion have to cross the territory of Midian north of the Gulf of Akaba. Everything therefore
points in favor of the assumption that Moses' negotiations with
his father-in-law are to be placed before the departure of the people from Kadesh.

The beginning of this story proceeds exactly like
Moses' conversation with YHWH in Exodus 33. For the passage
through the wilderness Moses wants to obtain a reliable guide; he

turns to his father-in-law, who knows the wilderness well, but he refuses outright. Once more Moses presses him strongly: "Do not leave us in the lurch." We need you as "eyes" in the wilderness! Here the story suddenly breaks off. What can its conclusion have been? Did Jethro give in? And if not, how does Moses find a way out of the difficulty?

We do not know. But as a continuation of the story the ark suddenly emerges and takes over exactly the role which Moses envisages for a guide through the wilderness; it travels in front of the people "to seek out a resting-place for them." In the deleted tailpiece, the story of how the ark came to the Israelites must, therefore, have been told; and it must have been one which offended the sensitivity of later generations and led to its deletion. The most probable assumption is that Jethro, as far as he personally is concerned, continues to refuse to go (for we hear in other stories nothing more of his accompanying them), but as a substitute he procures the ark for them. And it is with the ark, as we shall see, that the deity marches. The substitute is much more important than the human guide for whom Moses had asked.

Here again is a complete analogy of this story to the preceding one, where, we concluded, the ark is introduced as a substitute. Here it is certain, when we consider the appended continuation that deals with the ark. For later generations the fact that the holy ark according to this story did not originate in Israel but apparently in Midian was objectionable. It is indeed a fact that no story of ancient times tells of any report about the origin of the ark in Israel.[88]

But perhaps going back from this point, which is the pivot of the story, we can gain a better understanding of the whole account. As the real significance of Exodus 18 is not the description of a family visit but the introduction of the sacrificial ritual and organized jurisdiction, so here the real significance of the story is that, from the beginning, the procuring of the ark from Midian was being described, and not a second visit by Jethro and the attempt to win him over as a guide.

What then was the ark and the significance of it? Which religious conceptions stand behind it? These questions are so important that we must deal with them fully.

The Ark of the Covenant[89]

The Exterior of the Ark: Form and Use.

As long as it was a matter of investigating legends and historical events, we could start with the reporting of the narrative texts. In the case of the ark the problem is somewhat different. Here we have a cult object of central significance that, according to all sources, dates from the Mosaic period, yet, as an existing object, it is historically attested to for centuries afterwards. There can be no doubt that the holy ark, of which the most ancient sayings from the Mosaic period brings us tidings, is the same that stood in the Temple at Shiloh; it is the same that was seized and then returned by the Philistines, and that David later solemnly led up to Jerusalem. It is the same that was brought by Solomon into the most holy adytum of the Temple and remained there until its destruction by the Babylonians in the year 587. Its history can consequently be traced for about 650 years. For this reason alone it would be significant as a renowned witness of the Mosaic period. Furthermore, it was considered at all times to be a most sacred object, which had a direct relationship to the deity. At this point it is important to be clear about the object itself, its form and function. That may appear a small matter, but it will be seen that this is the only way to arrive at a real understanding of the literary texts and thereby of the inner problems.

Even when we assume that the ark was hardly visible to human eyes, after it was taken into the adytum of the Solomonic Temple, it was previously a well-known and frequently observed object; we may thus expect to find good descriptions of it. In reality we obtain valuable information in two passages only: a description of the ark and the cherubim in Exodus 25:10-22, and statements about the building and the opening of the Solomonic Temple in 1 Kings 6:23-28 and 8:6-9. The statements from the Solomonic period can without hesitation be accepted as reliable accounts of eyewitnesses. But how are we to assess Exodus 25 which purports to give a description of the ark from Mosaic times? If we were really obliged to seek a testimony from Mosaic times, it would be difficult, for Exodus 25 is much later. But for centuries (at least 250 years) the ark could be seen by any spectator, and the possibility of obtaining a reliable report about it thereby becomes considerably greater. The description of the ark in Exodus 25 is preserved in the Priestly Code (P); the older narrative accounts do not give any such descriptions. Here, however, P apparently draws on genuine ancient sources. It is dealing in its own special field with a cult object to which its interest is completely devoted; its credibility is not impaired because the description is given in the form of a divine command addressed to Moses in order to render the "Mosaic milieu" more lively. The ark (*aron*), as its name indicates, is a chest meant to contain the two stone tables of the law. This chest was made of acacia wood (*shiṭṭim*), the very light and at the same time extraordinarily durable wood of a species of acacia found in the Sinai peninsula. (According to the description in P the ark was overlaid inside and outside with gold; for our purposes that is not important.) It had the usual form of a chest: two and a half cubits long (ca. 49½ inches), one and a half cubits deep (ca. 29½ inches) and just as high (Exodus 25:10).

An important consideration must now be discussed. A chest meant to receive some object must have a cover. This cover rests above; it must be possible to open it from the long side. Any other arrangement is technically impossible.[90]

At the four upper corners of the ark, rings were attached through which carrying poles were passed for transporting it. Not to obstruct the cover these carrying rings had to be attached to the two short edges and the poles had to be parallel to the short edges. Consequently the ark was carried cross-wise, as is fitting for a chest. Since the poles, as we are expressly assured, were never removed (25:15), the ark, even when it was resting at its place, always stood with its long side across. That, as we shall see, is important for understanding the function of the ark.

In the cult object which enjoyed veneration, however, the ark is only one part, and in a certain sense not even the most important part. To the ark of the Covenant also belong the two cherubim and the *kapporeth*, "covering slab"; both parts together are designated as *merkabhah*, a "vehicle of the deity." The kapporeth, which is not described in more detail in Exodus 25, is a kind of covering slab lying above the ark and in size corresponding to the cover of the ark. There is a cherub on each side firmly attached to its narrow ledges. According to all we know, these cherubim are winged beings of composite bodily form, numerous examples of which we know particularly from Assyrian plastic art. The cherubim placed on both sides of the ark spread their inner wings so as to overshadow the covering slab from both sides, with the faces of the cherubim turned inward and looking down upon the kapporeth from above.

The most important statement is contained in verse 22: "I will speak with you from above the kapporeth, from the place between the two cherubim." Here then, in the space which is limited beneath by the kapporeth and the wings of the cherubim resting upon it, and on the two sides by the cherubim, here according to this conception the deity is to be located.

The kapporeth is frequently thought to rest directly above the cover of the ark. That is impossible. In order to make it possible to open the ark cover (and it must be opened if the ark has some content), the kapporeth must lie some 29½ inches above the cover of the ark, since the cover is that wide. The space between the kapporeth and the ark is that high. If the cherubim have the height of a human being, their wings spreading inward horizontally from their shoulders lie at a height of about 59 inches above the floor. The ark itself is 29½ inches high; there remains in fact the space calculated here.

A picture quite different from this "older" comprehensive structure of the ark is obtained from the Solomonic one. Solomon had the merkabhah constructed anew. A brief consideration shows that that was necessary. The ark was, we know, often carried into battle — but only the box of the ark, because only this was made portable by means of the poles. On such an occasion the merkabhah remained behind. The Philistines captured the chest of the ark only, and thereby it was preserved. The merkabhah, however, which remained behind in the Temple of Shiloh, was destroyed with the Temple.

The merkabhah, which Solomon constructed anew, had colossal measurements. The cherubim were about 16½ feet high (1 Kings 6:23). Their wings were extended horizontally, each 8⅓ feet broad; the inner ones touched each other in the middle, the outer ones touched the wall. This "wing-ledge" was probably about 13⅓ feet above the ground. Thus, underneath the wings of the cherubim there was a kind of chamber, 16½ feet wide and 13⅓ feet high. And in it, quite small, on the floor, stood the ark, 29½ inches high. Above the wing-ledge of the cherubim right up to the ceiling of the Holy of Holies, was a clear space of about 20 feet high.

The most striking difference between the Solomonic merkabhah and the ancient one is that in the former the kapporeth is missing altogether. The wings themselves are here the kapporeth. The free suspension of this ceiling high above the ark again favors the assumption that in the old merkabhah the kapporeth also hung free at a certain height above the ark.

How is the relationship of the deity to the ark conceived? Most scholars see the ark as the deity's throne. Torczyner[91] was the first to recognize correctly that, among the component parts of the ark, it was the merkabhah which represented the chariot of the deity. The deity was conceived as sitting upon the wings of the cherubim (or, what is the same thing, upon the kapporeth). But even Torczyner could not arrive at a perfectly clear conception, because the relative position of ark and merkabhah in space was not clear to him. Since the deity was seated invisibly upon the wings of the cherubim, the ark was under its feet. The ark was the deity's footstool, not its throne.

During the whole biblical period this conception remained alive and fully accepted. We find it expressly corroborated in the later strata of biblical literature, in which the ark is designated outright as "the footstool of his feet." Ps. 99:5: "Exalt ye YHWH our God, and prostrate yourselves at the footstool of his feet!" Ps. 132:7: "Let us go unto his dwelling-place, and let us prostrate ourselves at the footstool of his feet!" Lam. 2:1: "He has cast down the beauty of Israel from heaven to earth and has not remembered the footstool of his feet in the day of his anger." 1 Chron. 28:2 "To build a house of rest for the ark of the covenant of YHWH and for the footstool of the feet of our God."

We shall soon see how significant this conception is for the understanding of the two sayings about the ark.

But something else also becomes clearer: the significance of the ark for the preservation of the tables. In the ancient Near Eastern world it was a firmly established custom to put solemn treaties "under the feet of the deity," which thereby became the guardian of the treaties.[92] The ark was the deity's footstool. The deity "enthroned above the cherubim" with its feet resting upon the ark, as it were, closed the lid of the ark, securing the covenant treaty.

The new construction of the merkabhah by Solomon did not change these conceptions; it did increase the measurements to a colossal size. The room of the Holy of Holies in quite a real sense remained "a place for Him to sit in" (1 Kings 8:13). The winged throne of the deity was now 16½ feet wide, 13½ feet high above the ground and had above it a space of 20 feet; but basically it remained the same as the primitive vessel of early days.

These remarks may sound brutal, heretical, and disrespectful, but we have to bear in mind that the ark was an object dating from the most ancient times, a remnant of the magic age, of the mythological prehistory of the Israelite religion. And let us not forget a second point: it is not really important what the people thought of the chest in which the tables of stone lay, nor are these tables important in themselves, because a man like Moses was allowed to break them into pieces. What is important is what was written on the tables. And this remains true even if the tables were never placed in the chest.

The Sayings over the Ark (Num. 10:35-36)

10:35. "It came to pass, when the Ark set forward, that Moses said, Rise up, YHWH, and let your enemies be scattered, and let them that hate you flee in your sight! 36. And when it came to rest, he said, Sit down, YHWH of hosts, the thousands of Israel!"

I am giving the text and translation of the two sayings essentially as rendered by Torczyner, who in his treatise "Die Bundeslade" has correctly explained their significance in the most important points. He has, like others before him, adopted in the second saying the reading *shebhah*, "sit down," instead of *shubhah*, "return," and I agree with him. But in one essential point, Torczyner is gravely mistaken and thereby has again hampered a real understanding of the sayings. He endeavors to show that *shebhah* is to be understood as "mount up," and that the second saying, like the first, was pronounced at the departure of the ark on its journey. It is awkward to contradict a clear tradition unless it is absolutely necessary. Here, however, we have quite a clear and uniform tradition: the first saying was pronounced "when the ark departed," the second, when it "came to rest." The complicated explanation given by Torczyner is not only precarious but also unnecessary.

When, however, the interpretation of the structure and use of the ark which we have given here is accepted, the understanding of the two sayings is so simple that one is almost ashamed to add another word of explanation. And the tradition is fully justified.

The first saying is manifestly a fighting slogan. The word *kūm* does not mean here to depart for a journey, but to go into battle. From repeated evidence we know that tne ark was taken into battle. But with the ark YHWH was meant to come, too! (cf. 1 Sam. 4:7). How did that happen? The deity was thought to be enthroned upon the merkabhah, the ark being beneath it as its footstool. When Israel went into battle, only the ark proper, the chest, was taken along; it alone was equipped for carrying (see above). Yet it was the footstool of the enthroned deity. The deity was, therefore, summoned: "Rise up, YHWH!" The conception is that YHWH, rising from his seat, stepped upon the ark as a footstool and, now standing erect but invisible, was carried into battle; through the terror spread by him, he put the enemy to flight. When the battle ended, the ark was returned to the merkabhah, put in its place, and the deity was requested: "Sit down, YHWH!" Not mount for a journey but take a seat upon your throne of cherubim. It is childlike and naive, but in itself a simple and clearly understandable process.

The sayings in their form and contents show clearly that they date from very ancient times, probably from the Mosaic period. Both sayings appear in rhythmic form. The first is a heptameter $(2 + 2 + 3)$,[93] the second a pentameter $(3 + 2)$.

While the first saying presents hardly any textual problem, the second is more difficult. Torczyner deserves considerable credit for its correct linguistic explanation, since all previous attempts were quite unsatisfactory. He first recognized that *rebhabhoth* as a genitive depends on YHWH: YHWH of myriads. That is also proved by the meter: the caesura of the pentameter lies behind *rebhabhoth*. Further he has clearly proved that *rebhabhoth* is here only a synonym for *ṣebha'oth*, commonly used elsewhere. His citation and evaluation of the mutilated verse in Psalms 68:18 are an achievement of unusual acumen and absolutely convincing. But in spite of that we cannot concur in his interpretation of the phrase *YHWH ṣebha'oth* or here *YHWH rebhabhoth*. If he thinks that such an association is impossible for a personal name and that therefore YHWH is here still to be understood in an appellative way as a preliminary stage of the name ("the roaring"), then we must object that the saying cannot pos-

sibly date from a period (if there ever was one!) in which YHWH
had not yet acquired the character of a name. The first saying, indeed, shows the contrary. And only a name can be introduced by
the request, Sit down! But the interpretation of *sebha'oth* or
rebhabhoth is to be rejected too. Like many other scholars, Torczyner sees in the *sebha'oth* or *rebhabhoth* a heavenly host ("the
wild host"), which drives along with a loud noise; or rather, he
translates the expression *YHWH sebha'oth* generally as "din of
an army," "mighty din." Our interpretation proves that to be impossible. For, with this interpretation the following phrase, *alfē
Yisra'el*, which curiously enough Torczyner does not discuss at
all, is without connection and becomes unintelligible. Rather,
there is one possible interpretation only: the *sebha'oth* or
rebhabhoth are *earthly* hosts, the hosts of the people whose war
god is YHWH, as the ark sayings show.[94] The phrase may here in
fact be taken generally as "hosts," as is suggested by Torczyner;
and precisely for this reason it is determined more closely by the
second apposition: the thousands of Israel. Moreover, *alfē* is not
a numeral but the military organization, the thousand, the regi-
ment.

The correct translation, and in the context of both sayings the only possible translation of the second saying, is, therefore, Sit down, YHWH of hosts, of the thousands of Israel.

When we consider from the point of view of the history of legend the two sayings about the ark in their context, one
inconsistency is striking. The two sayings are throughout war
slogans; they speak of YHWH only as Israel's war god. For the
introductory legend, however, YHWH, and with him the ark, is
first and foremost the guide through the wilderness. When the
mutilated form of the stories is considered, it can be suggested
but no longer proved that perhaps we have here the revision of a
still more original legend. A palladium similar to the ark, which
was carried into battle and at the same time served as a guide in
the wilderness, is also known from other Bedouin tribes (the
Rualla) residing in the Sinai peninsula in our own time. This use
of the ark as a palladium of war is no doubt the more original and
older version (it continued to exist in later times too). Its role as a
guide through the wilderness is a theological reinterpretation. We

could perhaps find out more about it if we were better informed about the origins of the ark.

We know very little about it, however. We saw above that several signs point to Midian for its origin: Jethro's connection with the first mention of the ark; Jethro's certain influence on other institutions of the cult and the law; and the apparently intentional deletion of the conclusion of the story. Far-reaching speculations have been associated with the Midianite origin of the ark, particularly by Gressmann.[95] He concludes that not only the ark but also its god, YHWH, came to the Israelites from Midian.

This conception, however, presents great difficulties. The real problem is merely shifted. How then did YHWH come to the Midianites? Was he their only god? What role did he play in their religious life? Why has this conception of God produced no effect at all in Midian, but has produced effects of world-wide import in Israel? Was Moses only a passive receiver? In that case why did Jethro not enter into the tradition as the founder of Israel's religion? Basically that "explanation" does not explain anything at all. Nevertheless, a strong Midianite influence on Israel's cult and law is undeniable and attested to precisely by our tradition. How is that to be explained?

To elucidate this phenomenon I will go back to the considerations to which we were led above concerning the prehistory and fate of the tribe of Levi. In ancient times the tribe of Levi as the owner of the oasis of Kadesh was the bearer of a definite legal and cultic tradition. The tribe was then scattered by a warlike catastrophe in which it lost Kadesh; thereby Moses' family apparently came to Egypt while other Levitic families went to other north Arabian tribes. Midian in its northern part is situated in the vicinity of the Kadesh area. What could be more plausible than that some Levites emigrated to Midian and took with them their own traditions? From this point of view it becomes more readily intelligible that Moses on his flight should have turned toward Midian; he knew he would meet tribal relatives, with whom he could find hospitality. (Similar occurrences still take place today, as we learn from the adventurous youth of Ibn Saud.) Here Moses, assimilated as he was to Egyptian traditions, could become better acquainted with the traditions of his own tribe and possibly for the first time make contact with their specific form of the worship of God, a YHWH service, the foundations of which he created anew and deepened by the originality and genius of his spirit. Here, tradition teaches, he had close connections with the priesthood, which as in ẹl-Ola may well have been a Levitic one, or at least strongly influenced by the Levites. Here he later turned to make available legal and cultic traditions of ancient Levitic composition, when he undertook the re-creation of his people in Kadesh. In this way too the transmigration of the ark could be understood quite freely; the same applies, as we shall see, to the connection with the Sinai traditions. The peculiar duality of the Mosaic creation, which contains in addition to the loftiest and purest ideas remnants of magical witchcraft, would in this manner become more readily understandable. YHWH, accordingly, was always the god of the Levites; he remained so in Midian and was amalgamated in Kadesh with the refined conceptions of God that Moses created.

The Golden Calf [96] (Exod. 32).

The story of the Golden Calf belongs to the group of Sinai legends because of its present place and connection. Without going into the question of that relationship now, we shall nevertheless deal with it here because it contains cult legends that are important for a complete understanding of the significance of the cult and religion.

The story is built up on the fairly uniform, continuous, and well-preserved ancient account; but it is expanded by some easily recognizable insertions. Small additions of this kind we will omit in the rendering of the text; that is justified by a mere textual comparison. But several larger insertions are listed here: verses 7-14 patently do not belong to the ancient account; they anticipate what follows, which makes Moses' sudden wrath unintelligible, since he was bound to know everything beforehand. Verses 15b and 16 give a description of the tables, which is to be eliminated. Verses 17-18, the interlude between Moses and Joshua, likewise do not belong to the ancient body of the story, which knew nothing about a companion of Moses.

The assessment of the three sections, 21-24, 25-29, and 30-33, is difficult (34 must be an addition). Considered by itself, verse 35 is the best direct continuation of verse 20. For there is an inner contradiction in the fact that in verse 28 the punishment of the people takes place through Moses and the Levites, while in verse 35 the punishment is inflicted through YHWH. In style and conception, nevertheless, these three pieces bear the distinct characteristics of the ancient account. The best solution of the contradictions is to treat these sections as semi-independent stories that circulated at the same time as the main account and were later united with it. When for the moment they are omitted, the result is a highly compact dramatic story. We shall discuss and evaluate them after presenting the basic account.

32:1. "And when the people saw that Moses delayed to come down from the mount, the people gathered themselves together against Aaron and said unto him, Up, make us a god who shall go before us; as for this man Moses who brought us up out of the land of Egypt, we do not know what has become of him. 2. And Aaron said unto them, Break off the golden earrings and bring them unto me. 3. And all the people broke off the golden rings, which were in their ears and brought them unto Aaron. 4. And he received this from them and fashioned it with a graving tool and made it into a molten calf; and they said, This is your god, O Israel, which brought you up out of the land of Egypt. 5. And when Aaron saw this, he built an altar before it; and Aaron made a proclamation and said, Tomorrow shall be a feast to YHWH. 6. And they rose up early on the morrow and offered burnt offerings[97] and brought peace offerings; and the people sat down to eat and to drink and rose up to indulge in misdemeanor. 15. And Moses turned and went down from the mount, with the two tables of the testimony in his hand. 19. And it came to pass, as soon as he came near the camp that he saw the calf and the dancing; and Moses became enraged and he cast the tables out of his hands and broke them beneath the mount. 20. Then he took the calf which they had made and burnt it with fire and scattered it upon the surface of the water and made the children of Israel drink of it. 35. And YHWH smote the people with a plague because they had made the calf.

Aaron's Excuse

21. "Moses said unto Aaron, What did this people do to you that you have brought a great sin upon them? 22. And Aaron said, Let not my lord be enraged; you know the people that they are unbridled[98] 23. So they said to me, Make us a god, which shall go before us; as for this man Moses who brought us from the land of Egypt, we do not know

what has become of him. 24. And I said unto them, Whosoever has any gold, let them break it off; so they gave it to me; and I cast it into the fire, and there came out this calf.

The Installation of the Levites

25. "And when Moses saw that the people were out of control (for Aaron had let them get out of control, a derision among their opponents), 26. then Moses stood in the gate of the camp and said, Whoso is on YHWH's side, let him come unto me. And all the sons of Levi rallied unto him. 27. And he said to them, Thus says YHWH, the God of Israel: Put ye every man his sword upon his thigh, and go to and fro from gate to gate throughout the camp and slay every man his brother and every man his companion and every man his neighbor. 28. And the sons of Levi did according to the word of Moses; and there fell of the people that day about three thousand men. 29. [99] And Moses said, You have today taken office on behalf of YHWH,[100] each man against his son and his brother to bring blessings upon yourselves today.

Moses' Intercession

30. "And it came to pass on the morrow that Moses said unto the people, You have been guilty of a great sin; and now I will go up unto YHWH; perhaps I can receive pardon for your sin. 31. And Moses returned unto YHWH and said, Alas, this people is guilty of a great sin in making for themselves a god of gold. 32. Yet now, if you will forgive their sin, [do so]; and if not, blot me, I pray you, out of your book, which you have written. 33. And YHWH said unto Moses, Whosoever has sinned against me, him will I blot out of my book."

The scene of the story is in the vicinity of Mt. Sinai. According to the introduction and to the later continuation of the story, Moses went up the mountain to YHWH to receive the tables of the covenant. Besides this motif, however, another presumably older one glimmers through the account: the people expect him to "bring" with him the god or, rather, to induce the god to lead the people on their way. Since Moses has not returned and perhaps has met his death, they demand the "making" of another god who is to lead them — that is, the same motif that we are familiar with from the other accounts.

With this demand the people turn to Aaron, who is now considered second after Moses, to be his given successor. Yet he is not, as in the fight with Amalek, simply one nobleman alongside others, but he is elected for the specific task, at the same time a priestly one, of giving the people a new leader god. Like Moses, Aaron must previously have been a priest and was most probably a Levite. But he was carved from different wood than Moses. He immediately yielded to the demands of the people; he did not lead, but was himself led. He made for them a "golden calf," that is, a young bull, from wood which was plated with gold. What sort of god was that? While announcing a sacrificial feast in honor of the god for the next day, he called it a "feast to YHWH." The image of the bull is meant to represent YHWH or, rather, to be a symbol for YHWH, and the people immediately recognize it as such.

From this it follows that the worship of YHWH under the image of the bull was familiar to the people. It was no innovation, but an old and well-known cult. The innovation, the world-shaking innovation, comes with Moses and his demand for an imageless cult. Aaron was a priestly representative of conservative views; he was a follower of YHWH, but a Levite of the old class, who had always worshiped YHWH in this way. That is likely to have been the external form of the cult in earlier times in Kadesh, Midian, and elsewhere after the Levites were dispersed, before the reformer Moses arrived. We are again struck with the analogy to the Kuraish of Mecca and the reformer Muhammad.

There is no trace whatever here that this Aaron was a brother of Moses. It is highly improbable. He was simply an opponent of Moses, separated from him by a world of ideas, a noble Israelite or Levite of the old school. There is nothing about him of the pious High Priest, as he appeared to people in later times.

The cultic feast which then follows exhibited features which are well-known from the bull worship in Canaan. After the sacrifices and the sacrificial meal, "the people rose to indulge in misdemeanor." The term used here, ṣaḥek,[101] is the same as that in Genesis 26:8, and there as here it has a sexual connotation. It denotes the sex orgies, which were frequently connected with these cults.

This scene — how Moses at the sight of the aberration of the people shattered the tables of the covenant in burning anger — has rightly become world famous. It is of august grandeur. Whether or not it is historical in the strict sense is unimportant; the idea underlying it has remained historically effective. At the same time it gives a lifelike portrait of Moses, as he remained in the recollection of his people. His wrath is as strong and elementary as the force with which he built up his life work. It is as powerful as the infinite patience he needed to overcome all resistance. How different from Aaron! He immediately yielded to a riotous mob. Moses, however, acted alone, facing the wild mass of the people, as if he had an army behind him, ruthless and with the self-assurance of a superior mind. That is why he carried the day; no hand was raised against him. He shattered the idol; no one blocked his way. He then submitted the people to an ordeal of God, similar to that of the ordeal of jealousy in Numbers 5:27-28: he made them drink the water which contained the ashes of the burned bull-image. And it is YHWH who punished the guilty.

Anyone who reads or hears the story must ask: And what happened to Aaron, the principal culprit? The short account in verses 21-24 speaks about that. How did he come before Moses? Humble and guilt-conscious, with threadbare excuses. He did not speak to Moses like an elder though guilty brother to the younger one; this account recognized no relationship between them. Rather, he stood like a trembling servant before his enraged master. And remarkably, as in Numbers 12, again nothing happened to Aaron. Again the conclusion of the story is missing. Here was the place to pronounce the judgment of death over Aaron; it is bound to have been here. Later hands have deleted it; they let Aaron, the poor wretch, die at a great age, the same death as Moses, the hero. Not quite the same, though, as we shall see later. They did not know how to give him the halo with which a true poet has transfigured the passing of Moses.

In our text, before the punishment decreed by YHWH over the people, Moses wrestles with YHWH to save the life of the people. The same applies to this scene as to that of Moses' anger: historical or not, it is profoundly real and of sublime grandeur. It too shows us the genuine Moses as the people knew him and as popular legend came to recall him.[102]

Moses — his sudden anger has cooled off — stepped before the deity not as an accuser of his people but rather as their advocate. The guilt is clear, it is undeniable; the punishment is well deserved. That is why Moses asked for no more than mercy. But —

and that is the demon in this man — he *demanded* it. He threw his life into the balance. He did not want to die *on behalf* of the people; he is thoroughly Jewish, there is no representative death. *To live* with his people was what he wanted, the people who are the work of his spirit and his will. If the people die, then his life has no value either: "blot me out of your book!"

Can there be anything greater? Yes, indeed! For now comes the climax of this dialogue, the reply of the deity. The deity, inflexible, far removed from man, is unflinchingly just, even though his beloved one is petitioning before him. Unswerving, he gives his reply: He who has sinned against me, him I shall blot out of my book! You desire mercy, O man? Leave mercy to me. Do not demand or coerce. I shall be just,[103] for I am God; you may then decide whether you can go on living, for you are man. But *I* shall not blot you out. That is a YHWH different from the night demon who went around attacking people; different from the omnipotent powerless one from whom Moses obtained the ark by a ruse. It is a god, conceived most deeply and spiritually, and a judge of men; a deity, which could come to men only after Moses had lived. In all simplicity, with the fewest possible words, the most stupendous scene of the Bible is depicted.

The election of the Levites to the priesthood has been joined to the story of the Golden Calf. As a rule one sees in this story the transition of the tribe of Levi from a worldly to a priestly one.[104] That, however, is not quite right. When the tribe of Levi was still living in Kadesh as a worldly tribe, it was at the same time a "priestly tribe," and apparently it served in this capacity for a wider area. But this priesthood was a traditional, primitive, innate one. Now, under Moses, came the day of decision for or against the purified new religion. Every single individual had to make his own decision. Only Levites who were proven became members of the new priesthood. That is why it is expressly stated here and in the Blessing of Moses that the faithful ones who followed the lead of Moses did not spare even their fathers and brothers. It may have been only a small number of families which flocked to Moses; for in the subsequent period we know historically that Levite priests only were the descendants of Moses and the Zadokites of Gibeon (later Jerusalem). It is a specially ironic aspect of history that these Zadokites derived their descent direct from the Aaron against whom the movement of the new Levites was bound to be directed in the first place.[105]

When in the subsequent period a "priestly tribe of Levi" is spoken of, it really concerns members of a tribe. It is a genuine genealogical relationship in the same sense as it would be with any other tribe, and not, as Eduard Meyer suggested, merely a guild with a fictitious relationship. In this purge and reformation of the tribe, those who did not perish but were withdrawn very likely lost their connection with the "priestly tribe" completely and were absorbed into the other tribes of Israel.

A second conclusion may with certainty be drawn from our story. The Levites who followed the lead of Moses actually became full priests. There is no trace of Levites being chosen for menial services only, while alongside and above them were special priestly families, as represented in later times. Indeed our account excludes such a procedure altogether. For the subsequent period down to Deuteronomy, the terms Levite and priest remain equivalent (although in an older period non-Levite priests also existed). The differentiation between priests and Levites is the result of a later development arising under special conditions.

Whether the installation of the Levites into the priesthood occurred on the occasion reported or at any other time is not important for a historical evaluation. It may be considered a historical fact that it took place in the Mosaic period and under Moses, indeed in a hard struggle against severe opposition. Of this we possess a later very impressive testimony in the Blessing of Moses. There it is said of Levi, like a poetic repetition of our story, "Who said of his father and of his mother: I have not seen them;[106] neither did he acknowledge his brethren nor would he know anything of his own sons. But they have observed your command and kept your covenant."

In the legendary tradition of the Blessing of Moses we learn something else that deviates from our account: the installation of the Levites is here associated with Massah and Meribhah; it consequently took place in Kadesh. It is clear that this is more likely and apparently also a more original element. Like many another legend this one also was subsequently transferred to the Sinai.

We have dealt with this account in such detail because it has been the subject of grave misunderstanding on the part of many scholars. Gressmann's interpretation is entirely misleading.[107] He assumes the faithful followers of YHWH to be any Israelites who were later made "Levites," that is, "priests," as a reward for their attitude; in this case (in agreement with Eduard Meyer's view) the Levites are only a professional guild. Quite apart from the fact that this interpretation contradicts the clear text of the tradition, it is impossible simply because the word *Levite* in itself does not signify priest but was associated with this notion only under certain historical conditions. Why then should those men ordained as priests be called Levites if they were not? Rather, Levi is a tribal name. It is correct to make a difference between Aaron and the faithful Levites. But this difference is not between priest and layman, but between an older stratum of more primitive Levites and a later one of Levites faithful to YHWH and to Moses. Because of his interpretation Gressmann is led to the entirely paradoxical opinion that Moses was not a Levite. If anyone was, according to all the evidence we have it was Moses. To think that the Levites had no family association at all, but were merely a professional guild, is a misunderstanding of the Blessing of Moses. It is not said here that they *have* no father but that they do not *recognize* father, mother, brother, and son out of their faithful adherence to YHWH; it is the same in our account.

What exactly the new course was to which the Levites subscribed on this fateful day is a question which touches on the essence of the matter. But we can penetrate it only after we have pierced through many a shell.

The Urim and Thummim[108]

The Urim and Thummim were an oracular vessel by means of which the deity was consulted and through which, in difficult cases, it announced its decision. They are at the same time an excellent example of the difference existing between true historical tradition and a priestly "tradition" artificially devised.

According to the representation of the Priestly Code dating from later times, the Urim and Thummim belonged to the high priest's vestments;[109] they were consulted only by the high priest and were handed down by heredity from Aaron, the first high priest, through all generations from father to son. The Code gives an exact description of how they were worn in the ephod and breastplate of the high priest (Exodus 28:4.30; Lev. 8:8), but not a word is said of the

Urim and Thummim themselves or the kind of use to which they were put. For at the time this account in the Priestly Code was written, the Urim and Thummim had been missing a long time and were totally unknown. When one of the priestly families returning from Exile could not prove its priestly descent, the governor decided (Neh. 7:65) that it should stay away from the priestly service "till a priest[110] will arise for the Urim and Thummim." How would that be possible, if the high priests had administered the Urim and Thummim in an unbroken tradition? Later the high priest wore the Urim and Thummim without exception in his breastplate. Here we are dealing with pure fiction.

The historical tradition is totally different. From it we know about two specimens of the Urim and Thummim. One was in the possession of the Danite priest, Jonathan, the grandson of Moses (Judg. 18); the other was in the possession of the Eli family of Shiloh, where it is expressly mentioned in connection with Ahijah (1 Sam. 14:3, 18, 37, 41), his brother Ahimelech (1 Sam. 22:10, 13, 15), and the latter's son, Abiathar (1 Sam. 23:6, 9; 30:7). All these persons are descendants of Moses. Accordingly the Urim and Thummim did not go back to Aaron but to Moses, and they were handed down by him as a family heirloom. Abiathar was the last to consult the oracle. On his deposition by Solomon he took his secret with him. After him the Urim and Thummim were never again consulted and sank into total oblivion, a mystery of antiquity.

Before investigating the origin of the Urim and Thummim we will first determine how they were consulted. We have several statements about this. The clearest is 1 Samuel 14:40, 41, only that here the masoretic text is mutilated by the omission of one line, which, fortunately, is fully preserved in the Septuagint. Saul says here, "If, Oh YHWH, God of Israel, this guilt is on me or Jonathan [my son], give Urim; but if this guilt is on your people of Israel, give Thummim."

From this follows:

1. The Urim and Thummim — substantiated also from all the other references — answered an alternative question only: yes or no, this or that. Questions which left a choice between many possibilities could not be decided by the Urim and Thummim (for example, the draw of Achan by lot, Josh. 7:14-18; the allotment of land among the tribes, Josh. 18:10 ff.; the selection of a tribe, Judg. 1:1-2; or the choice of Saul to be king, 1 Sam. 10:20-21).

2. The oracle consisted of two recognizable, marked lots, one of which was called Urim, the other Thummim.

3. It had to be precisely fixed in advance which lot would signify the one and which the other case.

We do not learn anything about the marking of the two lots. But to know and to interpret these marks correctly was the secret of the oracle-giving priest. Having recourse to the Urim and Thummim was explained by the expression "to consult God." This vessel then served to ascertain the will of the deity in certain cases by "technical means," even without any special revelation.

According to all the accounts we have, the Urim and Thummim can be traced back to Moses. How did he come to be in possession of this important vessel?

It might be expected that there would be a special legend to inform us about it, for example, that he obtained it from the deity itself. But just as in the case of the ark, we are disappointed here: such an account is not recorded. The reason, presumably, is the same as for the ark; once upon a time there was such an account, but because its character was objected to by later generations, it was deleted. Only one passage escaped this censorship and from it we learn something significant: Deuteronomy 33:8 in the Blessing of Moses. Although we dealt with this passage earlier, we will again examine it:

Your [that is Levi's] Thummim and Urim belong
To the men [or sons] of your faithful one.
Whom you did prove at the spring of proving.
With whom you did strive at the waters of striving.

Here it is confirmed that the Levites ("the men of your faithful one") received the Urim and Thummim from Moses. When the Urim and Thummim are named as the chief distinguishing mark of the Levirate, the Levites and they only are thereby designated as those who are in possession of the Urim and Thummim. We now know that this circle was very narrow: the descendants of Moses and those who followed their lead. They were at the same time those who were to hand down the law, to make known the divine instructions (toroth), and to offer up the sacrifices (v. 10). They had opponents (v. 11), who contested their claim and were forcefully cursed.

The "faithful one," Moses, however, who acquired the Urim and the Thummim, was characterized as the man "whom you did prove at the spring of proving, with whom you did strive at the waters of striving." This cannot be only an incidental praising of Moses, but must have a special reference to the Urim and Thummim. Yet what does that verse mean? When and how did God prove Moses at the spring of proving? When and how did God strive with Moses at the waters of striving? Apparently this alludes to legends which told of such things. But there is not a single one in the stories about Moses.

Nevertheless the meaning of the words is quite clear. God strove with Moses (or Moses with God) at the waters of Meribhah. Yet, the meaning becomes twisted and misleading when, trying to smooth things over, it is often translated, "*for* whom you did strive at the waters of striving." The words cannot mean that, nor is anything about that known to us. There must have been legends according to which a real struggle or at least a trial of strength took place between God and Moses. The idea is not as monstrous as might appear at first sight, for similar events are repeatedly reported elsewhere: the circumcision scene in Exodus 4:24-26 and the outwitting of the deity by Moses in Exodus 34. The preceding words "whom you did prove at the spring of proving" show that an intellectual competition was meant, a contest of wits and acumen. That is stated for the glorification of Moses, for he has passed the test. The way in which we have to imagine such a "proving" is shown by a later stratum of the manna legend in Exodus 16. Through a miracle, at the daily collection of the manna, each person found just as much as he needed. But on the sixth day of the week the Israelites found double the amount and on the seventh day nothing at all. They did not understand and consulted Moses. He, however, with his penetrating mind immediately recognized the "proving" and solved the riddle; he "discovered the Sabbath" before it was commanded on Mount Sinai. Such a contest had its prize — if the human being was victorious over the deity. In the account of Exodus 34 this prize, as we have shown, was apparently the ark. In the allusion in the Blessing of Moses the prize is perfectly clear: it is the Urim and Thummim which on this occasion Moses gained from the deity. There, the conclusion of the story, which reported it, has been deleted; here, the entire legend, which once upon a time recounted it, has been deleted. The conclusion that such an account did exist has been made certain by the simple fact that the

Urim and Thummim were oracular vessels which really did exist and were historically traceable. How they came into the possession of the priests surely *had* to be told; their authority and the recognition of their Mosaic origin rested positively on this account. We shall see that there were legends of such origin for all cult objects, but almost all of them have suffered the same fate of mutilation and deletion by later censors.

Can we form any idea of what the Urim and Thummim were like? At the manipulation of the oracle they were always named together with the ephod so that this also was bound to have been part of the oracular vessel. The owner of the oracle was called a "bearer of the ephod" (1 Sam. 14:18, according to the LXX). In the case of the priest of Dan, the Urim and Thummim are not expressly mentioned, but only that he has the ephod and "consults God" (Judg. 18:5, 14, 20). When Abiathar escaped from the blood bath of Nob, there was "the ephod in his hand" (1 Sam. 23:6); immediately afterwards it is related (23:9) that he consulted the oracle on behalf of David. The ephod consequently belonged to the oracle of the Urim and Thummim. In the opinion of most scholars it was a pouch in which the Urim and Thummim were kept. They, accordingly, were a kind of lot of which each, on coming out, answered a definite question, namely, one of two alternative questions.

What was the procedure of drawing a lot? Most authors think that the pouch of the ephod was shaken until one jumped out. In opposition to this view I think that the lot was *drawn out*, which is more natural. He who consulted the oracle said to the priest: *haggishah ha-ephod*, "bring hither the ephod" (1 Sam. 14:18 and 23:9). When Saul became impatient, he said, *esof yadekha*, "withdraw your hand!" (14:19). Consequently the pouch with the lots was held out and the questioner drew one lot.

What do we know about the kind of lots used? There is first of all the name: *urim we-thummim*. Each of the words denoted one of the lots, as we see from 1 Samuel 14:41. Although these words apparently have a plural form, they are not properly plurals but old word formations ending in mimation like *mayim*, *shamayim*, *tummim*, *rekam*, *hinnam*, *terafim*, etc. The two words are without doubt derived from *or*, "light," and *tam*, "complete," "finished." They are mostly interpreted as symbolic expressions like "revelation and truth." But that does not agree with the time from which they date. I should like to make a suggestion pointing in another direction.

The two words begin with the first and last letters of the alphabet. In this sense the names may be interpreted as "rising" or "beginning" and "completion" or "conclusion," namely, of the alphabet. The one represents the aleph, the other the taw. It may be presumed that they consisted of two little tablets on one of which an *aleph* was inscribed and on the other, a *taw*.

This is a period when writing with letters, that is, with an alphabetic script,[111] was just emerging. The assumption, formerly current, that the Phoenicians were the inventors of the alphabetic script is becoming more and more improbable. More and more indications support the assumption that the spread of the alphabet started from the Sinai peninsula. Through the discoveries of Sir Flinders Petrie we have come to know a script which perhaps was not yet an alphabetic script, but contained the formal elements of north Semitic letter writing in a primitive form, with a manifest leaning toward hieroglyphic models. The decisive factor, however, in the invention of letter writing is not the external form of the signs, but the discovery of the consonants: the discovery that the human language is composed of few and ever-recurring elements. Moses was in Egypt; he had the opportunity while on the Sinai peninsula to become acquainted with the Sinai script. It is tempting to think that such a genius might succeed in discovering the consonants. In that case the secret of the oracle of the Urim and Thummim would be understandable in that the signs upon the lots were intelligible only to him and a few initiates.

The Brazen Serpent[112] (Num. 21:4-9)

The story of the brazen serpent is based on two motifs: (1) the often referred to grumbling of the people and their punishment; (2) the healing of snakebite by some magic means. The beginning of the story has been revised by later hands, but its content is not likely to have been changed much. 21:6. "And YHWH sent fiery serpents among the people, and many people of Israel died. 7. And the people came to Moses and said, We have sinned, because we have spoken against YHWH and against you; pray unto YHWH that he take away the serpents from us. And Moses prayed for the people. 8. And YHWH said to Moses, Make a seraph [a fiery serpent] and set it upon

a pole; and if anyone that is bitten looks at it, he shall live. 9. And
Moses made a serpent of brass and set it upon the pole; and if a
serpent had bitten any man, he would look at the serpent of brass and
recover.

This is not just any miracle story, but one which is closely
connected with cultic functions. For the brazen serpent really is an
existing object, about which we have an interesting piece of news
from the time of King Hezekiah of Judah (727-699). In 2 Kings 18:4 we
read: "He [Hezekiah] broke in pieces the brazen serpent which
Moses had made; for unto these days the children of Israel used to
burn incense to it, and it was called Nehushtan."

This notice is informative in several respects. First, it
confirms the Mosaic origin of the serpent. The question arises, how
did the serpent come into the Temple of Jerusalem? The way can be
none other than the one in which the ark and the Urim and Thummim
got there: from the sanctuary of Shiloh and the family of the Elides,
whose last known descendant, Abiathar, was, under David, the first
priest of the Jerusalem sanctuary. This cult object too had been an
heirloom handed down in the family of Moses.

We learn further that the serpent had a special cultic
name. It was called *nehushtan*. The name, which has an antiquarian
form, contains a twofold allusion: to the word *serpent* (*nahash*) and to
the word *bronze* (*nehosheth*). Its actual meaning is *brazen serpent*
and confirms the tradition which dates the story back to the time of
Moses.

Finally, a most important aspect, the notice relates that a
special cult was devoted to the serpent. That is why it fell victim to the
reform efforts of Hezekiah. According to the wording of the text, that
was not a later aberration but a cult which apparently existed as far
back as men remembered. Possibly, even at the time of Hezekiah, the
brazen serpent was credited with special healing powers; the essential thing was not this, but the cult devoted to it.

When we consider the ancient account in this light, it also
shows features which suggest that the same assumption can be made
for the Mosaic period. In spite of the framework it is apparent that not
only is a healing miracle related here but in addition cultic features
glimmer through the account. First of all, mention is made not simply
of serpents but of particular demonic beings, the *serafim*. According

to the representation given by Isaiah (6:2), they were hybrid creatures with wings, of a semi-divine character; according to the belief of later generations — and probably of the ancients also — they belonged to the god's retinue as his servants. To ward them off, the serpent symbol was set up. In Numbers 21:8 this symbol itself is designated as a "seraph." It consequently represented a semi-divine being that was entitled to be worshiped in its own right.

Further, the way in which it was set up also points in this direction. It was not simply placed upon a pole; this would be sufficiently designated by *makkel* or simply *'es*. Rather, it was connected with the "flagstaff." We recall that such a flagstaff was mentioned in connection with the story of the fight with Amalek. Here it is a sacred object in front of which people swear an oath, and it is named "flagstaff of YHWH."

The impression we are left with is that the oldest account arranged and rearranged the subject matter to fit it smoothly into its own time. It speaks of an object dating from Mosaic times, which then enjoyed special veneration and apparently had a special mythological significance. In order somewhat to veil this significance, which went back to primeval magic conceptions, the cult symbol was made more innocuous by representing it as a memorial of a healing miracle. The cult object itself, the flagstaff with the seraph, points to a period and a religious stratum which are older than the days of Moses. It was probably a survival from the ancient Levitic cult of Kadesh. Like many other antiquities, it too was taken over by Moses, adapted to the YHWH cult, and reinterpreted by a new legend. For the healing miracle in itself did not require the serpent-staff; could not YHWH, who sent the serpents directly, bring about the healing from the snakebite? And why should those perish who could not gaze upon the serpent-staff because they were too far away or because it was dark? So then, not the healing miracle but the cultic serpent-staff is the core and original element of this legend.

Moses' Mask[113] and the Teraphim[114]

In Exodus 34:29-35 a remarkable story of the "mask of Moses" has been handed down to us. It presents particular difficulties for analysis because it belongs to accounts which have been thoroughly revised. From several examples, however, we now know what that means: here aspects that were objectionable from a later point of view have been obscured and reinterpreted. But just such stories are the ones that supply especially instructive information about the original phases and early stages of religion.

34:29. "And it came to pass, when Moses came down from Sinai that Moses did not know that the skin of his face was radiant since he had spoken with Him. 30. When Aaron and the children of Israel saw Moses, behold, the skin of his face was radiant, and they were afraid to come nigh him. 31. And Moses called to them; and Aaron and all the rulers of the congregation returned to him, and Moses spoke to them. 32. And afterward all the children of Israel came nigh, and he commanded them all that YHWH had spoken to him on Sinai. 33. And when Moses had finished speaking with them, he put a covering on his face. 34. And when Moses came before YHWH to speak with him, he took the covering off each time, until he came out again; then he went out and spoke to the children of Israel what he was commanded. 35. Then the children of Israel saw the face of Moses that it was radiant, and Moses again put the covering on his face until he went in to speak with Him."

From a formal point of view the story is now found in the framework of the Priestly Code. But behind its present form, which is the result of a revision, is an account that in style and contents deviates completely from all that the Priestly Code reports elsewhere; it is related to the accounts of the ancient stratum. The revision is betrayed by a number of contradictions. The story begins by relating an event that occurred once but which the later storyteller transferred to Sinai; owing to Moses' long dialogue with the deity, a reflection of the divine radiance remained upon Moses' face. This reflected splendor[115] is imagined as real radiance from which the others flee in terror. From verse 34 onwards, however, quite a different situation is presupposed; here Moses' regular communication with the deity is spoken of, that is, in the Ohel mo'ed, the Tent of Meeting. The event, occurring once, has become a permanent institution. Moses' precautionary measure is represented in a contradictory manner also. When Aaron and the nobles were afraid to approach Moses, Moses called to them reassuringly; they came up, he spoke with them, and *then only* did he lay a covering upon his face. This he also did later after his regular meetings with YHWH.

The result is the strange phenomenon of Moses' face remaining concealed from the Israelites for forty years; only when facing the deity did he uncover his face. Properly speaking, one should expect the opposite: when man steps before the deity he veils his face. So it is in the revelation at the burning bush (3:6), at the theophany in Exodus 33:22, and also with Elijah in 1 Kings 19:13. As a matter of fact events were apparently told in this way in the original version of the ancient account. When the late redactor — for reasons which we shall learn later — reversed the sequence of events, he was obliged to find a new motive for the veiling and he introduced the fear of the radiance of Moses' face. But he was not consistent for, in spite of the radiance, Moses spoke with Aaron and the princes and only then did he put on the covering.

What was it in the ancient account that caused the revision? We assume that once upon a time it was related as follows: When Moses entered the tent of God, he put a covering on his face; he took it off when he came out. To a later writer what could be objectionable in this? Only one thing: the *kind of covering*. In our text a special term for covering is used, *masweh*, which occurs nowhere else. The stem means to "enwrap," to "veil," from which comes the antiquarian and rare word *suth*, "garment" (Gen. 49:11). The ancient word is chosen here with reason; it has quite a specific meaning, which is translated by the word "covering" only in a preliminary way. As we can still recognize from comparison with the Aramaic *maswen*, it denotes the mask.

That of course would cause objections later. What would it mean that Moses stepped before the deity clothed with a mask? We shall discuss that presently. But we are now asking, What would be the meaning, according to our text, if Moses permanently walked about with a mask on his face? That really makes no sense, and there would certainly have been better means for veiling the radiance than a mask, unless the redactor of the story had been bound to use precisely this word. But just the senselessness of this representation is the strongest proof that our suggestion is justified: namely, that here once upon a time the contrary was told.

Covering the face with a mask for purposes of divine worship is a custom occurring with many peoples and is true today with a number of primitive tribes. It still existed with the Greeks of classical times and from it there developed, from cultic roots, the

stage play. Symbolically, the mask signifies the assimilation to the
deity. The priest put it on when he stepped before the deity, and took
it off when the cultic ceremony was over. It is quite understandable
that the retention of this very ancient usage in our story caused
offense later. Here the same development is traceable that, in the case
of the brazen serpent, induced a reformer like Hezekiah to abolish an
ancient usage, without regard to its Mosaic origin; that usage no
longer corresponded to the views of his time. And likewise in the case
of the cultic mask, which is a survival of prehistoric religion, we are
fully entitled to ascribe it to the ancient Levirate before Moses.

The cultic mask, it seems, was preserved to more recent
times in yet another form, and it was called *teraphim*. Formerly the
teraphim was thought to be a house god, in the manner of the lares and
penates among the Romans, because it is repeatedly named as an
object in the house without any connection with the public cult; it was
thought to be a small statue of a deity, such as has been frequently
discovered in excavations in Palestine. But that certainly is not right.
Generally, in the period which can be historically grasped by us,
representations of the deity do not occur with the Israelites. It would
be remarkable indeed if that one exception to the general rule had to
be made.

In the story of Jacob's flight from Laban's service (Gen.
31), Rachel stole her father's teraphim. To escape discovery at the
examination of the tent she put it under a saddle of a camel and sat
down on it. If then the teraphim was an idol, it must have been one of
those little figures that have been found in great numbers, since it
could be placed under the camel saddle. That, however, fits very
badly with the story in 1 Samuel 19, in which the teraphim again
played a part. When Saul sent his bailiffs to arrest David, David's
wife, Michal, let him escape through the window; putting a teraphim
in the bed she covered it up and indicated to the messengers that
David was ill. In the half-light they believed that the figure in the bed
was David. Here the teraphim is bound to be life-size. An unbridge-
able gap appears to exist between the two stories, which disappears,
however, when we assume that the teraphim, as has been repeatedly
suggested, was a face mask. This can give the appearance of a man
and can also be placed beneath the saddle of a camel. If this suggestion is correct, we then have the thread which connects this cult
object with the story of Moses' mask.

What we know about the use made of the teraphim agrees perfectly with this assumption. For the prophet Hosea (ca. 740), the teraphim is still an object of self-evident and justifiable veneration, which could be missed only with difficulty. (From this alone it becomes clear that it cannot be an idol!) By way of a threat he says (Hos. 3:4): "For the children of Israel shall sit solitary many days without a king and without prince and without sacrifice and without pillar and without *ephod and teraphim*." In this connection the teraphim was an object of the public cult and closely connected with the ephod. We find the teraphim again connected with the ephod in the second passage, where historically it is mentioned with the priest of Dan (Judg. 17:5; 18:14; 18:20). Here the kind of relationship between the two becomes even clearer: like the ephod, the teraphim belonged to the oracle.[116] What function the teraphim had here is scarcely in doubt: when the priest wanted to consult the oracle, he girded himself with the ephod, put on the face mask, and then stepped before the deity. At a later time people took offense at this (a time in which the Urim and Thummim had fallen into oblivion and the teraphim had become independent) and declared the teraphim to be idol worship.

But for us the history of the Moses' mask has now become perfectly clear. When Moses entered the tent of God to consult the deity, he put on the face mask, the teraphim, and — we may add — girded himself with the ephod, as was done for centuries after him. The remodeling of our story is likely to be later than the time of Hosea.

The mask, which appears here in the public cult only, passed over into the family cult. Whether this was the case in very ancient times, we cannot decide. The two stories in which the teraphim occurs, Rachel and David, bear the character of fluctuating legends. The first was written down in the time of David, the second later still. Only for this period is there evidence that the teraphim was used in a private house. The evolution of the teraphim is also found with other nations: the transition from the public cult into the house cult; then to a spectral tool; and later still to a comical one that, however, continues to have a glimmer of the sinister old aspects.

The Sacred Tent[117]

At first glance one has the impression that the ancient

accounts about the sacred tent do not relate any story at all (the name of the tent is either YHWH's tent or tent of the dwelling, tent of the law, tent of the testimony, most frequently *Ohel mo'ed,* that is, "tent of appointment," of meeting, encounter, assembly). But that is impossible, for such a sacred tent *must* certainly have existed. It is needed as the abode of the ark and of the other sacred objects like the Urim and Thummim, ephod, teraphim, serpent, and flaggstaff. The fact is that all the information handed down to us about the tent dates from comparatively late strata of the tradition. That is also what has induced a great scholar like Wellhausen to declare the tent of meeting, *Stifts-Zelt* (Luther), and its description to be an imaginary product of the later priesthood.

This point of view is untenable. For, as we shall soon see, the sacred tent was an object that can be proved to have really existed until the time of Solomon. The accounts about the sacred tent in the wilderness are, it is true, mainly preserved by the Priestly Code, but undoubtedly they go back to ancient accounts. The detailed description of the tent, given by the Priestly Code, in all probability goes back to eyewitness descriptions, although certain embellishments have been added.

What became of this tent of God when the Israelites invaded Canaan? The tent and the sacred objects which it contained were separated; while the ark, the ephod with the Urim and Thummim, and the brazen serpent were set up in the Temple of Shiloh, the tent remained in Gibeon. We have quite unequivocal reports about it through the Chronicler whose work, otherwise historically worthless, as is well-known, contains a number of very reliable, ancient pieces of information. He relates (2 Chron. 1:3): "Solomon went to the high place that was at Gibeon; for there was the Ohel mo'ed, which Moses, the servant of God, had made in the wilderness."[118] 1 Chronicle 21:29 is just as clear: "The tabernacle [*mishkan*] of YHWH, which Moses had made in the wilderness, and the altar of burnt-offerings were at that time on the high place in Gibeon." Since we know from Joshua 9 that the first sanctuary of YHWH on the soil of Canaan was erected at Gibeon, this information is well confirmed.

It appears that the tent as such did not play a special role in the Mosaic period. It is mentioned in the older sources only twice: Exodus 33:7-11 and Numbers 12. In both passages it is suggested (by the Priestly Code) that the tent was set up outside the camp. That, however, is surely a later alteration of the real circumstances in order to attribute a particular sanctity to the tent as such, which it did not have according to the ancient sources; for here the Priestly Code contradicts itself. It reports (Exod. 33:8-10) that each time Moses went into the tent, the Israelites standing in front of their tents watched him until he disappeared within. That is possible only if the tent stood in the midst of the camp, otherwise it could not be seen from everywhere. Accordingly, Exodus 25:8 commands: "Let them make me a sanctuary, that I may dwell among them." Above all, however, the "camp-order" of the tribes (Num. 22), given in detail by the Priestly Code, is expressly based on the assumption that the tent is *within the camp* and the tribes "pitch round about the Ohel mo'ed."

According to the original conception YHWH, as we have seen, permanently dwelt in the tent enthroned upon the wings of the cherubim, with the ark as his footstool. This very anthropomorphic conception also caused offense later; each time YHWH wants to speak with Moses, the Priestly Code has him descend from heaven in the pillar of cloud and after the speech ascend. It can hardly be said that this conception is less anthropomorphic than the original one.

In any case it is evident from these accounts that in the Mosaic period there really existed a tent of God for the sacred vessels, which would be expected. Its name, Ohel mo'ed, "tent of meeting," has had many interpretations. Gressman decided that here YHWH met in deliberation with the angels. But this conception is very artificial and has no support whatever in the sources. Rather, we have seen that the phrase "YHWH of hosts" refers to the military hosts of Israel. It thus follows quite naturally that the tent, in which the ark stands, was the place at which YHWH met with the Israelites or, if you wish, with the elect, who came to consult with him. There neither is, nor was, any account about the tent with a primitive or mythological bent; precisely this fact proves that it was an object with a purely practical use, namely, the housing of the sacred vessels. Only when the tent had come to stand in Gibeon devoid of its contents did the Zadokites, officiating in it (1 Chron. 16:39), surround it with a new halo of special sanctity, which then passed from it to the Temple in Jerusalem.

6

Sinai [119]

‒‒‒‒‒‒‒‒‒‒‒‒‒‒‒‒‒‒‒‒‒‒‒‒‒‒‒‒‒‒‒

The Oldest Account and Its Characteristics

The core and soul of the Mosaic period, according to the prevailing tradition, were the giving of the law on Mt. Sinai. And rightly so. On Sinai Moses received the fundamental law of the Ten Commandments, the foundational document of Israel's religion.

There arise two problems which are closely connected with one another: the first is the external place of this giving of the law, the site of Mt. Sinai, and its proper frame within the desert march; the second is the inner place of this legislation and its relation to that of the law of Kadesh.

There is no part of the Bible which has been so skillfully and so frequently revised as the narratives about Mt. Sinai. This episode has a very strong influence on the other narratives. It happens repeatedly that the account of an event has been transferred to the Mt. Sinai cycle or has been brought into association with it, whereas intensive research shows that it belongs to Kadesh. It is as if Mt. Sinai was the mysterious magnet mountain which draws everything toward itself. Indeed, the later the accounts, the more they are centered around Mt. Sinai.

These circumstances make it even more necessary to penetrate as far as possible into the oldest form of the account. While critical analysis of the texts is here specially difficult, it is also very rewarding. Only after uncovering the oldest form of the account can both problems be traced back to their simplest form or can we succeed in finding a solution for them.

The textual material, which we will examine, is surprisingly limited. It comprises no more than chapters 19, 20, and 24 of the Book of Exodus. Before this Sinai cycle are narratives from Kadesh (chap. 15:22 to the end of chap. 18); between chapters 20 and 24 is

inserted the Book of the Covenant, and from chapter 25, which
without doubt belongs to P, we have the minute description of the
mishkan, the "Tabernacle." Thus a limit is given, clear and free from
objection.

Chapter 19 is the introduction to the giving of the law on
Mt. Sinai. If we regard this chapter as a unit, it gives rather a grotesque picture of the external events. In verse 3 Moses climbs the
mountain in order to receive a statement from the deity; in verse 7 he
descends and reports it to the people. At the close of verse 8 he again
ascends the mountain in order to receive ceremonial instructions; in
verse 14 he again descends. In verse 20 he ascends the mountain for
the third time, while already the theophany appears in full majesty —
but still the revelation[120] does not come! In verses 21 and 24 he once
more receives an express command to descend in order again to
ascend with Aaron. He descends (v. 25), and now, while he is below,
follows the proclamation of the Ten Commandments! (20:1-17). For
what purpose is the ascending and descending repeated three times?
That is hardly tenable. No uniform account would describe events in
such a manner.

This grotesque form of the account has arisen only because many hands worked over the oldest, simple narrative; ever
new details of embellishment were added in order to heighten the
solemnity and grandeur of the event. The proclamation of the law is
postponed for three days, so that the people may first "consecrate
themselves." The multiplicity of the accounts leads to other repetitions: the appearance of the mountain is twice described, verses 16
and 18; the prohibition about approaching it is given twice, verses 12
and 21.

The oldest account, however, is quite short and simple.
19:18. "Now Mt. Sinai was altogether in smoke,[121] and its smoke
ascended as the smoke of a furnace, and the whole mount quaked
greatly. 20. And YHWH came down [122] on the top of the mount, and
YHWH called Moses to the top of the mount, and Moses went up.
20:1. There YHWH spoke the following words. Now follow the Ten
Commandments." The Ten Commandements are found today in the
account of E. But there can be no doubt that J also handed them down
(see 34:28). In the Hebrew text of 20:1, Elohim, "god," is found; but
the LXX and Targum read YHWH, and that is surely a more original
reading.

After the Book of the Covenant which is inserted here
(chap. 21-23), this ancient account is resumed again with a short
narrative. In it, Aaron, Nadab, and Abihu are inserted and so is a
covenant-sacrifice (24:2-8). The narrative itself goes: 24:1 "And unto
Moses he said, Come up unto YHWH, you and the seventy elders of
Israel. Then Moses and the seventy elders of Israel went up. 10. And
they saw the God of Israel; and there was the likeness of a pavement
of sapphire under his feet, and like the very sky for clearness. 11. But
against the nobles of Israel he did not raise his hand. They beheld
God, and ate and drank."

A third short piece is immediately added to this, again
interrupted throughout by numerous additions that are obviously
later because of repetitions and colorful imagery. The last words of
24:18 are taken up again by 34:28, which belongs to this account as a
direct continuation. 24:12. "YHWH said unto Moses, Come up to me
into the mountain and be there, and I will give you the instructions
and commandments so that you may teach them.[123] 14. Then he
spoke to the elders, Tarry here until I come back unto you;[124] Aaron
and Hur are with you, whoever has a lawsuit let him go unto them. 15.
And Moses went up into the mountain, and the cloud covered the
mountain. 18b. And Moses was on the mountain forty days and forty
nights. 34:28. And he was there with YHWH forty days and forty
nights; he neither ate bread nor drank water, and he wrote upon the
tables the words of the covenant, the Ten Words."

On this occasion only one special point shall be mentioned
in which the tradition wavers: whether the stone tables were inscribed by God or by Moses. The usual interpretation is that the
original tables were inscribed by God himself and that the second
tables were inscribed by Moses; they were prepared by him after he
had smashed the first in his anger over the Golden Calf. The existing
testimony for the first tables is dubious, because the writing by the
deity is found only in later additions: it is, first, an announcement in
24:12, where the word order shows that the words "which I have
written" are an addition; then, as a completed procedure in 31:18,
which quite outside the context is again handed down in P (characteristic of it is the expression "tables of the testimony"). The tradition for the second tables is not uniform either. In a later account
(34:1) Moses receives the command to prepare two tables and bring
them up into the mountain, so that the deity may inscribe them with

his own hand. In the execution of the work, however (34:27 and 28), it was Moses who put the writing on the tables.

In the oldest account no difference is made between the first and second tables. The second are the only tables, as 34:28 joins immediately with 24:18. The episode of the Golden Calf is interpolated later and duplicates the event.

We shall see that these three short pieces, which constitute the oldest layer of the Sinai narratives, are not consecutive. The first and third sections obviously belong together. There follows first the proclamation of the "Ten Words" as the foundation of the covenant between God and the people, then the writing down and at the same time the further instruction of Moses during forty days.

A different atmosphere is felt in the second section. What is happening here? Moses and the elders of the people are summoned by YHWH to the mountain. There is nothing here of fire and clouds. "They beheld the God of Israel, ate and drank." What is presented in a very ancient form and in entirely mythological terms is the conclusion of a covenant between God and people. The narrative is not a supplement to the other two pieces, but a second, independent account running parallel to them. It is as it were the primary rock of the tradition; it narrates the conclusion of the covenant in the most rudimentary form. The representatives of the people are summoned, as is proper for a solemn treaty. The appearance of the deity is not described, but is presented in quite a human and mythological fashion. It is twice reported that the elders beheld the deity. The surroundings of the deity are depicted with the features of heaven: shining blue stone beneath, clear as the heaven itself. Those invited are so near the deity, they behold it so closely that they must fear for their lives; hence the peculiar assurance: against the nobles of Israel he did not raise his hand.

The meal is the culmination of the scene. The deity is the host. The guests who eat with god thereby enter into unity with him. The primeval ideas expose the bedrock of the language. *Berith*, "covenant," signifies properly "the meal"; *kārath berith*, "to conclude a covenant," means properly "to carve the meal." That is what we see here. Otherwise man is wont to offer up a sacrifice to the deity, and while cutting up the animal for the sacrifice, he gives the deity its portion and solemnly consumes the meal in its presence; he thus comes into communion with the deity. That is why the covenant-sacrifice in the text immediately preceding is nothing other than a later variant of our narrative. But in this case it is not man who brings the sacrifice. The deity itself gives the guests hospitality in its lodging; they eat with it in its presence.

That is the deepest covenant-communion which human beings can achieve. That at the same time is the most rudimentary representation, yet a stratum older than the oldest of the other Sinai narratives. In this oldest story of all, however, we find a different scene of action. We shall speak still further about the milieu of the Sinai stories. But the mountain, which is described in the story of the elders, is not the volcanic Sinai. Here there ascends "no smoke like the smoke of a furnace." Here there is no thunder and no lightning. Here is shining light and clear azure in a festive but peaceable place for a sacrificial meal. The mountain is evidently the dwelling place of the deity. But *this* Sinai may be situated anywhere, at Kadesh or any other place; it is plainly the mountain of God.

We acquire from this an important piece of knowledge: in the oldest stratum of the tradition, the seat of God, Sinai, is not yet associated with the idea of the smoking, volcanic mountain. This is as true as it is in the revelation at the thornbush which, according to the interpretation of E, likewise belongs to the mountain of God, Horeb (Exod. 3:1), or as it is in the miracle of the spring at Massah-Meribhah, where, according to the same E, a rock in the neighborhood of the spring bears the name Horeb (Exod. 17:6).

It has now become essential for us to try to locate the place of the revelation, that is, the site of Mt. Sinai.

Where Was Mt. Sinai Situated?

The biblical statements about the location of Mt. Sinai are very vague and can hardly be placed geographically. The Priestly Code locates it in the "wilderness of Sinai," which does not help us very much. The Code distinguishes it from the "wilderness of Sin," but that, for purposes of determining the location, cannot be pinpointed more closely either. Of somewhat greater significance is that the Code repeatedly mentions a third name, a "wilderness of Zin," and according to all the statements, that is situated in the neighborhood of Kadesh (Num. 13:21; 20:1; 27:14; 33:36; 34:3-4).

We know E does not call the mountain of God Sinai, but Horeb. This, according to the allusion in Exodus 17:6, appears to be located by E in the region of the springs of Kadesh. J usually calls the mountain merely "the mountain" or "the mountain of God"; the name *Sinai* occurs in J only in Exodus 19:18, and there without any definite statement of the locality.

Since direct geographical statements are lacking, we are thrown back on conclusions made from indirect reports. These follow essentially from two aspects: the name and the descriptions of the mountain.

We have already said something about the name *Sinai* in chapter 2. The name is not to be separated from the rare word *sẹneh* for thornbush. It means therefore either "mountain of the thornbush" or "the thorn mount, the pointed mountain."

A name for a mountain similar to Sinai is found once again in the Bible, in 1 Samuel 14:4: *seneh*, and it also means the same, for it is here expressly denoted as *shen ha-sela'*, "rock-tooth" (also the word *shen* is to be regarded as related to *sn* and *ṣn*). Thus its name means "thornrock" also, and it can just as well be called Sinai.

We have seen that the burning thornbush as the dwelling place of YHWH has to be located in the district of Kadesh; accordingly, Mt. Sinai is to be sought there too. The rest of the statements agree with this. The name of the desert *Zin*, in which Kadesh is situated, means the same, "thorn."[125] The name Horeb must be interpreted as "swordrock," thus corresponding with the "thorn rock" which, according to E, lies near the springs of Kadesh.

It now becomes clear that for this stratum of our tradition Mt. Sinai is a mountain in the vicinity of Kadesh or in Kadesh itself. If, then, the "Sinai accounts" have been distinguished from the "Kadesh accounts," for this stratum of our tradition the two groups fall together. The giving of the law on Mt. Sinai and the giving of the law in Kadesh are for these sources not a contradiction but two different records of the same event.

The great difficulties of the problem emerge when we approach the description of the mountain and the procedure of the giving of the law, as they are described in the first and third sections of the ancient account. Here another picture arises: it is bound to be another Sinai which is being referred to. Whoever lets the description of the mountain and the giving of the law influence him impartially, even without the individual embellishments of the later accounts, cannot doubt for a moment but that it is the description of a volcano erupting. "The mountain was altogether in smoke and its smoke ascended as the smoke of a furnace, and the whole mountain quaked greatly." This natural phenomenon has nothing to do with storm, thunder, and lightning; it is more nearly the description, entirely accurate, of the outbreak of a volcano. Verse 24:15 agrees with it when it says: "The cloud covered the mountain."

But if the Sinai described here was an active volcano, it cannot be a mountain near Kadesh or in Kadesh. For, not only is no volcano found there today, but — and this can be said with complete certainty — there never were any volcanoes there. On few matters does geology give such complete information as about volcanic formations. Not only Kadesh but the entire Sinai peninsula also has never had volcanoes. This "smoking mountain," the eruption of which is described in colors which have been actually observed, must be sought elsewhere. Where?

The introduction to the Blessing of Moses (Deut. 33:2) suggests a definite place where Mt. Sinai can be sought. There it is said, "YHWH came from Sinai, and rose from Seir unto them. He shone forth from Mount Paran and came to Meribhath-Kadesh." Here a definite route is described, which the deity traveled over between Mt. Sinai and Kadesh; Mt. Sinai is far removed from Kadesh. If we take the route in reverse and draw a line from Kadesh to the Seir range (on both sides of the Southern Araba), this line leads into the district east and southeast of the head of the Gulf of Akaba.

At one time numerous volcanoes existed there. Inland from the east coast of the Red Sea stretches a long range of extinct volcanoes, the Harras. At least one of them in the neighborhood of Medina was active in the post-Christian era. Of others it may surely be taken for granted that they were active in an older historical period. Here, and only here, the volcanic Mt. Sinai of Exodus 19 must have been situated.

The district where we will seek it is the territory of Midian. That is a very important fact for the linking together of our tradition. It is indeed quite certain that the Israelites had connections with Midian. The question that has to be clarified is how an account about a volcanic eruption in Midian came to be admitted into Israelite tradition. We shall speak of this presently.

We seem to be faced with an insoluble contradiction. There are many indications that Mt. Sinai is to be sought near Kadesh and that "law and justice" were also proclaimed in Kadesh; another series of unmistakable signs connects Mt. Sinai to Midian. There is apparently no reconciliation between these contrasts and, in fact, numerous scholars, among them Gressmann, have endeavored to reach a decision in favor of one assumption or the other.

But we are not dealing with a genuine contrast at all, a real alternative. I should like to explain the situation as follows: *one* line of tradition knows of a Mt. Sinai near Kadesh, the dwelling place of YHWH with the burning bush. Another, entirely independent tradition tells of a volcanic mountain in Midian, which is likewise called Sinai and is regarded as the dwelling place of YHWH. Its eruption is viewed as a revelation of the deity and is brought into association with the law of the Ten Commandments. The antithesis is not a real one, but one existing only in literary history. There can be no doubt about it, within the Moses traditions of Sinai the Kadesh tradition represents the oldest stratum. The complication arose because the tradition of the fiery mountain in Midian has gradually attracted to itself a series of the Kadesh narratives; the later the account the more narratives there are.

More precise examination shows that this contradiction still exists within the Sinai tradition itself. Of the three sections, which deal with the conclusion of the covenant on Mt. Sinai (chaps. 19; 24:1-11; 24:12-18), only two are associated with the idea of a volcanic mountain; the middle section speaks of a mountain that is not a volcano but the seat of the deity. This section, which is the most ancient, belongs to Kadesh, whereas the two others are located in Midian. How has this Midianite tradition become part of our Moses tradition?

Through thousand-year-old conventions our ideas have become so fixed that any change of thought will be very difficult. In spite of this it must be pointed out with all possible precision and clarity that since the fiery Mt. Sinai must be situated in Midian and can be nowhere else, the Israelites on their desert march were never at that Mt. Sinai. Even the late list of stations in Numbers 33, which with unrestrained imagination has the Israelites wander through the wilderness for forty years in all directions, does not assert that they were in Midian. Therefore, attempts have been made repeatedly to identify Mt. Sinai with this or that mountain on the Sinai peninsula proper — a useless endeavor. But the Israelites were not in Midian, where the mountain must have been. If they had been there, Jethro would not have felt it necessary to visit his son-in-law Moses in Kadesh (and according to the later tradition to bring his family to him), but on the contrary Moses would have come to him, to Midian, and there have been his guest. It is then not possible that this Sinai tradition is the result of a national experience, such as, for example, the tradition of the exodus from Egypt and the catastrophe at the Sea of Reeds.

But beyond doubt, Moses himself was in Midian before he undertook his life's work. It is therefore quite conceivable that he knew about the active fiery mountain, which undoubtedly was known among the Midianites as the mountain of god. But there is indeed nothing, nothing at all which can prove that for the Midianites YHWH already was this deity, that they were "followers of YHWH" (Gressmann). It is, however, perfectly possible that Moses, who knew about an old Levitic tradition, recognized YHWH in this deity of the fiery mountain, indeed that he had there an experience of God similar to that of the burning thornbush, an experience that then was re-echoed in Exodus, chapter 19. For a spirit like Moses', just such an experience could be the means of freeing himself from the age-old belief in the locally restricted nature of the deity and of advancing toward the idea of the universality of God. In any case YHWH had to detach himself from this mountain if he wanted to come to the help of his people in Egypt (cf. Exod. 3:8). He did so in the form of the pillars of fire and of cloud, which bear features pointing to the god of the volcano; in this form YHWH led them to Kadesh. However, it is true, the other view is plausible and conclusive that the god, who appeared to Moses in the thornbush near Kadesh, hastened from Kadesh to assist his people in Egypt and, with them, returned from Egypt to his seat.

Furthermore, a second possibility, which satisfactorily explains the facts of the tradition, appears to me the more probable. In Midian there was, we suggested, yet another group of Levites who, following the catastrophe of the tribe of Levi, had drifted out to this place. They, basically, were adherents of YHWH, but they brought with them older and more primitive views of YHWH, traces of which we find again in the opposition of Aaron and Miriam to Moses. They no doubt saw YHWH as the deity of the fiery mountain, thus endowing him with traits which remained operative as undercurrents in the Israelite religion. When they joined with Israel at the rally of the people in Kadesh, they brought this Midianite-shaded Sinai tradition with them and effected its union with the older tradition of Kadesh. The picture of the fire-spitting Sinai, when compared with the modest mountain of God at Kadesh, appealed more and more to the senses and imagination, and gradually moved into the center of the narratives about the revelation, the giving of the law, and the covenant.

This is an attempt to gain an idea of the development that we can only infer from its literary strata. But there can be no doubt about the phenomenon itself, the double thread of the Sinai tradition, on the basis of the particulars found in our sources.

7

The Departure to Canaan

If the traditional conception is taken as a basis to explain the historical events, the forty years' stay of the Israelites in the wilderness of the Sinai peninsula remains completely unintelligible. If the children of Israel departed from Egypt in order to turn toward Canaan, which they could reach in ten to eleven days, why did they finally turn toward this objective after forty years? It is clear that the attempt of the tradition to explain that this was because of the disobedience of the people, resulting in their aimless wandering until that generation had died out, is historically quite unsatisfactory. But if one accepts, as we are doing, that the objective of the exodus was Kadesh, then there arises a second difficulty: why did the Israelites eventually leave the fertile oasis, in which they had found a secure home, to turn toward Canaan?

Two good reasons may be adduced for that. The first is the natural increase of the population in Kadesh. A Bedouin tribe, living under the favorable conditions that would be probable in the rich oasis, would show vigorous growth in spite of the high child mortality that existed in a primitive people and in spite of the losses through attacks and raids. Even if we take as a basis the present-day increase among the Arabs living in Palestine, under bad hygienic conditions, 2½ percent per annum, the population of the oasis might perhaps be doubled in the course of forty years. But second, we have to consider that related tribes would join the people under the firm guidance of Moses, the leader of genius. We need not suppose that all these tribes demanded and received admission to the oasis. In the vicinity of the oasis a number of tribes (as was the case later at the time of Muhammad) joined the original tribe in religion and politics and were ready for every warlike adventure; this fact suffices for the historical effectiveness of that factor. Kadesh became too small for the Israelites. The leader faced a decision of enormous gravity.

If the course of events was such as we are suggesting, we will be full of awe and admiration for Moses' greatness. He had already solved some gigantic tasks: the liberation of slave tribes from Egypt; the finding of a firm and secure home for them; and their transformation into a people through a national religion and wise laws. But now as an old man he started the greatest task of his life with fresh courage and a plan of genius: to give this new people a greater land, which alone would enable them to mark out their course toward a historic future. They stood on the southern border of this land, the land of Canaan, the longed-for goal of the Bedouins residing in the area. How Moses led the people into the Promised Land is told by the last Moses stories in the fourth and fifth books of the Torah.

The Story of the Spies [126]
(Num. 13 and 14)

The account of the sending out of the spies is now set in a remarkable context. Not very long after the exodus from Egypt, after the Israelites had arrived in Kadesh and had remained there for a while, Moses decided to send out spies, instructing them to bring back a report about the land of Canaan. The spies returned, but their report discouraged the people, who now preferred to return to Egypt rather than to march on. As a punishment for this faintheartedness and disobedience against the divine command, they had to wander in the wilderness for forty years.

The spies are sent out from Kadesh, and return there. But the event takes place at the beginning of the desert period and not at the close. That, however, is impossible; the sending out of the spies must immediately precede the occupation of the land of Canaan, or it would have been necessary to send out a second group of spies when the people were ready to depart (for what use was the information of forty years earlier?). We have already seen that the purpose of antedating the time was to find a plausible explanation for the fact that between the departure from Egypt and the entry into Canaan forty years passed. But this explanation is not a valid one, for in reality the Israelites remained in Kadesh during this period.

Still a second problem, which usually receives little attention, demands a solution. The spies set out from Kadesh northward to explore the land of Canaan and at least its southern portion. But when the Israelites set out on the conquest of the country, they did not go the way the spies took at all. According to the tradition before us, they did not march from Kadesh toward the north for several days (they could have been in Beersheba, at the border of the permanently cultivated land, in three days!), but instead they made an enormous detour which took them first into East Jordan and then into Canaan proper at Jericho. That would be so extraordinary that either it can hardly be believed, or a very detailed explanation for it has to be expected. Neither, however, does apply. That march is not only credible; it is a historical fact; and we do not get the slightest explanation for this curious direction of the march. We shall see that an analysis of the narratives, joined with the rest of the historical information that is preserved to us, shows a very complicated relationship between tradition and historical reality.

The account about the spies is in all sections thoroughly revised; at times so much so that the ancient kernel can be extricated only with difficulty. The copious additions and expansions belong mostly to the Priestly Code. The characteristics of the ancient account are: 1. Kadesh is properly situated in the wilderness of Zin, now, as in the Priestly Code, in the wilderness of Paran.

2. The work of the spies, which lasted forty days, extends only into the area of Hebron. The later redactor, however, made them cross on foot the entire land, as far as the sources of the Jordan in the north. Only the ancient version agrees with the available time indicated. The march to the sources of the Jordan alone would require at least thirty days, there and back (over 434 miles). The route, as far as the area of Hebron (about 112 miles) is concerned, requires about seven days on the basis of an average marching day and the same for the return journey. With the caution demanded of spies who march mainly at night and avoid the villages, one can reckon twelve plus twelve days, so that the other sixteen days could be used for inquiries and digressions from the shortest route. This corresponds roughly to the given circumstances.

3. In the ancient account only Moses is mentioned. He sent out the men, he received their report. Later, Aaron's name was inserted several times.

4. The original account does not contain the names of the spies, which is not a matter of great concern. Caleb in 13:20, if the name is original here, could be intended as gentilitial for the tribe.

The additions in chapter 13 are otherwise easily separated.

Part 1

13:17. "And Moses sent them [the spies] out to spy out the land of Canaan and said to them, Get up into the Negev and go up the mountains, 18. and see what kind of country it is; and the people who dwell in it, whether they are strong or weak, whether they are few or many, 19. and what the country is that they dwell in, whether it is good or bad and what cities they are that they dwell in, whether in camps or fortified places. 22. So they went up into the Negev and came to Hebron[127] (23. and they came unto the brook-valley of Eshkol; they cut down from there a branch with a single cluster of grapes and it had to be borne on a pole by two of them). 25. And they returned from spying out the land at the end of forty days, 26. and they went and came to Moses at Kadesh and reported and showed him the fruit of the land. 27. And they told him and said, We came into the land to which you sent us, and surely it flows with milk and honey, and this is its fruit. 28. Only the people who dwell in the land are fierce, and the cities are fortified and very great; and moreover we saw the descendants of Anak there, 33b. and we looked like grasshoppers to ourselves, and so we looked to them."

Part 2

14:2a. "The children of Israel murmured[128] against Moses and said, 3. Why does YHWH bring us into this land to fall by the sword and our children to become a prey? Is it not better for us to return unto Egypt? 4. And they said one to another, Let us make a captain and let us return unto Egypt! 26. Then YHWH spoke unto Moses saying, 27b. I have heard the murmurings of the children of Israel which they keep murmuring against me. 28. Say unto them, As I live! says YHWH, as they have urged me, so will I do to them! 29. Your carcasses shall fall in this wilderness. 31. But your children of whom you say, They will become a prey! Them I will bring there, and they shall conquer the land, which you have rejected. 39. When Moses spoke these words to the children of Israel, the people mourned greatly."

Part 3

40. "In the early morning they got them up to the top of the mountain saying, Lo, we are here and will go up unto the place which YHWH has commanded, for we have sinned. 41. And Moses said, 42. Do not go up, for YHWH is not among you, lest you be smitten down before your enemies. 44. But they presumed to go up on the top of the mountain, though nevertheless the ark of the covenant of YHWH and Moses did not depart out of the camp. 45. Then the Amalekite and the Canaanite, who dwelt in that hill country, came down and smote them and dispersed them even unto Hormah."

An analysis of the text discloses that in 13:1-16 the Priestly Code gives a detailed list of the names of the spies; the beginning of the actual account is verse 17. Verse 20 repeats verse 19 and anticipates verse 23. Verse 21 gives the later point of view, already proved above as incorrect, according to which the land is explored as far as the sources of the Jordan. Verse 24 is a gloss on the name Eshcol. Verse 29 is an ethnographic gloss. Verses 30 to 33 present the internal contradictions among the spies, which for the result, the impression on the people, are immaterial; the purpose of the addition is above all to give a special place to Caleb.

14:1 is the later version of the Priestly Code, as is borne out by the expression 'edah; the same holds for 2b, the essential content of which is repeated in verse 3. Verses 5 to 25 in the style of P give long-winded discussions between Moses and the people and Moses and YHWH, and in conclusion a prophecy about Caleb. Verse 27a is impossible beside verse 27b, from which, moreover, some words have slipped into the wrong place — at best, the beginning of verse 29 is an old constituent; the remainder including verse 30 belongs to the Priestly Code. Verse 32 repeats verse 29a; verses 33 to 35 are the subtle explanation of the Priestly Code for the forty years of wandering in the wilderness, because the spies took forty days! Verses 36 to 38 contain a personal judgment on the ten spies who criticized the country unfavorably. In verses 40 to 45 we have eliminated slight additions and repetitions.

Now for the matter itself. The oldest attainable account is very simple. The spies press in as far as the Hebron district and, returning after forty days, give their report: the land is good, but difficult to conquer. The people are becoming fainthearted; divisions appear, one section of the people wants to choose a new leader. By way of punishment they are condemned to remain forty years in the wilderness. Full of repentance they now want to start on the conquest against Moses' advice, but north of Hormah they are defeated.

A closer look, however, shows that this form of the tradition, which we have inferred as being the oldest attainable here, can hardly be the original one. Very different historical facts appear indistinctly through it.

The main problem seen historically is not that of finding an explanation for the forty-year stay in the wilderness. We have this explanation (namely, the continuing stay in Kadesh), but it is not very helpful. If we put the story of the spies at the end of the wilderness period (and precisely then!), there remains one great riddle.

The entire account presumes as self-evident that the invasion of Canaan is to come from the south. That is why at the close of our account the people mistakenly make the advance in this direction. If the report of the spies had turned out well, if the people had been ready for the invasion, Moses would have had to continue the march northward. Why then did he make the gigantic detour by East Jordan? Also, following tradition, at the second, final departure they could immediately have taken the nearest road! The disobedience of the people and the new way are not connected at all! In the present form of the tradition there is an inner contradiction: Moses, who accepts the report of the spies, afterwards follows another route; the people, who do not accept the report, in spite of that go the direct way, even though they are unsuccessful.

This suggests that the disagreement was really of a different kind. If Moses chose the detour, he must have devised this plan earlier, for indeed it does not depend on the spies' report. In that case, therefore, he would have had no need whatever to send out the spies, since the south country as far as Hebron would interest him little if he intended to break through at Jericho. On the other hand, if we were not influenced by the way tradition presents it, the simplest assumption would be that the section of the people which really made the sudden advance from the south had planned from the beginning to go in this direction and for that purpose sent out the spies. According to this theoretical consideration, the contrast would then be: a section of the people went against Moses' will, the south-north route. Do we then have traces of such an original basis for our account? There are in fact such traces.

At the conclusion of our account we are told that the people undertook an advance to the north, setting out from Kadesh, but were repulsed "even to Hormah." Accordingly the battle took place north of Hormah. As the Israelites returned to Kadesh, according to our account, they gave up Hormah too or did not conquer it at all. A parallel to this account telling of the same event is in Numbers 21:1-3. This account says (after making some small corrections of the text):[129] 21:1 "When the Canaanite, who dwelt in the Negev, heard that Israel was coming by way of Tamar, he fought against Israel and took some of them away captive. 2. And Israel vowed a vow unto YHWH: If you give this people into my hand, then I will place their cities under the ban. 3. YHWH heeded the plea of Israel and gave the Canaanite into its hands, and they placed them and their cities under the ban. Therefore the name of the place was called Hormah, 'city of the ban'."

This account, which is completely independent of the saga about the spies, is in several respects very interesting and important. First of all, Moses is not mentioned by a single word. The actor is "Israel." Israel fights, promises to keep the ban, and conquers Hormah. That fully agrees with one presupposition of our theory. We have before us here, proceeding independently, a section of the people with whom Moses is not present. In addition, the different outcome of the battle is very remarkable.

In the story of the spies the Israelites suffered defeat north of Hormah and returned to Kadesh; in the independent account they conquered Hormah and other cities of the district. And yet, in both cases only one and the same event is being dealt with. There can be no question of an attack on the Negev taking place twice in the time of Moses. Only the representation of the event is very different. While in Numbers 21 the battle for Hormah is a stage in the advance of the tribes into Canaan, in Numbers 14 it is a misguided act of disobedience, which must therefore fail. It is immediately clear that Numbers 21 is nearer to historical reality, and that the connection of the story of the spies with the march to Hormah is artificial.

But most important is the view that this short narrative opens up. What became of the conquered city of Hormah? What did the Israelites do after the conquest of this district? Of this nothing is reported here. The conquest of Hormah appears as an isolated action without any further consequences. That, historically, is impossible.

THE STORY OF THE SPIES

If linking it to the story of the spies is merely artificial, we should expect the advance of the Israelites into Canaan from the south to follow on the conquest of Hormah.

There is in fact a third and most important source that gives Hormah a place in this connection: the account of the conquest as given in Judges, chapter 1.

It would take us too far afield to give an exact analysis of this fundamental historical document which I have discussed previously.[130] Indeed, in this document the advance of the Israelites into Canaan from two directions, the south and the east, is reported as a fact. There, once again, a notice about Hormah is found in Judges 1:17: "Judah went with Simeon, his brother, and they smote the Canaanites, who inhabited Zephath, placed them under the ban and called the name of the city Hormah."

Here again the same event only can be meant, for the city cannot be twice "banned" and destroyed. This is assured by the mention of the ban and the renaming of the city as in Numbers 21. From this we learn the former name of the city, Zephath, "watch-tower." But above all, now the event stands in a clear historical context. At the invasion of Canaan a section of the tribes marched from Kadesh directly northward, and the capture of Zephath-Hormah was only the first step to the final establishment in the Negev and the mountains of Judah. The general expression *Israel* in Numbers 21 likewise carried here a particular limitation. At the conquest of Hormah two tribes were named, Judah and Simeon. But still other tribes had a share in the total enterprise. Of these, two at least can certainly be determined: Ḳayin (1:16) and Caleb (1:20). Most probably the tribe Rechab also had a share. It remained in the south and in the later history of Israel again played a part. Finally, we know that a section of the Levites also went with Judah and his "brethren," for in Judges 17:7, a generation later, we hear of Levites from Bethlehem-Judah; the Levite mentioned here is a grandson of Moses descended from Gershom. Thus we learn from these accounts that a coalition of five tribes, almost half of the people, undertook the conquest of the country from the south — contrary to the will of Moses.

Now we have attained a clear picture of the events which lie behind the story of the spies. At the departure from Kadesh a division of the people took place. The leader Moses along with the larger section of the people, and with the sacred objects, chose the route eastward; but a considerable section of the people, parting from him, went separately and were successful in the conquest of southern Palestine. The rupture reached even into the family of Moses: the branch of Eliezer, from which the priests of Shiloh are descended, went with Moses; the branch of Gershom, from which the priests of Dan are descended, went with Judah. That is the "disobedience" which is mentioned in the story of the spies. Now we can understand the peculiar transformation that the events have suffered in our tradition. The undertaking of the southern tribes could not be concealed entirely, but it was not allowed to succeed because it was undertaken against the will of Moses. The first step in this transformation and veiling of the events is the narrative of Numbers 21:1-3, an isolated success without further consequences. The second step of the transformation is the narrative of Numbers 14:40-45, a failure as a punishment for disobedience. We now understand the thorough revision of the story of the spies, the oldest attainable stratum of which is still far from the historical facts. But we have seen that the original course of events still allows for a restoration through the parallel accounts that have been preserved.

The problem we had at the beginning still remains: Why did Moses not also proceed to the direct conquest of Canaan from the south? Why did he choose the detour by East Jordan?

Here we can hardly do more than make conjectures. The best course may be to try to conclude from the subsequent events what were the motives. The southern tribes with their procedure had only a very limited success. The obstacle of the fortresses of Jerusalem-Gezer, which they could not overcome, called a halt to their advance. These are the "great fortified cities" that are mentioned in the report of the spies. So it came about that by a strip of Canaanite territory the southern tribes remained completely shut off from the northern tribes for two hundred years. With superior insight, Moses clearly recognized and rightly assessed that obstacle; he decided to circumvent it from the east in order to secure for his people the best part of the land north of that ring of fortresses.

Yet another reason for the route by the east is suggested. The territory of East Jordan underwent a lively change. Amorite tribes had broken into East Jordan territory from the north earlier. They were sections of the Amorite kingdom situated in Syria, of which we know through the Tell-Amarna letters,[131] and had probably yielded to the growing pressure of the Hittite empire in Asia Minor. One group had established a kingdom in the district of Bashan between the Jarmuk and Hauran; a second displaced Moab from the northern part of its territory between the Arnon and the Jabbok, and advanced as far as the Jordan. The news of such a displacement of peoples circulates in the desert from mouth to mouth and from tribe to tribe with astonishing speed and accuracy. Until a fresh balance in the population was achieved, here was a favorable opportunity for a determined advance of nomadic tribes intending to exploit the confusion in their own interest and to force an entry into West Jordan territory. That is likely to have been Moses' plan. If he had been able to carry it out with the full might of the entire people, which had become impossible by the secession of the southern tribes, success would surely have been even swifter and more complete than it was already. At all events, the march to the east bears the stamp of a plan devised sagaciously and on a grand scale, worthy of a leader like Moses.

The March into East Jordan

The direct route from Kadesh into East Jordan territory goes through the district of Edom. According to a fortuitous and therefore quite authentic notice (Num. 20:16), this district at that time stretched northwest into the region of the oasis of Kadesh. If the Israelites wanted to march through this district they had either to push their way by force of arms or to open negotiations. They had no reason to let it develop into a military conflict, for they did not intend to settle in this district; they had to reserve their forces for battles to come. Besides, Edom was a very noteworthy opponent, who at this time had already achieved a firm political organization (Gen. 36:31-39). The Israelites therefore attempted to open negotiations; this is reported in a short narrative in Numbers 20:14-21.

Here two sources are interwoven, which is immediately evident from several repetitions. The oldest account is quite short. 20:14. "Moses sent messengers from Kadesh to Edom: 16b. Behold, we are in Kadesh, the city on the borders of your territory. 17. We should like to pass through your land; we will not pass through field or through vineyard, neither will we drink of the water of the wells; we will walk only along the king's highway until we have passed your border. 18. But Edom said unto him, You shall not pass through what is mine, lest I come out with the sword against you.21:4. So they journeyed by the Reed Sea route in order to compass the land of Edom. 10. Then the Israelites marched on and camped at Oboth. 11. They journeyed from Oboth and camped at the Abarim springs. 12. From there they journeyed and camped in the brook valley of Zered. 13. From there they set out and camped on the other side of the Arnon."

While the later account (it names as the leader of the negotiations not Moses but "Israel") interpolates a long and moving speech, in which Edom[132] is appealed to as the "brother," the older account is short and factual. Moses made his overture. Edom rejected it curtly, emphasizing the refusal by a clear challenge. Moses made no attempt to force a passage through, but marched round the territory of Edom, turning toward the southeast almost as far as the Gulf of Akaba and then bending northward into the caravan route.

The account bears the stamp of complete historical authenticity. Its two essential points could not have been invented: the retreat before Edom (a later writer would have invented here the fiction of a splendid victory) and the strange detour toward the south. Even on this route the Israelites still had to cross the Edomite border district; but the Edomites allowed them through, glad to have turned aside the hungry landseekers. By itself the detour did not play an essential part in the march of the Israelites; it lengthened their route by about five or six days' marching. Thus they came to the Arnon, now the boundary between the territory of the Moabites and the Amorites.

The battle with the Amorites under King Sihon follows as the second stage of the march. The account about this (Num. 21:21-26, 32) has been revised by a later hand, following the model of the account about Edom. But its basis is in every respect historical. Israel defeated the Amorites at Jahaz on the border of the wilderness and took possession of the country between the Arnon in the south and the Jabbok in the north. It is not probable, though, that the Israelites now colonized the cities in this territory; a farseeing leader like Moses must have realized that every weakening of the impetus of his people by such a splintering, before the people had achieved their proper military objective, the conquest of West Jordan, was dangerous. The account about Gad and Reuben, discussed below, deals with this problem.

It may, however, be considered as certain that in this district Israelite tribes, precisely the tribes of Gad and Reuben, were already settled and had intermingled with Moabites. The Mesha inscription[133] (about 840) says of Gad, "The people of Gad dwelt in Ataroth from of old."[134] The Moabites considered the original inhabitants to be these Israelites, because they were already there when the Moabites invaded the land. Since the Moabites occupied the land before the time of Moses, the tribe must have set foot in East Jordan territory considerably earlier, presumably with the movement of the Habiru about 1400. We have no such clear and direct testimony about Reuben. But this tribe, which played a very small part in the subsequent period and at the time of the Blessing of Jacob (about 1000) was near extinction, passed into tradition as Israel's "firstborn." In the absence of other distinctions this title has been traced back to Reuben as an "old" tribe that dwelt for a long time in East Jordan. Since both tribes, Gad and Reuben, were by tradition reckoned to be the "sons of Jacob," there remains only the assumption that they joined the Israel coalition at the time the related Israel tribes under Moses appeared in East Jordan.

In the account of the victory over the Amorite King Sihon,[135] an interesting song is inserted (21:27-30), which has given rise to many discussions.

27. Come ye to Heshbon!
    Let the city of Sihon be built and established!
28. For a fire is gone out of Heshbon,
    A flame from the city of Sihon,
    It has devoured the cities of Moab,
    It has swallowed up the heights of Arnon.
29. Woe to you, Moab!
    Lost, the people of Chemosh!
    He has given away his sons as fugitives,
    And his daughters as captives.
    [The rest is mutilated and unintelligible.]

Numerous theories have been advanced about the meaning of this song and its historical background; almost all start from incorrect presuppositions. It is neither a satirical song of Israel about Moab, nor is it one about Sihon; it is not a reflection on the battles of Israel with Moab in the ninth century either. If we do not let ourselves be swayed by any prejudice, it can only mean one thing: it is a victory song of the Amorites over Moab, a glorification of Sihon, preserved by a strange coincidence and become immortal by its acceptance into the Bible. The correct explanation, as we give it here, is found earlier (v. 26), added by a later hand: "For Heshbon is the city of Sihon, the king of the Amorites; who fought against the former king of Moab and took all his land out of his hand as far as the Arnon. The singers sang about this!" Here the song is given. These singers are the singers of Sihon; the song itself is a mocking song of the Amorites about the Moabites.

It seems that the invasion of the Amorites into Moab and the destruction of their kingdom by the Israelites followed each other closely in time. The same King Sihon is named as conqueror and opponent of Israel, and we have no reason to doubt this statement. The land between the Arnon and the Jabbok, which the Israelites took away from him, then remained the center of discord between Israel and Moab. Israel never gave up its attempts to colonize it; Moab never gave up its right to own it.[136]

After the battle with Sihon there follows (21:33-35) a short account of the battle with the second Amorite kingdom, that of Bashan. This too is preserved only in a later revision; its kernel is likely to be historic. The battle was presumably engaged in only by a northern tribal group, Naphthali and Zebulun, which then invaded Galilee through the Jarmuk valley. It did not lead to the immediate colonization by the Israelites in East Jordan territory, but it did force a passage through to West Jordan territory. The final settlement took place two generations later through Manasseh clans.

There is no reason now to discuss the Balaam legend, since it has no connection with the Moses stories. One thing may be mentioned, however, that an analysis of the Balaam story leads us to locate the magician in Edom (instead of in Aram as is often the case). If that is so, this Balaam ben Be'or is apparently identical with Bela ben Be'or, King of Edom, mentioned in Genesis 36:32, which gives us an important clue for determining the chronology of the list of Edomite kings.

The story of the settlement of the tribes of Gad and

Reuben in East Jordan has no more need to be discussed here than the
Balaam legend. No part of the account in chapter 32 goes back to
actual old accounts. The fact was that the two tribes were living east
of the Jordan, and people sought to explain this from the events of the
Mosaic period. In reality, this presentation of the course of events is
quite impossible. It relates that the two tribes demanded the allotment
of territory in East Jordan, because "they had much cattle." Here
cause and effect are interchanged. How would only these two tribes
have much cattle after forty years of wandering in the wilderness?
They are granted the land after first pledging to cooperate in the
common conquest of Canaan. They agree, build pens for their cattle
in East Jordan, and leave behind their wives, their children, and their
cattle, while they cross the Jordan with the other tribes. How un-
worldly and without regard to the actual conditions is this presentation! The helpless families and the cattle would, of course, immediately become the booty of hostile raiders. Since this version is
impossible and we hear nothing of a later migration of the two tribes
into East Jordan, it again follows that at the time of Moses they were
already living there.

Baal Pe'or
(Num. 25)

The last story before the death of Moses is located at the
boundary of the Promised Land, at Beth Pe'or, in Shittim in the
Jordan valley according to a probably later localization. It is only
partly preserved in its oldest form; it is methodically inadmissible to
supplement it by the later expansions. For the deletion of the old
conclusion does show that the story contained something other than
the later continuations that have replaced it. 25:1. "When Israel dwelt
in Shittim, the people began to commit harlotry with the daughters of
Moab.[137] 2. They invited the people to the sacrifices for their gods,
and the people did eat of them and worshipped their gods. 3. And
Israel coupled itself in honor of Baal Pe'or. Then YHWH was in-
censed with Israel. 4. And YHWH said to Moses, Take all the chiefs
of the people and hang them up unto YHWH in the face of the sun.[138]
5. And Moses said unto the tribes of Israel, Slay everyone his people
who have coupled themselves in honor of Baal Pe'or."

It is not of great significance whether this story took place in Shittim or Beth Pe'or; the geographical situation of both is not very different, and the scene is generally clear. We find ourselves on the easterly, Moabite range of mountains at the Jordan valley, somewhere opposite Jericho, immediately before the entry of the Israelites into Canaan proper. Cultivated land is everywhere, and the Bedouin group of the Israelites are for the first time confronted with the life of the settled peasants. The Israelites, it is true, are Bedouins no longer in the full sense of the word. For a generation the will of the leader has kept them in one place where they could sow and reap, grow fruit trees, and keep domestic animals. But throughout those forty years they were isolated, as on an island; the mighty spirit of their leader used this period to bind them to the worship of the invisible and imageless God, and to hammer into them the elementary commandments of justice and morality. Now for the first time they come among other men; the "civilization" of their environment is about to overwhelm them. Here begins the tragic entanglement of Israel — tragic because inevitable — which continues during its entire history; its essence is the struggle between the desert-ideal and the assimilation to the events of daily life and the environment.

In Moab, Israel became familiar with the "Baal cults" of the Canaanite peoples. They were sensual peasant cults of fertility bound up with luxurious sacrificial banquets, drinking bouts, and sexual orgies held in honor of the deities, who were symbols of procreation and growth and abundant fertility. The question whether or not this Baal Pe'or is identical with Kemosh, the god of Moab (Gressmann), is immaterial. For these deities have no personal names, scarcely any personal individuality at all; they are simply called Baal (meaning "owner") of the cult place concerned.[139] This first encounter of Israel is the content of our short, mutilated story. The "harlotry with the daughters of Moab" is not simply "immorality" (a notion which, in the field of sex, is altogether remote to people of this ancient period) but signifies cultic prostitution, the self-abandonment of the woman in the service of the fertility god, a practice found in all the cults of the ancient east. Cult and sexual licentiousness in such a case belong together (as in the story of the Golden Calf); whoever submits to the one, surrenders to the other. This connection is expressed quite clearly in the story. The Israelites were seduced by the women to take part in the sacrifices: "then Israel coupled itself for, i.e., in honor of, Baal Pe'or." More is at stake than correcting a misdemeanor; it is historically a world decision. That is why Moses intervened with inexorable cruelty. The chiefs of the people, to the extent that they were accomplices, died a cruel death but with religious ceremonies. The rare expression *hoḳe'a* is used here for the first time (from the root *yḳ'*, "to dislocate;" cf. Gen. 32:26 and, in the same sense, 2 Sam. 21:6,9,13). It denoted a special kind of death that served as the expiation for a sin and was carried out with religious ceremonies. The bodies were set out in the open air "before God" or "in the face of the sun." Because of the basic meaning "to dislocate," I suppose that this is a case of crucifixion, in which the body was hung up in an unnatural attitude, that is, dislocated. Moses further gave the order to slay all those who "have coupled themselves for Baal Pe'or."

With this the story abruptly breaks off. We learn no more about the carrying out of the command and nothing about the consequences. The continuation in the Priestly Code (25:6-18) no longer has anything to do with this story and stands in flagrant contradiction to it. If the slaying of *all* the guilty was ordered by Moses, it is hard to see why the killing of *one* guilty person by Phinehas[140] should avert the punishment from the people. The episode is only understandable by the reward which Phinehas received for it: the hereditary priesthood. That, however, is superfluous; it had already been granted to Aaron and then been expressly assigned to Eleazar, the father of Phinehas (Num. 20:25-28). Moreover, the Priestly Code created a completely different milieu for the story. The opponents are suddenly Midianites — we do not know why — and the seductive women are Midianites; the whole is the devilish plot of Balaam, which becomes clear in the continuation, especially chapter 31. Also Balaam suddenly becomes a Midianite and is slain with "the five kings of Midian," he himself being one of the five. But at least three of the names of the five kings are Edomite (Rekem and Zur are names for Petra, Hur is taken from the tribe of the Horites); the fourth is called Reba' (the fourth), and the fifth, Balaam, as is well-known, is found in the list of the kings of Edom. From this it is clear that the whole story related in the Priestly Code is a bungling piece of work, and has not the slightest thing to do with the ancient story.

We can only surmise why the conclusion of the ancient account has been deleted. If we scrutinize what the Priestly Code has substituted, we cannot but suppose that originally the contrary was related: it was not the ostensible descendants of Aaron who were invested with the priesthood and those holy objects but the descendants of Moses, the ancestor of Eli of Shiloh, who, we later find, was in possession of those holy objects. That, however, had to be deleted because it was fatal to the claim of the Zadokites. But these are merely suggestions on our part.

Moses' Death[141]

Even the superman Moses one day had to suffer the fate of man and die. He died before the final, crowning achievement of his gigantic life work, before the conquest of Canaan, before the crossing of the Jordan. This can be concluded from all traditions as a certainty. The deep tragedy which lies in this has continued to occupy the thought and poetry of his people. Why must Moses die before the entry into Canaan? We say soberly: he was an old man and had to die sometime. But the people were not satisfied with this simple answer. The writer of the late Priestly Code seeks and finds a reason by casting on Moses the ugly shadow of disobedience — unjustly, as we have seen. The oldest narrator, a genuine poet, speaks of such great things, of the death of the greatest one, with the simplest words. Moses died not because the enormous vitality of this giant was exhausted; he appeared to be almost immortal. He died a special death: the deity summoned the loved one to it. God ordered him to die, and die he did in full vigor. The narrator has in great simplicity molded this into a powerful image.

Deut. 32:48. "YHWH spoke unto Moses, 49. Ascend this mountain of Abarim, unto Mount Nebo, and behold the land of Canaan, which I am giving the children of Israel for a possession, 50. and die on the mountain, whither you go up, and be gathered unto your clans. 34:1. And Moses went up from the plains of Moab unto Mount Nebo. And YHWH showed him all the land, Gilead as far as Dan, 2. and all Naphthali, and the land of Ephraim and Manasseh and all the land of Judah as far as the distant sea, 3. and the Negev and the Jordan district, the depression of Jericho as far as Zoar. 4. And YHWH said unto him, This is the land which I have sworn unto Abraham, unto Isaac and unto Jacob, saying, I will give it unto your seed. I have let you see it with your own eyes, but you shall not go over thither. 5. So Moses the servant of YHWH died there in the land of Moab at YHWH's command. 7b.[142] His eye was not dim, nor his life sap fled. 6. He buried him there in the valley in the land of Moab over against Beth Pe'or. And no man knows his grave unto this day.''

That is a strikingly simple and moving account, which has become a symbol down to our own day. Moses saw the land of his longing, but he may not enter. God showed it to him. Now he can die; of the future of his people he was certain. He departed in full vigor of spirit and of body. He was spared the fate of seeing the completion of his work as a frail old man or of outliving his usefulness. For the people there remained the longing to be with their great leader, who appeared tireless even to the very last. There remained about him the feeling of the enigmatic, the demoniacal, the strange that always surrounded him. He came from a foreign land to his own people, as a miracle; he went from his people into the unknown. His death is already enveloped by legend. No veneration at a hero's grave will coarsen and turn into idolatry man's respect in the presence of his greatness: no man knows the location of his grave, even to the present day!

8

The Work of Moses

The Ten Commandments[143]

The Ten Commandments which Moses brought from Mt. Sinai — according to tradition spoken and written down on the tables of stone by the deity itself — belong to the superlatively great events of the human race. We should speak of them only in the simplest words, because not even great words can glorify them. They are the kernel and the soul of Moses' life work, the foundation stone of the religion of Israel through which they have become the basic law for the moral development of all mankind.

It is recognized today by all serious scholars that this law actually dates from the time of Moses and therefore can be rightfully ascribed to the lawgiver Moses.[144] The Ten Commandments are, apart from occasional remarks in the stories, our most important source for recognizing the spiritual content of Moses' life work. Before throwing light on the inner meaning, let us deal with the external form of the Ten Commandments.

The law of Moses is, according to all traditions, collected in the form of Ten Commandments. This form is no chance one, but neither is it conditioned by its special contents and fitted only for this law. After several further "decalogues" were discovered by Goethe, Budde, and Gressmann, I have shown recently[145] that the regular and general form of the laws of Israel in olden times was in the form of ten commandments. The entire Book of the Covenant consists of ten commandments, as does a great part of the Holiness Code in the third Book of Moses (Leviticus). That the law of Moses should be in the form of ten commandments is then not strange or distinctive in any way. Ten commandments deal with the law of slavery, enumerate the bodily defects which a priest must not have, or list the measures for the prevention of infection. But there is one aspect in which the Mosaic Decalogue rises above most of the rest: it makes no threats of punishment but only normative regulations.[146] Thus it is not the form which constitutes the special features of this law but its contents.

It is easy to understand why all these old laws are arranged in groups of ten. In a period in which people did not write at all or wrote little, this form served as a memory aid for learning things by heart. People could always count on their fingers a group of ten.

The demarcation and division of the Ten Commandments are not as fixed as one might think, and this question is not immaterial for the evaluation of the contents. The Jewish and Christian traditions number the commandments differently — neither correctly. The difficulty lies in the demarcation of the first commandment. The Jewish tradition takes as the first commandment the statement: "I am YHWH your God," etc. In spite of all attempts at an explanation, that is not a commandment but merely a statement. Instead, the "second" commandment contains two clearly different commandments: 1. "You shall have no other gods before me." 2. "You shall not make unto you any image of God." The uncertainties in the last commandment will be presently discussed.

Now for the important question about the form in which the Ten Commandments have been handed down to us. It is well-known that they are in two versions, Exodus 20:2-17 and Deuteronomy 5:6-21. These two versions differ so strikingly from one another that important conclusions emerge. The two versions set side by side follow.

Exod. 20:2-17	Deut. 5:6-21
1. I, YHWH, am your God, who brought you out of the land of Egypt, out of the house of slaves.	1. I, YHWH, am your God, who brought you out of the land of Egypt, out of the house of slaves.
2. You shall have no other gods beside me.	2. You shall have no other gods beside me.
You shall not make unto you a graven image of God nor any manner of likeness, that is in heaven above and the earth beneath and that is in the water under the earth. You shall not bow down unto them, nor serve them. For I, YHWH your God, am a jealous God, visiting[147] the iniquity	You shall not make unto you a graven image of God nor any manner of likeness, that is in heaven above and in the earth beneath and that is in the water under the earth. You shall not bow down unto them nor serve them. For I, YHWH your God, am a jealous God, visiting the iniquity of the

Exod. 20:2-17 (contd.)

of the fathers upon the children, even to the third and fourth generation of them who hate me; but showing love to the thousandth of them who love me and keep my commandments.

3. You shall not take the name of YHWH your God for an unworthy purpose; for YHWH will not leave unpunished one who takes his name for an unworthy purpose.

4. Remember[148] the Sabbath day to keep it holy. Six days shall you labor and do all your work. But the seventh day is a Sabbath for YHWH your God. You shall not do any manner of work, you nor your son nor your daughter, nor your manservant nor your maidservant nor any of your cattle nor your sojourner,[149] who is within your gates. For in six days YHWH made heaven and earth, the sea and all that in them is, and he rested on the seventh day. Therefore YHWH has blessed the Sabbath day and hallowed it.

5. Honor your father and your mother, that your days may be long upon the land, which YHWH your God gives to you.

6. You shall not murder.

7. You shall not commit adultery.

8. You shall not steal.

9. You shall not bear false witness against your neighbor.

10. You shall not covet your neighbor's house. You shall not covet your neighbor's wife nor his manservant nor his maidservant, nor his ox nor his ass nor anything that belongs to your neighbor.

Deut. 5:6-21 (contd.)

fathers upon the children, even to the third and fourth generation of them who hate me; but showing love to the thousandth of them who love me and keep my commandments.

3. You shall not take the name of YHWH your God for an unworthy purpose; for YHWH will not leave unpunished one who takes his name for an unworthy purpose.

4. Keep the Sabbath day to make it holy. Six days shall you labor and do all your work. But the seventh day is a Sabbath for YHWH your God. You shall not do any manner of work, you nor your son nor your daughter, nor your manservant nor your maidservant nor your ox nor your ass nor any of your cattle nor your sojourner who is within your gates, so that your manservant and your maidservant may rest as well as you. And remember that you were a servant in the land of Egypt and YHWH your God brought you out from there by a strong hand and by an outstretched arm. Therefore YHWH your God commanded you to keep the Sabbath day.

5. Honor your father and your mother, as YHWH your God has commanded you, that your days may be long and that it may be well with you upon the land, which YHWH your God gives you.

6. You shall not murder,

7. and you shall not commit adultery,

8. and you shall not steal,

9. and you shall not bear false witness against your neighbor,

10. and you shall not covet your

Exod. 20:2-17 (contd.)   Deut. 5:6-21 (contd.)

                                          neighbor's wife, neither shall you
                                          desire your neighbor's house, his
                                          field and his manservant and his
                                          maidservant and his ox and his ass
                                          and anything that belongs to your
                                          neighbor.

A peculiar unevenness within the two versions strikes us immediately. Commandments six to nine are quite short, ten is somewhat longer but comprises only the commandment itself. One to five,
however, contain besides the commandment an added reason in two
and four in a very detailed form. That alone suggests that all the
commandments in their oldest form had the concise brevity of six to
nine. This becomes a certainty when we see that precisely in these
motivations the two versions to some extent deviate very strongly
from one another. These deviations are not small differences, as
happens frequently in the Bible when texts are given twice; here they
are entirely different texts. In the fourth commandment in particular,
the argument in each text is substantially quite different. The fifth
commandment too shows strong differences. From this it is evident
that people did not dare to alter the laws themselves, so that there are
only insignificant variations. But the motivations were apparently
not considered inviolable because they were not part of the text
proper.

        The tenth commandment holds a special place. The others
command or forbid some action. The tenth commandment prohibits a
desire. What does it mean that a man should not desire his neighbor's
ass? If he wanted to appropriate it, that is already forbidden by the
eighth commandment. If he wanted to take his wife, that is already
forbidden by the seventh commandment. In Exodus the house comes
first, in Deuteronomy the wife. Why the enumeration at all? The
conclusion is a sufficient reason: you shall not covet what belongs to
your neighbor. The conclusions which can be drawn from these
striking peculiarities of the tenth commandment will be discussed
when we examine the contents of the commandments.

        Prior to the two very different versions of today, there is
an archetypal form used in common which is a very short form of the
Ten Commandments without any motivation or explanation, found in
the sixth to ninth commandments. At the same time it is clear that the

beginning of the second commandment has to follow the first.[150] The original form presumably is somewhat as follows:

1. I, YHWH, am your God; you shall have no other God beside me.
2. You shall not make unto you a graven image.
3. You shall not take the name of YHWH your God for an unworthy purpose.
4. Remember the Sabbath day to keep it holy.
5. Honor your father and your mother.
6. You shall not murder.
7. You shall not commit adultery.
8. You shall not steal.
9. You shall not bear false witness against your neighbor.
10. You shall not covet any house.

We will make a few remarks about that part of the *contents* of the commandments of which the meaning is not entirely clear. We will assume from the start that such a law must be very easily understood by everyone in the community, for it is devised as the basic law for a primitive people and as the principal rule for their religious and moral conduct. Complicated explanations or those derived from philosophical notions are not in place here. The plain sense of the words has to be our ultimate guideline.

The first commandment determines that YHWH alone is the God of Israel. Therefore the translation "I am YHWH, your God" is meaningless. YHWH does not need to make himself known or introduce himself. It must mean, according to the strict literal sense of the words, "I, YHWH, am your God," no one else. Therefore, because YHWH is in apposition, the absolute pronoun *anokhi* is used here; "I am YHWH, your God" is conveyed by *ani* YHWH *elohekha,* as it is usually expressed in Leviticus. Precisely this (it is remarkable how rarely it has been recognized!) is what the famous Credo of the Jews expresses in somewhat different words: "Hear, O Israel, YHWH is our God, YHWH alone."

The second commandment forbids any representation of the deity. From the exposition it must not be concluded that every figurative representation of living creatures is altogether forbidden. Rather, the exposition is merely a detailed explanation of what is to be considered a *pesel:* every figurative representation of a living creature, so far as it is intended to be a representation of the deity.

The third commandment presents great difficulties for our comprehension. I have the impression that many interpreters of this text had no clear conception of its meaning. When we read in Buber, "Do not bear his name in delusion,"[151] I freely admit that for me the words are not understandable, nor can I imagine that Buber has given an understandable meaning to them. Most interpreters hold the view that the commandment forbids misusing the name of God which would give sanction to something false. Rashi says that here swearing falsely is forbidden. But that is almost covered by the ninth commandment and could have been expressed much more simply and clearly. Others think it forbids cursing; that too does not follow from the wording. Again, others maintain that one should not pronounce the name of God loosely and thoughtlessly for all kinds of inconsequential purposes. But is that a matter which belongs within ten basic laws for mankind? Above all, I insist that the lawgiver must have expressed something that was clear to the people and immediately understandable.

First, let us understand the wording correctly. The "name" of YHWH, as we shall see, is not mentioned here incidentally. At this time something special and mystical attaches to the name of the deity; whoever has the name at his disposal can through its enunciation exercise a definite and powerful influence upon the deity (see chap. 2). What does the expression *nasa' eth ha-shem* imply now? It occurs only in this passage. *Nāsa'* means "to lift," "to lift up." Usually the phrase is *nāsa' ḳol,* "to lift up one's voice" (in order to weep or to speak). Nearest in relation to our passage is the phrase in Numbers 23:7 *wa-yissa' meshalo,* "he took up his parable" (Balaam). In all these cases the verb *nasa'* indicates the beginning of the speech and stresses the emphatic intention. In the third commandment, if we wish to get exactly the right sense, we have not only to understand "whoever pronounces the name of YHWH" but also something like "whoever enunciates the name of YHWH" with conscious intent or solemnity. Finally, what does *la-shaw* mean? The word is found once again in the ninth commandment. Here its meaning is quite unmistakable; it means "false," which the parallel in Deuteronomy proves. In this sense it is also used of the "false" or "sacrilegious" oath. Thus also a *minḥath shaw* (Isa. 1:13) is a sacrifice which is offered in an unworthy frame of mind. Only in later

parts of the Bible (Job, Psalms) does the word at times get the
meaning "void," "vain," almost like *hebhel*. In more ancient times,
however, it always had the connotation of something morally inadmissible.

We therefore have to understand the third commandment
thus: "You shall not enunciate the name of YHWH for an illicit (or
unworthy) purpose." In that case it is immediately clear what it
means and what it intends to forbid. The name of God is uttered,
permissibly and legitimately, when a man turns to him in prayer. But
in the course of the development this usage became even rarer, for the
awe of the name became ever greater; the fear of misuse finally
became man's fear of any use at all. After some centuries the point
was reached where only the High Priest might still enunciate the name
in a specially solemn manner; in all other connections the name was
replaced by different words like Elohim, Adonai, etc. And finally,
remarkable in the history of religion, it happened that the name of
God, which at the time of the revelation to Moses was the central
point of the religion, became completely forgotten and unknown.

The misuse of the name developed because whoever
knew and pronounced the name could thereby attain a magical effect,
not only an effect on material things (see the legend of the Exalted
Rabbi Löw) but an effect even upon the deity itself. By pronouncing
the name it became possible to coerce the deity by magic. Therefore
Jacob, Gideon, Manoah, and Moses struggled to acquire the knowledge of the name. This use of the name of God is forbidden by the
third commandment. Thereby everything "magical" was banished
into the sphere of the unlawful and prohibited. That this was possible,
that Moses in one of the basic commandments undertook to eradicate
this general belief of his time and of the following centuries by
forbidding its practice, is an astonishing sign of how far ahead of his
time he was in his inner religious development. Indeed, according to
the legend, Moses was actually the first to transgress this commandment, to make use of the name for coercing the deity; for the scene in
Exodus 34 cannot be understood in any other way.

This explanation of the third commandment shows all
signs of being correct: it agrees fully with the wording; it shows that
this wording must have been understandable to every Israelite of the
time; it exhibits a content which was important enough to be included
in the Ten Commandments.

The fourth to ninth commandments need not be discussed at this point although their inner significance will be discussed later; but they are clear and require no elaboration.

The tenth commandment, on the other hand, is rather obscure. We have given a few references to it above. Even the outward form differs from that of the rest of the commandments. While with the more detailed commandments (two, three, four, and five) it is immediately clear that an original commandment of concise brevity has been lengthened by an interpretation, that does not appear to be the case here. We indeed assume, that, following the general law of formation, this law too was once upon a time quite short; but what was its original content? A number of things are enumerated that should not be coveted. In Exodus the house is first listed, in Deuteronomy the neighbor's wife. Which was the original? If it were the wording of Deuteronomy (the wife), a change in this order would be quite unintelligible. If, however, the house was originally listed first, we can well understand that later, at the time of Deuteronomy, people took offense at this and the wife was then put in first place. Originally, therefore, the house came first. But how is it possible that the wife could *ever* rank after the house? And still more, what sense had such a prohibition in Mosaic times? It was only under the settled conditions of Canaan that there was any occasion for a transgression. Houses in the wilderness? Or in Kadesh? Oxen and asses in the wilderness?

All difficulties disappear when it is assumed that originally only the house was named in the commandment. The oldest form was *lo' taḥmod bayith,* "You shall not covet any house." That, however, is a commandment, which fits exactly with the spirit of the Mosaic period. It is the brief expression of the "desert-ideal," the tenacious adherence to the forms of nomadic life that alone were considered worthy of men and pleasing to God. In the settled life of the peasants the Bedouin sees a moral and social decline in contrast to the free life of the desert. In his opinion, the possession of a solid house draws other evils to it, not only restraint but also possessiveness, proneness to a life of ease, cowardice, relaxation of tribal loyalty, dissolution of pure moral customs.

The tenth commandment of the Decalogue, thus understood, does not stand alone. From the ninth century, four hundred years after Moses, we hear of the tribe of the Rechabites, who resided

in the Negev and were zealous YHWH worshipers. Their leader
Jonadab ben Rechab, named in this passage (2 Kings 10:15), is again
mentioned in the time of Jeremiah (Jer. 35:6) as the ancestor of the
tribe, who left them an inviolable law: "You shall drink no wine . . . ,
neither shall you build a house, nor sow seed, nor plant a vineyard
. . . , but all your days you shall dwell in tents." Here we have the
same demand as part of a program of a conscious nomadic life with an
Israelite tribe which pitched its tents in the immediate neighborhood
of Kadesh.

Some nine hundred years later we have from almost the
same district, the northern part of the Sinai peninsula, a Greek
account[152] regarding the Nabataeans, in which it is said: "There is a
law amongst them, neither to sow corn, nor to plant fruit trees, nor to
drink wine, nor *to build a house."* This sounds like a translation of the
account about the Rechabites. The great similarity is not accidental
because it is the expression of a common outlook on life, which was
native to all the tribes of this district. Early Islam had similar tenden-
cies also. Wherever this commandment was found, it served as a
basic commandment of life.

If our interpretation of the tenth commandment is right,
this commandment is the clearest proof for the origin of the Ten
Commandments in the time of Moses. For, at a later time such a law
was unthinkable, since it condemned and forbade the settled life. The
time of its composition might be fixed even more exactly. At the latest
it must have arisen during the Israelites' stay in Kadesh, when the
Israelites still led the life of Bedouins in an oasis. As soon as the
decision about the conquest of Canaan was made, such a law could
hardly be devised: a farsighted leader like Moses would have recognized without further consideration that under the conditions of a
settled life that law was not practicable. In reality, that plan for the
conquest of Canaan existed no earlier; it was drawn up toward the end
of the Kadesh period!

It was inevitable that the tenth commandment soon had to
undergo a change because after a few generations in Canaan it was no
longer understood. It could not be eliminated — ten was a fixed
number for the commandments — but what would people have put in
its place? It was treated as a purely moral commandment; first, "the
neighbor" was introduced. This completely changed the sense. Expansions were bound to follow. Why should only the house of the

neighbor not be coveted? Other possessions might be. Thus were added the wife, the field, the manservant, the maidservant, the ox, the ass, and finally everything that belonged to one's neighbor. That, logically, was an inevitable development. Thus, that commandment became a foreign element among the Ten Commandments. Misunderstood and unintelligible it was transmitted over the centuries, with painful attempts at explanation by the theologians. Our understanding is made possible only by going back to its original form.

The Confederation of the Twelve Tribes[153]

Whoever piously accepts tradition just as it is presented has an uncomplicated position enviable in its simplicity in the face of many problems; they do not exist for him. There is for him no problem about the twelve tribes: the twelve tribes, the descendants of the tribes' ancestor Jacob, went down into Egypt, then came out of Egypt and formed the covenant union, called the people of Israel.

In reality we are confronted by very difficult and involved problems, as soon as we consider events with the tools of historical criticism. The problems are in fact so difficult that historical research cannot give as simple and complete an answer to all questions as does the traditional point of view.

But is the picture that tradition hands down clear and without contradiction? By no means. The simple question about the number of the tribes cannot be answered without contradictions. Jacob had twelve sons; but among the tribes there were two who were not "sons" but "grandsons" of Jacob, Ephraim and Manasseh, while a tribe of Joseph never existed. Thus, the number of the tribes in the tradition became in reality thirteen. In all the lists concerning the desert wanderings there were thirteen tribes: Levi occupied the middle of the camp around the sacred tent, and the twelve tribes camped around him. In the "Blessing of Jacob" a way out of the difficulty was found by including Ephraim and Manasseh in *one* tribe of Joseph; but there never existed a "Joseph tribe." The confusion became still greater in the "Blessing of Moses" (Deut. 33) for, even including Levi, only eleven tribes were enumerated; Simeon was omitted altogether. To add up to the number twelve, Joseph was again divided into Ephraim and Manasseh in a late addition to the text (v. 17b).

One thing stands out clearly in the examination of this

tradition: The number twelve is a given number. Again and again tradition endeavors to reach this number, and indeed speaks of twelve tribes when there are not twelve at all, because the confederation of twelve tribes in the Moses period is an undeniable fact of every tradition. It is the task of a historical investigation to clarify the contradictions as far as possible and to ascertain which tribes came to join this coalition, that is, historically to define the concept of "Israel."[154] That, however, requires quite a different method: we must proceed from the historical statements about it in order to clarify the range of this concept; we have to become acquainted with the members of this coalition and grasp with certainty any changes it may have undergone.

In this way surprising results develop. The oldest and most important testimony of this kind is the account of the Conquest in Judges 1:16-36. The significance of this document for our problem is that it demonstrably dates from the time shortly after the immigration of the Israelites into Canaan;[155] it consequently is a historical source of first-rate importance.

In Judges there is a list of the tribes of Israel giving their conquests — a very remarkable list. The names of the tribes are: Ḳayin (i.e., Kenite), Simeon, Judah, Caleb, Manasseh, Ephraim, Zebulun, Asher, Naphthali, Dan.

Only ten tribes are named. Among them are two who do not appear again in any of the later lists: Ḳayin and Caleb. No fewer than five of the "Sons of Jacob" are lacking: Reuben, Levi, Issachar, Gad, and Benjamin. Precisely these marked deviations make the list worthy of a detailed study and show its great significance for our historical understanding. All these deviations have good reasons for being.

Levi was not named because he did not have a share in the land settlement. This was a tribe of priests, but not a tribe which possessed any real estate. For the Mosaic coalition he had, of course, to be counted in, as he was its bearer. Reuben and Gad were not named because they were already settled in East Jordan territory before the immigration of the Israelites, and only afterwards joined the coalition of "Israel." Gad, according to the testimony of the Moabite Stone ("the people of Gad dwelt in the land of Ataroth from time immemorial"), was in East Jordan before Moab settled there; and Reuben, in spite of his political insignificance, was considered to be the "firstborn" of Israel[156] because he had been there the longest. Finally, Issachar and Benjamin were not named because these two tribes were established in the land of Canaan only by being detached and separated from the Joseph tribes. Consequently, only one of the tribes of the five missing here, Levi, can have been a member of the tribal coalition in Kadesh. But the same holds good as much for Asher as for Reuben and Gad: indeed Asher at the time of the Tell Amarna letters (beginning of the fourteenth century) was settled in Galilee as part of the Ḥabiru immigration,[157] and therefore he cannot have been a member of the Kadesh coalition. How can it be explained that in this list we find tribes that have never been reckoned among the "Sons of Jacob"?

We have known for a long time that there was a group of tribes who were faithful servants of YHWH and on friendly terms with Israel, without later being reckoned as belonging to the people of Israel. All these tribes lived in the south of the country on the boundaries of the sedentary colonists. Of these Caleb[158] reached furthest to the north, namely, as far as Hebron. In the story of the spies and in the conquest of the land this tribe is so closely associated with the rest of the Israelite tribes that without difficulty we can consider it a member of the old coalition. It was not reckoned among "Israel" later because, for the most part, it was absorbed into the powerful tribe of Judah (Simeon was also, and was therefore absent in the list of the tribes in the Blessing of Moses because his district was regarded as part of Judah's).

The tribe Ḳayin, reckoned to Israel in Judges 1, has later, without qualification, been looked upon as Israelite. It had its location in the extreme south, together with Amalek. Before beginning his campaign against Amalek, Saul warned it as a friendly tribe and induced it to leave the battle area (1 Sam. 15:6). David also reckoned it to Israel; before the Philistine king he boasted of his reputed raids against Kayin as against Judah[159] and Jerahmeel (1 Sam. 27:10), and the tribe shared in his spoil (30:29). Kayin pitched their tents as far as the Plain of Jezreel (Judg. 4:11). A later tradition (Judg. 1:16, 4:11) has even made Moses' father-in-law a Kenite, contrary to the clear statement of the old accounts, apparently in order to give Moses an Israelite wife. The presence of Kayin in the list of tribes in Judges 1 makes it therefore certain that we should count it as a member of the Kadesh coalition.

But there are two more tribes not named in the list which have to be reckoned here. One is Jerahmeel. It is "officially" not reckoned to Israel, but David counts it among the tribes in the two passages mentioned above in connection with Kayin (1 Sam. 27:10; 30:29). That is understandable only if the tribe had in the past belonged to the Israel coalition. In the post-exilic period, as the genealogical trees of the Book of Chronicles show, Jerahmeel was again entirely merged with the Judeans. It would certainly not have been admitted in this period, exclusive as it was in matters of religion, if its members had not been zealous YHWH worshipers, and if the tribe had not always passed as Israelite.

That is the case in still greater measure with the tribe of Rechab. The Rechabites were especially fanatical adherents of YHWH worship (2 Kings 10:15-16;23), which among them retained the original coloring of the desert ideal (Jer. 35). Whence did they get this religious attitude? It can date only from the Mosaic period, during which they belonged to the Israelite coalition. Therefore they were always considered as an Israelite tribe and in the post-exilic period were without hesitation allowed to amalgamate with the Judeans (Neh. 3:14; 1 Chron. 2:55). What is common to all these southern tribes is that they were always looked upon as Israelites and yet, in the final fixing of the tradition in the form which we have, were not included among the Sons of Jacob. The reason is because in their way of life they remained nomads and semi-nomads, which thereby separated them from the life of the nation that was developing into a sedentary peasant nation. But in the Mosaic period they all were close neighbors in the coalition formed in Kadesh and associated themselves with its religious and national outlook. We can imagine that in the migration and events of the conquest they scarcely had any connection with the rest of the tribes. They were settled in the Negev and remained in the Negev; only Kayin and Caleb, dependent on Judah, pushed forward somewhat further north.

When we consider the information we have gleaned from the oldest historical accounts about the members of the Kadesh coalition, we have before us a list of tribes that is quite different from the one familiar to us as the Sons of Jacob. These tribes are: Levi, Kayin, Caleb, Rechab, Jerahmeel, Judah, Simeon, Zebulun, Dan, Naphthali, Ephraim, Manasseh. We now have exactly twelve tribes, as is required by tradition. These twelve tribes, in all probability, were the members of the Kadesh coalition.

Not all these tribes were in Egypt; a section surely joined the coalition in Kadesh. But any possibility of discovering that relationship for the individual tribe eludes us. The idea of this confederation of tribes proved to be fruitful. It became and remained the foundation upon which the people of Israel arose.

The Contents of the Covenant

Our task is now to comprehend the intrinsic value of this covenant and thereby the real life work of Moses.

The federation of Israelite tribes, whose first obvious objective was the conquest of Canaan, was not an isolated phenomenon. In the great movement of the Ḥabiru, we see a similar association of Bedouin tribes which one hundred fifty years earlier led to the conquest of a large part of Syria and Palestine. They were Hebrew tribes, with whom some Israelite tribes had apparently already arrived in Canaan. The migration of people, which shortly after the Israelites brought Greek tribes, the Philistines,[160] Takkal, Carians, and others from Crete to Palestine, shows strong similarities in this respect.

These alliances are distinguished from those of the Israelites in that they were set up only with the material object of the conquest of territories, without — as far as we know — a spiritual bond uniting them intimately. The consequence was that, after achieving their first objective, almost without resistance, they succumbed to the influences of their new environment, and thus quickly disintegrated from within and drifted apart. When the Israelites came to Canaan one hundred fifty years later, scarcely any trace of the Ḥabiru was left, and even the Philistines, who had a brief period of brilliant ascendancy, were unable to create an enduring cultural and government structure.

The Greek amphictyony in its inner structure came much nearer to the Israelite confederation of tribes. It was an association of tribes based on a strong religious foundation and grouped around a common central sanctuary, with the members obligated to unite for peace and arbitration and mutual assistance. The obvious similarity with the Israelite confederation of tribes led Martin Noth[161] to assume that the analogy applies to all the details; indeed, on this basis, he even postulates phenomena in the political and cultural life of Israel, which have not been handed down by tradition. We know that suppositions are often advanced in place of actual facts, but Martin Noth, besides the undeniable similarities, has overlooked two fundamental differences between the Greek amphictyony and the divine covenant of Israel.

The first fundamental difference is because the Greek amphictyony never had the effect of forming a nation. There were several amphictyonies living alongside each other and following one another; they were formations of an ephemeral kind. But the Israelite federation of tribes was from the beginning the constitutive element of the nation. It *was* the nation. Only what belonged to this tribal alliance was reckoned as being part of Israel. All changes in it were renewals, revivals, reinforcements, and developments of the old Mosaic union. The one ancient alliance always remained in force.

The second fundamental difference is that the religious substratum of the Greek amphictyony was not its distinguishing element. Its cults did not distinguish it from the rest of Greece; there were no religious conflicts at issue which would have resulted in the formation of the amphictyony. The Israelite federation of tribes, on the other hand, was the bearer of a special religion, which made it distinctive in its surroundings, and set it militantly against this environment. The Israelite federation was not only of a national but also of a religious and national character.

There is only *one* really complete analogy to the Israelite federation of tribes and that is the movement which Muhammad set in motion. It is also a truly religious movement, which for the first time led to the formation of an Arab nation. Correspondingly, the role which the oasis of Kadesh had was the same role which Mecca played in that movement. The tribe of Levi, even in astonishing details, found its analogy in the tribe of the Kuraish as possessor of the sacred places; there Moses emerged as a reformer within his tribe, here Muhammad; and each was at the same time political leader, lawgiver, commander of the army, founder of a state, and indeed prophet as well.

The primary condition of an alliance, indeed its precondition, is the suppression of blood feuds and the prevention of quarrels among the members of the alliance. The existence of the oasis of

Kadesh in itself demanded a truce of God for all those visiting it; but that alone is not meant here. A real alliance of tribes had to have as its foundation an enduring peace among its members. Once more early Islam provides the best known historical parallel. The commanding position held by Muhammad in Arabia in its beginnings arose above all because he appeared as arbiter between the Arab tribes, became more and more recognized as such, and ended their eternal feuds. For the Israelite tribes also the alliance was first a blessing in this respect. Our accounts are so incomplete that it is not surprising that we know little about the alliance from the Mosaic period. But even two hundred years after the conquest of Canaan feuds between the tribes were extremely rare events. Properly speaking, we know of one case only: the dispute between Gilead and Ephraim (Judg. 12:1-6). In two other cases we learn of steps taken by the federation of tribes against members who transgressed the ordinances of the alliance ("one does not so do in Israel"): the legendary story which is told of the battle against Benjamin[162] (Judg. 19-21) and the curse[163] against the city of Meroz (Judg. 5:23). But these examples show clearly how strong was the idea of the sacred alliance; even the Ephraimites reproach Jephthah only with his failure to summon them for help, according to the alliance. The great moral strength and authority governing the alliance can hardly be demonstrated better than by this enduring tribal peace, when the latter is compared with the endless feuds existing among isolated Bedouin tribes.

To attain such solidarity the alliance must be founded on an inviolable law. It is remarkable that, properly speaking, we do not have any definite information about this basic law of the Israel alliance. In the oldest passage telling us about the alliance, no law is mentioned (Exod. 24:11) and, in the passages where the oldest law of the Two Tables is proclaimed (Exod. 20:2-17), the alliance is not mentioned. Later hands filled this gap by additions. But there can be no serious doubt that the Ten Commandments were the basic law, which the tribes, in concluding the alliance, pledged to observe.

This law contained only the simplest and most general stipulations natural for a basic law. We will soon discuss how the individual laws can be explained and evaluated. But above all we must keep in mind that the purpose of the law was to regulate the life of a community that out of a tribal union was intended to develop into one people. If we approach that basic law with the demands of a far-reaching humanity or the needs of the introspective individual soul in mind, we will fail to recognize the historically conditioned essence of that law.

Further, for the federation of tribes a common law[164] and legal organization were necessary. It was one of the great achievements of Moses that he enforced this uniformity among the unruly tribes. He created the corporate body of the elders, who were at the same time judges. According to several traditions they numbered seventy (or seventy-two) in the time of Moses: that may correspond entirely to the facts, indicating the numerical insignificance of the population, as we have stressed. Each of these "elders" may have had some fifty families under his jurisdiction. According to all the sources we have, Moses functioned as the chief judge. Difficult legal questions which could not be decided by the testimony of witnesses were brought by him "before YHWH," that is, he decided by the oracle of the Urim and Thummim.

We have no contemporary accounts about the contents of the law. The Book of the Covenant, Exodus 21-23, is without doubt a collection from a much later time (although earlier than the time of the kings); it is just as certain though that many regulations laid down here fundamentally go back to the time of Moses.[165] The fact that there was a uniform law for all the tribes of the coalition is historically of great significance and one of the most important means for the formation of a unitary nation.

Outwardly the most conspicuous effect of the alliance was its political aim and the realization of it: the conquest of Canaan. But it is difficult to say whether this goal was originally a foundation of the alliance. The probability is that Moses, with the nucleus of the tribes who followed him out of Egypt to Kadesh, first pursued patiently the formation of a homogeneous people. But the strong attraction which this nucleus had for the environment of the related tribes, and the union of those tribes with "Israel" by the ensuing increase in military power, created the possibility and perhaps the necessity of fresh and larger plans and more far-reaching aims, which included the conquest of Canaan.

The way in which this conquest was set in operation later, after the death of Moses, makes it certain that underlying it there was a general and well-considered plan; it was not the individual actions of a number of tribes acting independently of each other. The broad

overall plan, it is true, was disrupted at one important point: the
southern tribes went their own way. But even so, the central thrust
out into the heart of the country from Jericho was strong enough to
give the Israelites, after a very short time, control over a great part of
the country. What extent these plans of conquest had in the original
commitment of the alliance's action may still be roughly inferred from
the notion of the ideal of a "Promised Land" that, in spite of the
manifold corrections of reality, was maintained with great tenacity
even down to later strata of the tradition. It did *not* include East
Jordan: this was at first only territory for marching through, and it
remained colonial land. But it did include the Phoenician coast
beyond Sidon (Judg. 1:31) and the entire coast of Canaan as far south
as Gaza (1:18). It then became decisive for the historical fate of Israel
that hardly anywhere did this advance reach the coast.

On the other hand, we have to reject the idea of later
generations that the individual shares of the tribes in Canaan, perhaps
going as far as drawing the boundaries, were fixed in advance by
means of "the lot."[166] That was physically and politically impossible.
Success of the venture was so incomplete that it would have led
directly to continued strife among the tribes. The peaceful acceptance
of their areas by the tribes shows at once that they established
themselves, as far as the fortune of war made it possible for them to do
so. The action itself had been centrally planned and carried into effect
by larger groups.

Although we have repeatedly stressed the similarities between the Mosaic coalition of the Israelite tribes and the Muhamma-
dan coalition of the Arab tribes, the fundamental difference must not
be forgotten: between these two alliances there is a period of almost
two thousand years. Moses is the creative genius of this idea,
Muhammad the imitator. The basic idea in the work of Moses, however, is not a political but a religious one.

The name *Israel* is introduced into the world arena with
the federation of Israelite tribes, and the name, a religious one, then
becomes that of the people, *Israel*. It means "God fights" for and
through the hosts which serve him in the alliance. It is the same idea
that appears, under the aspect of the divine, in the second saying
pronounced over the Ark of the Covenant as the name of the deity:
YHWH of hosts, of the thousands of Israel. What is very striking
about the name *Israel* is that in it the divine name YHWH is not used

but that El, the general term for a deity, is found. This is so, perhaps, because the full form of the name of God might be used only in a direct invocation; the short forms, however, were used for the names of persons (cf. also chap. 2). But this shows at once that the two names were felt to be fully equivalent. The theory of a preceding "Elreligion" of the Israelites is pure imagination; the new religion established by Moses would not have carried such a remnant over into a central concept like that of *Israel*. Nor would Moses have named his son Eli'eser. The name of God can drop out entirely, which happened with personal names (Ahaz, Nathan, etc.), and thus the short form Jeshurun arose (Deut. 32:15; 33:5; 26; Isa. 44:2), which rather more correctly may be read as Yisrun or Yisron.

An alliance is a two-sided obligation. Two princes may conclude an alliance with one another, each charging the other with mutual responsibility. If, however, the alliance is not concluded between equals, both parties are not equally charged. When such an alliance is concluded between a prince and a military group or a bodyguard, the weight of the obligation is shared differently. The prince, it is true, binds himself to care for the well-being of his soldiers and to stand by them; the soldiers, however, undertake to be loyal with a far higher stake, their entire strength and even their lives.

Here, however, where the covenant is concluded between the deity and a group of men who submit to authority, we can hardly speak of reciprocity—at least not in the case of a covenant which Moses concluded as the people's herald and mediator. Here, at the foundation of the covenant, lies the nucleus of one of the most tremendous advances in the thought of the human race. The age of magic which extended to Moses' time was overcome only by him; in that age an agreement between a people and their god in which the deity too undertook definite obligations was conceivable and often enough real! If, in the opinion of the worshipers, the deity did not observe those obligations, then they were free. It still happens with primitive peoples that the perfidious deity, which does not bring the promised rain, is punished by having its image flogged. Xerxes had the Hellespont lashed. Some seven hundred years after Moses, Rab-shakeh, the commander of the Assyrian king Sennacherib, still lived in the age of magic: he wanted to persuade the Judeans of Hezekiah to surrender because their God had failed them. At this stage of primitive religion people believed that they possessed means for compelling the deity to fulfill its obligations: magical means, sacrifices, and exorcisims, in which the name of the deity played a special part.

No trace of all this was left in Moses' covenant with God. At the revelation to Moses the deity promised of its own free will to liberate the people from Egypt and give them a good land. But in the obligatory law of the covenant, the Ten Commandments, the deity continued to appear only as an assertive power. Only when man has satisfactorily lived up to all the demands of the deity can he *hope* that the god will look upon the people as his own people, and show himself gracious to them. This was clearly expressed in a somewhat later exposition before the proclamation of the Ten Commandments (Exod. 19:5): "If you will harken unto my voice and keep my covenant, you shall be my treasured possession." The decisive point is that one partner of the covenant, the people, did not yet exist as such; we see the people in the making; only by entering into the covenant of God did a people develop. The covenant of God is the element constituting the nation of Israel. There were Israelite tribes which might conclude and again dissolve alliances with each other. The people of Israel developed only through the covenant of God and as part of it.

This fundamental significance of the idea of God for the covenant enables us to understand that, in the meager number of ten commandments, no fewer than three were devoted to obligations toward the deity. We will not discuss the religious conceptions which form their basis, but their general character must be emphasized. They contain fundamental demands which the deity placed on the partner to the covenant.

1. I, YHWH, am your God; you shall have no other god:
2. You shall not make for yourself an image of God.
3. You shall not pronounce the name of YHWH for an unworthy purpose.

All three are necessary in order to establish from the beginning the special relation of this people to their God. First of all, the question of any other God for Israel can never again be in dispute. Whether this implies merely the exclusion of other deities or God's absolute uniqueness is not under discussion here. It is sufficient for the covenant that the thoughts of the people were directed toward YHWH only.

Any representation of God in an image[167] was forbidden. That means not only that YHWH himself cannot be represented but any figurative symbolic representation meant to stand for the divine was also forbidden. Any contingent representation of foreign gods was already excluded by the first commandment. The name of the deity was definitely reserved only for the sphere of the sacred; any kind of magic, any spell was thereby forbidden. Here too we are confronted by one of the great milestones on the road of human civilization. An age of great antiquity was concluded and a new age began.

Commandments now follow in the law of the covenant; their leading idea, common to them all, has had the most far-reaching consequences for the development of human civilization. The fundamental laws for the attitude of man to man are given, and their common idea is that the fulfillment of these commandments is also a prerequisite for the divine covenant. A people of Israel, which was manifestly going to be created through this covenant, could exist only when it took these commandments upon itself. There was no divine covenant and no people of Israel without these laws. This explains the tremendous obligatory power of these laws for Israel. The inseparable ties existing between God, the people, and morality — that is what is unique in this design, and what constitutes the distinctive character of Israel in the world.

At the transition from the "divine" to the "human" commandments there stands the Sabbath.[168] In this collection of a few basic laws, in this deed of the covenant, in which nothing cultic is otherwise mentioned, the Sabbath cannot be thought of as a festival and cult-prescription. Otherwise additional festivals would be named, as we find in the "cultic" decalogues in Exodus 23 and 34. Rather, here the human significance of the Day of Rest is consciously stressed. The two versions of the Ten Commandments, Exodus 20 and Deuteronomy 5, deviate markedly from one another in the motivation given for the Sabbath, but they are in full agreement on its definition and elucidation: "Six days shall you labor and do all your work; but the seventh day belongs as a day of rest to YHWH, your God." This unheard of innovation was perhaps the most original element in Moses' law of the covenant. For all the rest analogies may be given; not so here. Here the bitter experience of the Egyptian slaves was spiritualized into an eternal charter of freedom for the working man. This day of rest for man has had from the first a religious sanction through its close connection with the deity: the day shall be "sanctified."

The other six commandments embrace the basic laws for human life, more correctly for the national community. Parents shall be honored; man shall not murder; he shall keep the sex life pure;[169] he shall respect property; as a witness he shall speak the truth; and he shall hold fast to the nomadic way of life.

It is no penal code which is given here; no threat of punishment accompanies it. Rather it is meant to be the guiding rule of conduct for a human and human-divine community. From an abundance of what is important, Moses has chosen only the most important, the most vital—so little, indeed, that it could be compressed into ten commandments which every child can and should learn by heart. The Ten Commandments contain a confession and an obligation. The confession reads: Israel has only one God, who cannot be represented and must remain withdrawn from every kind of magic. The obligation reads: Whoever belongs to Israel must respect the rights of his fellowman.

The Religious Work of Moses: Monotheism[170] in Israel

The peculiar aspects and incompleteness of our sources about Moses make it very difficult to attain clarity about the religious outlook of this man, to assess aright the real content of the ideas underlying his work, and thus to recognize, in addition to his time-bound achievement, his eternal one. It is much simpler to give a description of the nature of Israelite monotheism as an overall phenomenon because numerous sources supply extensive material about it, above all, the prophetic books and the Psalms. Many authors studying this field, especially Jewish ones, have viewed that material as homogenous and, without hesitation, have drawn conclusions about the older period[171] from more recent ideas. They thus succeeded in presenting the religious views of the Mosaic period as a wonderfully complete system, to which people in subsequent centuries found scarcely anything to add or change. Others, above all Christian theologians of the critical school, in opposition to this, strictly speaking saw only in the prophets of the eighth and seventh centuries the creators of monotheism, with Moses at best a precursor, representing a rather primitive preliminary stage containing remnants of polytheism, demonism, and animism. The same difference arose in the treatment of ethical problems. We should like to make the daring attempt, in the light of the material handed down to us, of ascertaining what we really do know about the religious and ethical horizon of Moses.

Decisive significance for evaluating cultural progress, or the man whose work it is, always lies in assessing correctly the level where this advance begins and in understanding the previous conditions and environment in which the new development becomes prominent. The present-day world boasts of mighty discoveries and inventions, which are transforming the appearance of our planet: we peer into the endless depths of the universe and into the workings of the atoms; we are spanning space and are making the most distant things audible and visible. But were not the discovery of fire, of the first artificial weapon, and the invention of alphabetic script far greater advances that, with one step, opened up new worlds to mankind? Things are no different in purely spiritual matters. The reflective work of a Spinoza, Kant, Darwin, or Freud has opened up for us new horizons of knowledge. But there are simple truths, which first had to be grasped and proclaimed, and which were far more revolutionary *in their time* because they inaugurated new epochs of the spirit.

We have to keep those facts in mind if we really want to grasp and appreciate Moses' work. We must understand the background from which this gigantic figure will arise. We have to understand the spiritual level of the surrounding milieu on which he created his work; what until then men to whom he turned with new ideas thought. Fortunately, we are not altogether helpless when confronted with these problems. In the legends which give an account of Moses, there are many features that characterize not so much him as his environment. And though we must be very cautious in making use of legends for the recognition of historical events, such legends are of great value for depicting the general historical and spiritual background of the period from which they date.

In the case of the Moses legends particularly, we have seen that there is a group of place and cult legends that point back to an Israelite period of great antiquity, to the time and places in which the work of Moses took place. In their spiritual content they are so different from other Moses stories that people have always been surprised that such curious contrasts should be placed side by side so abruptly: the most lofty and most primitive appear indissolubly mixed. But it is less a *beside* one another than an *after* one another. Here two periods elbow each other, the period before Moses and Moses' own time.

The deity of this period was called YHWH: more correctly perhaps Yahu or Yah (cf. chap. 2). But what a different deity that was! YHWH in the older stories was confined throughout to a definite place where he had his seat; and, as far as we can see, it was always the same place: Kadesh. Another thread of the ancient tradition leads to a different place, to the volcanic mountain in Midian, which was later called Sinai. There, too, the deity had its fixed residence. A later legend tried to reconcile these two traditions, but was confined entirely to their conceptual world; YHWH came from Mt. Sinai and traveled by a fixed route in order to reach Kadesh (Deut. 33:2; Judg. 5:4).

In both places the deity resided in a fiery flame; at Mt. Sinai in the eruption of the volcano, at Kadesh in the flame of the burning bush. In both places the god also became embodied in the pillar of smoke, which, dark in daytime, appeared fiery in the night. By the pillar of smoke he could travel. These ideas are largely materialistic. There is no reason to refine them by a reinterpretation, as has been attempted again and again by the later strata of our tradition. It is much more important to recognize clearly these conceptions as distinguishing marks of a primitive period which had, and could have, no other ideas of the deity. Only when we keep this in mind can we understand and evaluate the fundamental change which took place here.

Equally drastic and human were the ideas about the deity in the cult legends that were linked to Moses. Moses demanded to see the face of the deity. That was denied him, not because in itself it would be impossible, or because the deity had no countenance, but because no man could look at the face of the deity without dying. But he was given permission to look at the "back" of the deity. Other legends tell us that God spoke with him "face to face," or "as a man speaks with his neighbor." The deity was not visible to every eye, but it had a voice, and this voice was audible to the entire people. The voice also presupposed a body; it is a no less crass anthropomorphism than is visibility.

The deity above the ark was imagined in the same way physically and corporeally. The deity was seated on the two outspread wings of the cherubim and had the ark under it as its footstool. YHWH was invited to arise and step upon the ark, and thus, standing invisible upon the ark, he was carried into battle. Afterward he was again invited to take his seat on his throne. When YHWH negotiated with Moses, he spoke "from above the kapporeth [mercy-seat], from the place between the two cherubim" (Exod. 25:22). He was consequently represented as actually sitting there.

In the oldest stories this divine being was a demon,[172] that went around at night and was dangerous to everyone it met. In the well-known story it suddenly attacked Jacob at the crossing of the river. But Jacob made it lame by a cunning blow on the hip, and overcame it. In Egypt it strode from house to house killing anyone it found, Egyptians and Israelites, if it was not dissuaded by blood on the threshold. It attacked Moses when, unsuspecting, Moses wanted to spend the night in its sacred dwelling ground, and due only to the prudence and quick resourcefulness of his wife was Moses' life saved. It spread terror among its enemies when it was carried on the ark into battle: the terror which went out from it when it looked at the Egyptians "out of the pillar of fire and cloud" plunged them into confusion and panic.

The conceptions held about this demonic god are not only largely human but also highly mythological. By magical agencies he may be influenced, paralyzed, overpowered. The blood, which was smeared on doorposts and thresholds, kept him at a distance; evidently the basic idea was that the demon thought it had already slain someone in that house. It allowed itself to be duped by Zipporah who by means of the bloody foreskin persuaded it that it had already satisfied its desire for her. Moses' raised flagstaff compelled the deity to give the victory to the warriors of Israel. Whoever gazed upon the brazen serpent was immune from the bite of the winged serpents which YHWH had sent. The magic of the divine name was particularly effective. Again and again the heroes of these ancient stories made an effort to discover the correct name of the deity so that they could, by this means, exercise a magic compulsion over the deity.

Jacob, Manoah, and Moses ask the deity for its name, but only Moses learns it. In fact, an old, greatly revised story (Exod. 34) reports that Moses made use of the name to wrest a wished-for thing from the deity. As Jacob by a ruse outwitted the deity, so Moses too, by his prudence, won the oracle of the Urim and Thummim (Deut. 33:8).

This deity of great antiquity distributed its gifts not on the basis of principles of equity or according to men's moral behavior but according to its own love[173] and hate. Because YHWH loved the patriarchs he led the Israelites out of Egypt and gave them a land flowing with milk and honey. At the time of the patriarchs he punished the innocent pharaoh and the innocent Abimelech with sterility, although the wrong lay in the patriarch's deceit.[174] By blackmail, Jacob underhandedly obtained the right of the firstborn; by deceit, the blessing of his dying father, but he remained the darling of the deity. When the people murmured because of the lack of water and food in the wilderness, by some accounts they were given food and drink in a miraculous way, by other accounts the wrath of the deity suddenly broke upon them and thousands fell because of the bite of serpents or contagious disease. The sudden anger of the deity was incalculable; a group of Israelites who revolted against Moses were swallowed up by the earth; two hundred fifty men who disputed the prerogatives of the priests were consumed by fire. It had nothing to do with right or wrong when YHWH suddenly attacked Moses in the night. Here the grisly idea glimmered through that the deity claimed for itself *ius primae noctis* with the young wife, and that circumcision was a magic rite to protect the young husband on this dangerous night. The patriarch Jacob without any reason was surprised by the deity at nighttime.

It is a curious, one may even say an oppressive picture that we obtain of the ideas of God existing for us in the oldest attainable cultural stratum of the Israelites. These conceptions are somber and primitive, offspring of the age of magic, faltering unclearly in the dim twilight of prehistoric times. So long as scholars attempt to balance these ideas with the religious ideas of the historic people of Israel, they remain incomprehensible and an exasperating encumbrance on the religion which is later called the religion of the prophets. When we consider them as what they really are: the prehistoric remnants of an age-old religious system, which is rejected and repressed on a later and higher stage of development; the religion of the uncultured tribes of Israel, as tradition expresses it, *lifnē mattan torah,* in the period before the appearance of Moses, then indeed they lose that vexatious character and appear as the natural result of time and place. They form the dark background out of which the life work of Moses emerges, the remnants of a past which, like all religious developments, do not vacate the field without any trace before what is new, but are taken over into the following period as something obsolete, forbidden, opposed, and gradually eliminated. Only this stratum of the religion of the primitive period permits us to realize fully what was new in Moses' creation.

The most important source of knowledge for the spiritual life work of Moses — besides the individual features in the stories — are the Ten Commandments, the only written document of which it can be said that it goes back directly to Moses. It is very short, but it still permits deep insights into the religious ideas of the founder of the religion of Israel.

Moses' idea of God, which we can infer from the Ten Commandments, is not laid down in philosophical definitions or enumerations of the divine attributes. Rather, it is embedded in three negative regulations: (1) You shall have no other god beside me; (2) you shall not make for yourself any image of god; (3) you shall not misuse YHWH's name.

The first then is the uniqueness of God. The form in which it is here postulated does not enshrine the idea of the absolute uniqueness of monotheism. It is merely laid down that *for Israel* there is only one God, and can be only one. Whether any other god exists or can exist is not determined. It does not seem to me permissible to explain away this fact in favor of a detached and absolute monotheism. What Moses thought we do not know; what he expressed refers only to the immediate, practical aim to rule out the recognition and worship of any other deity in the spiritual sphere of Israel.

If we would rightly assess the magnitude of this attitude, we must look back into the past. It is a remarkable phenomenon that in none of the accounts or tales from Israel's remote antiquity do we find even the slightest trace of any deity other than YHWH. The patriarchs are YHWH worshipers, and even in the ancient legends, according to which we have just ascertained the ideas of God in the period before Moses, no deity other than YHWH occurs. This cannot be explained away by saying that the stories about this period have been revised and "purified." When we see that the archaic features of the pre-Mosaic YHWH remain fully preserved, in spite of all later censorship and revision, it is impossible to think that so basic a fact as the worship of another deity could have been entirely effaced. Even the theory of an "El-religion" of the patriarchs is only a theoretical construction; nothing of that kind has ever existed. If YHWH had stepped into El's place, Moses would not have called the divine covenant "Israel" nor his son Elieser.

Critical scholars through their efforts to prove the existence of YHWH among non-Israelite peoples, especially the Midianites, at the most ancient period have indirectly confirmed the exclusive existence of YHWH worship. Those attempts have failed. They are rather an expression of the fact that we have to assume the existence of pre-Mosaic YHWH worship. The pheonomenon is all the more striking because of all the related tribes concerned it is confined exclusively to the Israelites. We possess a document perhaps a generation older than the exodus of the Israelites, in the treaty between Ramses II of Egypt and King Hattushil of Hatti territory, in which the "gods of the Hebrews" *(ilani ḫabiri)* are invoked as numerous others are. Here there is no trace of YHWH. There remains no other explanation than that actually, in a group which is represented by the "patriarchs," an exclusive YHWH worship had existed for a long time and continued to be transmitted through the generations until Moses.

If this is the position, what then is new? What advance beyond the present did the proclamation of Moses bring? It is first of all the absoluteness and range of the demand: YHWH was for Israel the absolute, unique God and remained so for all time. Thereby, the way was prepared for a further deepening and development of the conception of God, which then, in fact, became the outcome of the spiritual history of Israel. But a far greater contribution to it was made by the inner content which the conception of God received through Moses.

For the second law was an innovation unheard of and, in the deepest sense, revolutionary: You shall not make for yourself any image of God. In the world of ideas existing in the magic age, the image of the deity was far more than an image and representation. It was part of the being and life of the deity; it was, as we would say today, "animated." The deity, who stood with its fearful powers above and outside the human sphere, lived in it through two of its attributes: the image of the deity and its name. The revolution of Moses was directed against both. Previously, the deity was, as we saw, throught of anthropomorphically. That is why the image of the deity was usually a human representation; at times, however, it was also symbolized by an animal:[175] bull, fish, serpent. In forbidding any representation of the deity on principle and for all time, Moses most incisively intervened in the magical conception of god itself and thereby enforced a development that was sure to lead to the idea of the invisible God, the God who is bound by no form and is not only unique but really the only One. The prohibition of any representation necessarily developed into the idea of the non-representable. The conscious renunciation of any representation of the deity is the decisive advance toward a new age of religion.

The objection that the reason for the prohibition of images lay only in the inability of the Israelites to make any images and in their lack of an artistic urge (Wellhausen, Gressmann, and others) is entirely out of place. When and where else has artistic inability among other peoples been a reason for such a prohibition? The crudest plastic representation of the deity suffices for worship. A wooden block with a rough carving that just hints at a face and limbs, a piece of stone on which a scoring indicates the neck and another the separation of the legs, these are sufficient for religious fantasy.[176] Primitive people are in this exactly like children who treat the crudest doll with the most ardent love. And the Israelites too could have manifested this in the early period. Their *ability* reached far beyond. If we look at the lion seal of Shema (eighth century) or the ivory tablets of Samaria (ninth century) we find highly realistic art combined with a strong plastic ability. It was not lack of ability which hindered the making of representations of God, but the determination which, implanted in the people by Moses, felt such a representation to be blasphemy, because through Moses the conception of the divine had been lifted to a new and higher level. We do not know what Moses thought, but we may make inferences from the consequences which his thought has had.

It was certainly not easy and not immediately possible to succeed in persuading the Israelites to abandon the wonted and well-loved representation of the deity. The recollection of this is preserved in the story of the Golden Calf in whose manufacture even

Aaron shared, Aaron whom we must consider to be a noble Levite. Again, two generations later, we find an image of God in the sanctuary of Micha, once more in the care of a Levite, Jonathan, a grandson of Moses, and brought along by him to the sanctuary of Dan, and again two hundred fifty years later under Jeroboam at Dan and in the temple of Bethel. In all these cases the image was that of a young bull, which would be regarded as an unobjectionable symbol for YHWH. That was not likely to be by chance; on the contrary it may be concluded that previously this representation was customary among the Israelites, before it was forbidden and cast away by Moses. But there can also be no doubt that from that time it was regarded as unlawful by the mass of the people and their spiritual leaders, and met with strong opposition. The few cases reported to us remained exceptions. All excavations in Palestine confirm the fact that representations of the deity did not occur among the Israelites; where they were found, they were Canaanite or introduced from foreign countries through the Canaanites.

Through this development, however, the God of Israel was not and could not be represented — an idea to which no other people of antiquity ever advanced. He thereby was lifted up to quite a different level in the consciousness and feeling of the people. YHWH was no longer one god among many but the only real God, in opposition to the "earlier" gods who were nothing other than imaginable and representable demons. In this way there grew out of the imagelessness of God the thought of the only God. Who would doubt that the idea of one God lay in the spirit of Moses, when he took the prodigious step of prohibiting the making of an image of God?

What was Moses' conception of the divine? This can only be deduced from the conclusions which he drew. Here was the most sweeping change brought by Moses not only to his people but also to all mankind.

In the world of great antiquity the deity was an extra human power, scarcely in touch with human affairs. Man, fearing[177] this power, sought to influence it favorably for himself by means of sacrifices, exorcisms, and magic art. But he never thought of planning his actions and his conduct toward his fellowmen in relation to the divine or of imagining that the attitude of the deity toward himself could stand in any fixed and legal relationship to his actions. The divine beings stood outside the norms which were set up for human conduct. Without restraint the myths related about murder, fraud, theft, adultery, and incest committed in the world of the gods. The gods were exalted above a conduct that men, in order to be able to live in a community, prohibited and avenged with severe punishments.

Here we are confronted by the fundamental difference which Moses' conception of God brought into the world. The moral demands that the Ten Commandments placed upon Israel were demands that Israel had to fulfill in order to enter into the covenant with the deity: they were *demands of the deity*.

Moses, for the first time, apprehended God as a moral being. It is the only determination of the divine essence which was given. The first commandments that speak of God gave only what was negative: no god apart from YHWH, no image, no misuse of the sacred name. But even later there were no other definitions of the deity and no other demands. No cultic service belonged to the conditions of the covenant; no belief in definite attributes of God was commanded, like his omnipotence[178] or omnipresence or omniscience or eternity. What was commanded were moral demands. Morality alone was the positive determination of the deity. Only what was moral was the bond between the divine and earthly spheres.

This idea, the singling out of *morality* among the practical relationships between man and man and its elevation into the sphere of the divine, was specifically Israelite. Or, more correctly, it has become a specifically Israelite idea since the time of Moses. For the effect of Moses on the nascent nation was so tremendous that it completely transformed the Israelite tribes, not only politically but also spiritually. The association of moral injunctions with religious ideas was not given intrinsically; it became so for mankind for the first time through Moses. This point must be completely clear to us because it was decisive for Israel's conception of God since Moses.

The commandments of morality are human matters developed by communities of men living together and necessary for the security of their group life. The horde of men existing in primitive times had first to become a peaceful establishment, adapted for the cooperation of communal forces by the individual abandoning the use of brute force against his companion in the horde. He did come to make sacrifices for the defense of his companions in order to obtain by it protection of himself by the others. We have accustomed ourselves to take the analogous process within our more limited family circle as a matter of course and a natural expectation; but the "ethics of the horde" developed entirely from the same roots.

When throughout many thousands or tens of thousands of years this adaptation of man to the forbearance and assistance of his "neighbor" and to the making of certain sacrifices in his favor is practiced, it finally becomes a strong and unconscious "instinct." At the same time, with the progressive concentration of men in larger groups, the validity of this impetus is extended. It thereby becomes the basis of a higher corporate life and the mightiest lever of a civilization striving for higher goals.

But now, a new and epoch-making development took place in Israel through the law of Moses. Man's moral relation toward his neighbor became *conscious,* and was made the absolute yardstick of human conduct. The demand came to exist in this people and their pioneering, enlightened spirit with an unheard of force, its substratum being unapprehended and unknown. This unknown force burned in Moses with a sacred flame; it became the basis of a covenant with God he kindled in the people created by him. That mighty force with which Moses wanted to forge together a people, impelled by a holy purpose, he called GOD.

The moral aspect, as we saw, was the sole positive determination of the divine being that emerged from the Ten Commandments. The deity was conceived as a moral being for the first time in the spiritual history of mankind. The deity demanded not only moral relationship; deity and morality were the same thing. The deity was the idea of morality. Only he who recognized the moral demands of the deity as obligatory, only he could enter into a covenant with the deity, and therefore these basic demands were contained in the Ten Commandments.

From this point on we can recognize more clearly Moses' ideas of God which in the beginning of the Ten Commandments were circumscribed in a negative way. God, who embodies the moral demand, can only be One. It is unthinkable that beside YHWH, whose essence is the moral law, other deities should be envisaged who have no share in it. He is absolutely unique, and unique not for Israel only. The secret and root of Israelite monotheism lies not in any philosophical reasoning about the conception of God but in the development of the God-idea from a moral urge. From the very beginning it was perfect monotheism, so perfect in the idea brought home by Moses that people in later centuries, who were in contact with the religious conceptions and rites of Canaan, found it difficult to maintain that monotheism in its purity and exclusiveness.

Here also was the fundamental reason for the prohibition of any kind of representation of God. The deities of the nations were closely bound up with the life of nature:[179] they were themselves objects of nature; they could be looked at and represented. The God YHWH, whom Moses comprehended, was no object of nature but an unseen spiritual principle. How would one and how could one represent or portray the moral law? What was most pure and profound in the human breast, the striving for what was good and true, became deified through Moses. Could one again fall back into representing the divine as human by giving it a human form? The attempt to represent *this* God was bound to appear not only inadequate but also absurd and blasphemous.

If YHWH was the embodiment of the right and the good, then it was also senseless to compose a mythology, to practice magic, to want by magic to extort or to coax him for something. Where there is only one God, the God of Justice, he can have no father, no mother, no wife, no sons and daughters; a mythology becomes senseless. In Israel too there were ancient stories of the "sons of God" (Gen. 6:2), of angels and of devils. But a clear mind like Moses' that had grasped the notion and composition of ten commandments, was sure to have rejected those elements and deemed them disposed of by the first commandment. They lingered on underground, however, and at the time of the Second Temple came to the surface again under Babylonian and Persian influence, together with the magic of a developed sacrificial and prayer ritual; the Second Temple saw a revival of the magical age throughout.

But it would certainly be a grave error (which the Jewish theologians jointly and severally commit) if one would simply construct a complete edifice of pure monotheism, maintaining that that was the teaching of Moses. There can be no doubt that in his religious system there were earthly remains, indeed that in much he was a son of his own time. No matter how commanding and superior a spirit he was, yet in many an aspect he remained in the grip of the habits and outlooks existing in the past, above all in cultic matters. And that is not astonishing, for the cultic is the sphere of religion in which things magical and out-of-date survive longest and most tenaciously. Moses fashioned the ark not only as the receptacle of the law but also as the throne-seat and footstool of the deity, who it is true remained invisible but was nevertheless anthropomorphized. He fashioned the brazen serpent—a relapse into the magic age. At cultic actions he made use of a mask—David still had it in his house, and the prophet Hosea still found it unobjectionable. He offered up animal sacrifices—a crass remnant of magical ideas of God; but who could expect and demand that a man of that time should suddenly advance as far as the pure monotheism of the eighth- and seventh-century prophets who were hostile to sacrifices?

It is through tradition faintly sensed that these features do not quite suit the image we have formed of the personality of the revolutionary innovator Moses. To be sure in cultic narratives an undertone repeatedly sounds indicating that Moses was not the original driving force. The first sacrifice in Israel was offered up not by Moses but by the Midianite priest Jethro. He too was apparently the one who came to fashion the ark. The cult was in general more an expression of what had been handed down, and the revolution consisted in giving it a new spirit.

But even if all these "earthly remnants" in the work of Moses are granted, his accomplishment remains incomprehensible and to an astonishing degree transcends his time. What momentum lies in the simple fact that, in the obligatory compact of the Mosaic covenant, the Ten Commandments, positive injunctions about the cult, were not included as conditions of the covenant! How far Moses was in advance of his time becomes clear when we compare this document with the two covenant documents of later periods. The covenant which Josiah concluded some six hundred years later (622) was essentially a cultic one; the restriction of the entire sacrificial service to Jerusalem, and the covenant of Nehemiah some eight hundred years later (445), also clothed in the form of "ten commandments," were almost entirely limited to what was cultic. Moses, the hero of antiquity, is far more "modern" in this than the later lawgivers. With full justification the great prophets (Amos, Micha, Isaiah, and Jeremiah) felt themselves to be his true successors and, in their struggle against the cult, appealed again and again to Moses.

At one point it might be thought that there was an excep-

tion and that a cultic element was included in the Ten Commandments, that is, the Sabbath commandment. But this is precisely proof
to the contrary. The ritual, which later outgrew the law of the Sabbath to an ever-increasing extent, had no place yet in the Ten Commandments. Although written later, the expansions and explanations
show what the commandment meant. In the motivation of the law
they differ, in the interpretation of its sense they agree. The Sabbath
on the seventh day, in regular weekly repetition, was meant to bring
relaxation and rest from the labor of the six-day week. The social
significance of this idea has frequently been discussed. But to comprehend the personality of Moses we must make clear to ourselves
the unprecedented originality of the Sabbath idea. It is one of the
grandest — the use of the word may be pardoned — "inventions" in
the history of civilization that a working man must rest one day in the
week; as a social idea this is perhaps more far-reaching than any
other. Although most peoples in one way or another have copied the
Sabbath of Israel, its most profound significance was surely comprehended and experienced in this people only. Its deepest sense was
a religious one, the command "to sanctify" this day. It was meant to
bring not only external rest to the weary but also a special consecra-
tion and spiritual tension, leading to what was loftier than the neces-
sities of daily life. That was what met an inborn need of this people,
and that was also, so we may conclude, the basic thought of Moses,
the main reason why he inserted the Sabbath law between the divine
and the human law.

  The moral commandments, which are inculcated as conditions of the covenant of God, were very few in number. Clearly
only those that are the most indispensable for forming a sacred
community of people have been deliberately chosen. There is not the
slightest doubt that in the time of Moses many more than those were
strictly enjoined and to some extent laid down in legal form. Witness
to this are the Book of the Covenant, whose roots go back into a very
ancient period, and several sections of the "Holiness Code" (Lev.
15-25),[160] which have been handed down in the age-old form of the
Ten Commandments.

  What gave the fundamental commandments of the Decalogue their special imprint, however, was the inseparable union of
religion,[181] morality, and law. The jurist smiles at it, and declares it to
be primitive and inadequate. But in truth herein lies the deepest sense

and the strongest power of Moses' teaching. With the peoples of antiquity (and this concept of *antiquity* applies down to the present day), the law, as a modern scholar has expressed it, is "the restriction of beasts of prey to their own hunting grounds." In the Israel created by Moses, the concatenation of law and morality and the inspiration of both by the divine spirit were a deep, even imperative need of the people's soul. Law can only be what corresponds to the demands of morality; and morality comes down to us from God and lifts us up to God. This special character was already imprinted onto the commandments by Moses, who in this was again pioneer and example to his nation.

Perhaps we are led still deeper into the essence of the matter and into the secret of Moses' thoughts by the prohibition of the magic use of the name of God.

In the thinking of this early period, image and name of the deity were almost body and soul of the deity. As the image of a god was not considered a dead object but its living representative, so the name was not a mere external denomination of the deity from outside but part of its spiritual personality, something that belonged to its essence. Therefore, whoever had at his disposal the real, genuine name of a god, to a certain degree controlled the deity itself and could coerce it. Only from this point of view can we comprehend why there are so many narratives dealing with the name of God. Tradition took it for granted that the real name of God was unknown to earlier generations and only Moses became acquainted with it through a special revelation. According to the belief of the magical age (which in many ideas survives still today!), a power was entrusted to Moses such as no man possessed before him. A unique account in fact reports (Exod. 34) that he once made use of the name ("he called YHWH by name," Exod. 34:5) to insist on the granting of his petition before YHWH. The third commandment on the contrary taught something different; it taught that Moses voluntarily renounced this power and forbade the use of the name of God for superstitious and magical purposes.

Our discussion has followed the ideas of that period: that magic power in reality did not exist; it was only believed in. The stupendous deed of Moses lay in his undertaking to uproot this belief in the world and forbid it. In order to achieve something like that, Moses must have outgrown the magic age. He had come to recognize, so we may conclude, that it was blasphemy to believe that any kind of coercion by magic could be exercised upon God through the misuse of the divine name. The name itself, as we saw above, was not a genuine name but an ingeniously arranged sound-group intended for the invocation of the deity. This name was used for the invocation of God only, and like the deity itself, the name thereby also became holy. By the prohibition and fear of any misuse, the sanctity of "the name" in Israel was enhanced to such an extent that any pronouncement of the name of God was gradually shunned and the name of God fell entirely into oblivion. In forbidding the misuse of the name of God for magical purposes, Moses made an end not only of the misuse but also of magic and witchcraft generally. What appears today to be a small thing was at that time a tremendous accomplishment, namely, that the spirit of one man could rise above solid age-old convictions. Moses could proclaim this prohibition only because he had attained to a new conception of the fundamental nature of the divine.

Moses was liberator, lawgiver, and leader of his people; he was not a religious mystic nor indeed a philosopher. The effect of his ideas was concentrated on actual conduct, not upon theory. That is why we find in the sources only practical injunctions and no definitions or speculations about the nature of the divine; those we have to infer only from occasional statements. The basic problems of ethics also are nowhere under discussion. God wanted man to do what is right and good. But how did evil come into the world? If YHWH was unique, and there was no other power beside him, why did he allow evil to exist?

Peoples with many gods solved the problem very easily. They believed that alongside the good gods there were one or more evil gods who led men astray. The responsibility for good and evil was thereby shifted from men to the gods. The Greeks had a goddess of discord and altercation, a god of theft, a god whose pleasure was war and murder, a goddess of sensual love who instigated adultery, a god who taught the art of the fraudulent oath. The Egyptians had their Seth, the Persians their Ahriman, the Teutons their Loki. Even the later Israelite development inclined at times in this direction. An evil spirit from God brought Saul to maddening rage (1 Sam. 16:14). "Satan" corrupted Ahab to make a fatal decision (1 Kings 22:20-22). "Satan" heaped misfortune on Job in order to mislead him to blasphemy.

In contrast, the outlook of the Mosaic period is characteristically different, simple and purely practical. The right action was commanded by God; the evil was *human,* it was disobedience against God. The full responsibility fell upon man, and upon him only. He had complete freedom of choice between good and evil. This conception was so firmly anchored in Israel from the Mosaic period onward, that it became the foundation of Israel's moral outlook on the world. All the conceptions of the later prophets were based on this outlook, and any view which restricted or denied the moral freedom of man, or taught predestination, led away from Judaism. It is clear that this postulate of the unconditionally free moral decision on the part of man stands in an insoluble contradiction to God's omnipotence and omniscience. It limits the omnipotence of God that man should have an absolutely free decision regarding his actions; and it limits the possibility of this being a free decision when its result should be known to the deity from eternity. It is instructive that this antinomy was not contemplated in Israel and was not even felt there. It substantiates what was pointed out above that Moses' and Israel's idea of God started from here, from what is moral. The moral is primary, the moral demand is absolute and superordinate. Morality is only thinkable when man's will has freedom of decision; the world picture had to be shaped with that freedom as a supreme prerequisite.

Moses taught nothing regarding the attributes of God. At least we do not know if he taught anything about them. We do not have from him, as from other founders of religion, sayings and parables from which we might conclude something about his opinions. Only here and there in the stories about Moses is there preserved a faint reflection of his conception of God.

The distinctive attribute of the deity in the religious sense is its righteousness. The God of Moses and of Israel, conceived and comprehended out of the moral feeling of man, gives every man his due. He loves and rewards the good ones; he hates and punishes the wicked. This is movingly described in the parable of how Moses strives to turn away from the people punishment for the Golden Calf. God is unflinchingly just, not only in that he punishes the people but also in that he declines, against the will of Moses, to include him in the punishment. Man should strive after God; therefore righteousness is the supreme human virtue.

The justice of God is not rigid like that of a hard judge; it is tempered by love. The liberation of the people from Egypt was the free act of God's love; because he loved the fathers, he rescued the children. But this love was no passport for sinners, no comfortable refuge for a bad conscience. It had to be earned again and again; neither could it set aside justice nor be a substitute for it. The later Jewish (and Christian) maxim that "repentance turns away the evil decree" is not an opinion from the oldest period. In spite of their repentance, the people were repeatedly punished (Num. 14:39-45), and so was David (2 Sam. 12:13-18).

God is almighty; all things go back to him, all that is and all that happens. "Who has made man's mouth, or who makes a man dumb, or deaf, or seeing or blind? Is it not I, YHWH?" (Exod. 4:11).

But from the omnipotence and justice of God there arose a new and difficult problem: How did suffering come into the world, and how was it compatible with God's justice and omnipotence? Every religion is based on the assumption that good is rewarded, and that evil is punished (whether in this world or in the next is irrelevant). Consequently where there is suffering, there is seeking for sin. But at no time could it escape man that not every affliction was the consequence of sin. Indeed man must reach the conclusion that most suffering and affliction come to him undeserved. But this entire approach to the problem was unfamiliar to the point of view of the Mosaic period; the problem of suffering and of its relation to God was not mentioned by a single word. This omission was soon felt. It was partially filled by the idea, expressed in an expansion of the second commandment, that God also visited the sin of the fathers on the children even to the third and fourth generation. But in reality this solution was not a solution, since even then the children did suffer innocently. By the death of his child a father can be severely stricken for his sin (thus David in 2 Sam. 12); but the child? Why does the child suffer? There are blind, deaf, invalid people; why do they suffer? Many centuries later an entire book of the Bible was devoted to the problem of undeserved suffering, the book of Job, but even here no solution is given. From the time of the classical prophets, especially after the Babylonian exile, the suffering of an entire people was accepted as a punishment for the sin of the fathers; but the suffering of the individual was not thereby solved and has never been brought into harmony with the notion of divine justice. Judaism has rarely acknowledged the bitter truth that sin and suffering are not commensurable and are not related to one another. How could we expect that in the early Mosaic period thoughts of this kind, which touch on what is deepest in religion, should find an echo in the narratives?

The teaching that Moses gave was directed throughout toward the actual and the practical. It called above all for one thing, obedience to God's commandments. That was the demand, which God laid down again and again. And this obedience to the commandments of God was indeed attained. Obedience to the law of Moses transformed the hordes of wild Bedouins into the people of Israel.

Summary

What are the results of our investigations? The question which initiated the investigation was: how close historically can we get to Moses by making a careful evaluation of the sources? The results must be evaluated from this point of view by linking together what is historically accessible in the phenomenon Moses.

1. Moses is a historic personality. He is an individual reality, not just a formation of legends. It is true that most of what has been handed down to us about him is in the form of legend. But numerous legends have been handed down, without our having reason to doubt their historicity, about other personalities who later lived in the full light of history (David, Elijah, Jesus, or Derrick of Berne). Moses has left historical testimonies, historical effects, and descendants. The largest part of the Moses legends is understandable only when we admit that they refer to a historical personality.

2. Moses was by descent a Levite. That he belonged to this peculiar "tribe of priests" is an inescapable presupposition of his special achievement and effect. On the other hand, the powerful historical role of the Levites in the development of Israel is only comprehensible because they consciously traced themselves back to Moses — whether physically or spiritually is not of decisive importance in this connection — and considered themselves heirs and executors of his work. Moses was a Levite, but at the same time strongly assimilated into the Egyptian environment. This too belongs to the prerequisites of his historical reality.

3. Moses' sojourn in Midian is probably a historical fact. From Midian stem substantial parts of the historical material which is connected with the work of Moses. From here originated the traditions about the volcano called Sinai, which have strongly influenced the conception of God in Israel. From here came the sacrificial ritual,

the sacred ark, and the judicial organization of the Israelite tribes in Mosaic times, as the analysis of the traditions shows — elements that, for the external form and historical persistence of the work of Moses, have become of the highest significance. But nothing indicates that the inner form, the thought-content of Moses' work, can be traced back to Midianite origin.

4. The exodus of Israelite tribes from Egypt must be considered a historic event. The silence of Egyptian sources about it is no argument to the contrary. In attempting to date this event, it seems best to place it during the long reign of Ramses II. A special event at the "Sea of Reeds" during the exodus also has to be considered historical. It is attested to by indubitable contemporary testimony, the Song of Miriam, which is only understandable from the circumstances of its origin at this time; as a later product it would be incomprehensible.

5. From the eastern border of Egypt the Israelite tribes headed immediately and directly for the oasis of Kadesh. Here they remained during the entire period of their stay in the wilderness. A "desert-wandering" in the sense of the later traditions never took place. The departure from Kadesh, about a generation later, was followed immediately by the march into East Jordan territory and the conquest of Canaan.

Traces of the most ancient traditions point to old pre-Mosaic connections of the tribe of Levi with the oasis of Kadesh. Probably the tribe of Levi at an early period was in possession of the oasis of Kadesh.

6. The goal of the exodus from Egypt was Kadesh and not Canaan. The plan for the conquest of Canaan arose only at a later time in Kadesh, presumably as a consequence of the overpopulation of the oasis.

7. The place- and spring-legends of Kadesh are older than Moses and originally had nothing to do with him. But a section of the Kadesh legends are genuine Moses legends containing a historical kernel. The cult legends of Kadesh also belong to the Moses legends.

From the place legends and the names of the springs it can be concluded that even before Moses the oasis of Kadesh was the center of a legal tradition.

8. The central role of Kadesh in the life and work of Moses becomes evident from the complete material. Kadesh was the

place of the giving of the law and the coming into being of the nation; here the "federation of the twelve tribes" was brought into being and given the name *Israel*. In both the national and the religious sense Kadesh was the cradle of the people of Israel. By far the largest part of all the Moses traditions goes back to Kadesh.

9. The divine name YHWH was first created by Moses as a symbol of a new religious epoch. It is an artificial product, neither needing nor open to any philological explanation. Even the name *Israel* is not an ethnic but a religious-political name of the tribal alliance and was created by Moses.

10. Aaron and Miriam were Levites and brother and sister, but not the brother and sister of Moses. They were opponents of Moses' reforms.

11. The Kadesh tradition and the Sinai tradition basically should be separated; they were only secondarily amalgamated with each other. The Kadesh traditions are the more original and important ones. The "mountain of the giving of the law" originally lay in Kadesh.

12. On the departure from Kadesh a division of the people took place. One section, under Moses, marched from Kadesh into East Jordan territory and conquered north and middle Palestine; the other section marched from Kadesh directly north and conquered southern Palestine. The attack from the east was strategically the better plan; but the division led to the conquest of all Canaan by Israelite tribes.

13. The Ten Commandments go back to Moses. They were the charter and substance of the federation of tribes. They were originally quite short and somewhat differently divided. The actual meaning of some of the Ten Commandments (the first, third, and tenth) has so far not been fully recognized in its true significance.

14. The twelve tribes of the covenant were not identical with the later "twelve sons of Jacob." On the immigration into Canaan new tribes (already settled or developed later) entered into the covenant; old ones (which did not get settled) had dropped out, but continued to be considered and recognized as members of the religious brotherhood.

15. The federation of "Israel" was a national one, but, more importantly, a religious one. In this it corresponded completely to the alliance of Arab tribes under Muhammad.

16. The basic religious idea of Moses was a genuine monotheism of great purity. It opened up a new epoch in the religious development of mankind. In cultic matters Moses took over ancient remnants of the age of magic.

17. Moses' work was new and revolutionary in the inseparable union of religion and morality and in the obligation of the federation to fulfill certain religious and moral demands. Moses was the first to be cognizant of, and to the present the most successful and effective founder of, a religion whose work has not been fundamentally altered by his successors.

As we emerge from the labyrinth of detailed investigations, the whole personality of Moses stands revealed. Moses was without doubt the most powerful genius brought forth by Israel. He was in his own time a solitary figure of greatness. The human material on which he worked was primitive, just awakening out of man's primeval period, still lacking any history, and only awakened to its own self-consciousness by him. A strange wonder in this environment was this giant, who alone, in place of the magical, somber, and bloody superstitions of his time, developed the sublime idea of a unique deity, which could not be represented and which demanded morality. He alone attempted to impose such a belief on a rude mass of slaves and Bedouins! In order to be able to achieve what he did, he possessed a variety of talents, which in their abundance and breadth have rarely been concentrated in one single man. The superiority of his spirit was so immense that it would not have been surprising if he had immediately been raised up as a god-man. At no time did he succumb to this temptation! And in addition he had to have all the ability of a statesman and army commander; he had to be able to assume the leadership of a people and to deal with the pressing dangers of every hour; he needed infallible judgment and the ability to make prompt decisions. He had to give the right command at the right moment. He required never-flagging power of will to carry things through, and the ability to probe into the smallest details in order to make possible their execution. He was unfeeling to the point of cruelty in order to break opposition and annihilate opponents. But he was not cruel; on the contrary he was just; violent in anger and "full of jealousy" when some principle was to be guarded and deviations from the novel way had to be averted. In addition he had infinite patience and forbearance[182] with the weakest of the weak who indeed were no giants as he was. A tireless teacher who by example and instruction so filled a new generation with his ideas that they endured after his death. And yet he was so close to the heart of the simplest one that all trusted his judgment and saw in him the father to whom they could come with all their trials, troubles, and disagreements. He "bore the burden of the people." He had to provide food and water. He had to give guidance on the way and provide security; he had to stem the careless selfishness of the people and within his community enforce subordination.

In his own mighty spirit he surveyed the entire vast route, from his world-fulfilling conception to its realization, through the action of each individual and each day. And he traveled that route with unerring certainty for forty years, day by day and year by year, until his work was crowned with success: such success that the coming generations felt themselves to be the heirs and successors of his course. With all the detail — and in small things lies the truly great! — he remained the prophetic visionary who conceived the final accomplishment and its continuance in a hostile world. He envisaged it as the objective and true service of God.

In the work of man, Moses was, through the grace of God, the artist who saw in the rough block not only the hidden, the perfect form; impatiently and patiently, he struck it out of the stone with a heavy hammer and smoothing chisel. He was man in his fullness, one in a thousand years. Where is there another who merges within himself this unique combination: a fundamental spiritual conception with practical effectivenss in action?

Moses is no doubt one of the greatest geniuses to whom the world has given birth.

References, Abbreviations, and Short Titles Used in the Notes

AAN—Miscellany in honor of A.A. Neuman, Studies and Essays, ed. M. Ben—Horin et al., Leiden, 1962.

AB—Attualità Bibliche, Rome

ABANE—Miscellany in honor of W.F. Albright, The Bible and the Ancient Near East, ed. G.E. Wright, London, 1961.

ABM—A. Altmann, ed., Biblical Motifs, Cambridge, 1966

ABR—Australian Biblical Review, Melbourne

Abr.N.—Abr Nahrain, Melbourne

ABS—A. Altmann, ed., Biblical Motifs and Other Studies, Cambridge, 1963

AER—American Ecclesiastical Review, Washington, D.C.

AGEP—Sir Alan Gardiner, Egypt of the Pharaohs, Oxford, 1964

AIBL—Académie des Inscriptions et Belles-Lettres. Comptes Rendus, Paris

AICO—Acts of the International Congress of Orientalists

AIPHOS—Annuaire, Institut de Philologie et d'Histoire Orientales et Slaves, Brussels

AKS—A. Alt, Kleine Schriften, Munich, 1953-59

ALBO—Analecta Lovaniensia Biblica et Orientalia, Louvain

Altertum, Berlin

ALUOS—Annual, Leeds University Oriental Society

An. Bib.—Analecta Biblica, Rome

Anatol. Stud.—Anatolian Studies, London

ANEP—J.B. Pritchard, The Ancient Near East in Pictures Relating to the OT, Princeton, 1954

ANET—J.B. Pritchard, Ancient Near Eastern Texts, 3d ed., Princeton, 1969

Anima, Freiburg (Switzerland)

Ant. Sur.—Antiquity and Survival, the Hague

Anthropos, Freiburg (Switzerland)

Antiquity, Gloucester

AnTR—Anglican Theological Review, New York

AO—Archiv für Orientforschung, Graz

ARM—Archives Royales de Mari. Transcriptions et traductions, Paris

ASAE—Annales du Service des Antiquités de l'Egypte, Cairo

ASF—Miscellany in honor of A. Silver, In the time of harvest. Essays, ed. S. Freehof et al., New York, 1963

ASTI—Annual of the Swedish Theological Institute, Leiden

AT—Altes Testament, Antico Testamento

ATR—Australian Theological Review

BA—Biblical Archaeologist, New Haven, Conn.

BAR—Biblical Archaeologist Reader, ed. G.E. Wright et al., 3 vols., Garden City, N.Y., 1961-70

BASOR—Bulletin. American Schools of Oriental Research, New Haven, Conn.

Bib.—Biblica, Rome

Bib. Or.—Bibliotheca Orientalis, Leiden

Bib. Sacr.—Bibliotheca Sacra, Oberlin

Bib. Sanct. Later.

Bible Today, Collegeville, Minn.

Biblos Press

BK—Bibel und Kirche, Stuttgart

BL—Bibel und Leben, Düsseldorf

BM—Beth Mikra', Jerusalem

BO—Biblia e Oriente, Genua

BR—Biblia Revuo, Moohee Ponds (Australia)

BS—Bibliotheca Sacra. Dallas, Texas

BSFE—Bulletin, Société Française d'Egyptologie.

BTS—Bible et Terre Sainte, Jerusalem

BVH—Miscellany in honor of A.W. Byvanck, Varia Historica, Assen, 1954

BZAW—Beihefte of ZAW (q.v.)

BZP—Biblische Zeitschrift, Paderborn

CAD—Chicago Assyrian Dictionary

CAH—Cambridge Ancient History, 3rd ed., Cambridge, 1970-

Cah. Hist. Eg.—Cahiers d'histoire egyptienne, Cairo

CAOB—Congrés d'archéologie et orientalisme biblique, Paris

CB, CBS—Cultura Biblica, Segovia

Cuad. B.—Cuadernos Biblicos

CBG—Collationes Brugenses

CBQ—Catholic Biblical Quarterly, Washington

CBS. See CB

CHM—Cahiers d'histoire mondiale. Paris

CJT—Canadian Journal of Theology, Toronto

CO—Correspondence d'Orient

Concilium, Mayence

Congr. Vol.—Congress Volume

CTM—Concordia Theological Monthly, St. Louis, Mo.

CV—Communio Viatorum, Prague

DBS—Dictionnaire de la Bible, Supplément

EB—Estudios Biblicos, Madrid

EBB—Enciclopedia de la Biblia, 2nd ed., Barcelona, 1969

EE—Estudios Ecclesiasticos, Madrid

EI—Encyclopaedia of Islam, 2d ed., 3 vols, Leiden, 1960, 1971,-

Eissfeldt-Ackroyd—O. Eissfeldt, The Old Testament. An introduction, trans. P. Ackroyd, New York, 1966; with additional literature, pp. 722 ff.

ELKZ—Evangelisch Lutherische Kirchen-Zeitung

ELW—O. Eissfeldt, Lesser Writings (Kleine Schriften), 5 vols., Tübingen, 1962-73

EM—Ensiklopediah Mikra'ith, Jerusalem, 1955-71, 6 vols. to date

Enc—Encounter

Er. Isr.—Eretz Israel, Jerusalem

ETL—Ephemerides Theologicae Lovanienses, Louvain

ETR—Etudes théologiques et religieuses, Montpellier

Eunt. Doc.—Euntes Docete. Commentarica Urbaniana, Rome

Evidences, Paris

Ev. Q.—Evangelical Quarterly, London

Exp. T.—Expository Times, Edinburgh

FBF—F. Baumgärtel, Festschrift, ed. L. Rost, Erlangen, 1959

FF—Forschungen und Fortschritte, Berlin

FNF—F. Nötscher, Festschrift, Alttestamentliche Studien, ed. H. Junker, J. Botterweck, Bonn, 1950

Franc.—Franciscanum, Bogotá

GHD—Miscellany in honor of G. Henton Davies, Proclamation and Presence, ed. J. Durham, J.R. Porter, London, 1970

GTT—Gereformeerd Teolog. Tijdschrift

GUOST—Glasgow University Oriental Society. Transactions

HHF—H. Hertzberg, Festschrift, Gottes Wort, etc., ed. H. Graf Reventlow, Göttingen, 1965

HJF—H. Junker, Festschrift, Lex Tua Veritas, ed. H. Gross, F. Mussner, Trier, 1961

HL—Das Heilige Land in Vergangenheit und Gegenwart

HMF—H.G. May. Festschrift, Translating and Understanding the OT, ed. H. Frank, W.L. Reed, Nashville, 1970

HR—History of Religions, Chicago

HSN—Donum . . . H.S. Nyberg, Uppsala, 1954

HTR—Harvard Theological Review, Cambridge

HUCA—Hebrew Union College Annual, Cincinnati

Hyatt—J.P. Hyatt, ed., The Bible in Modern Scholarship, Nashville, Tenn., 1965

IJT—Indian Journal of Theology, Serampore

Int.—Interpretation, Richmond, Virginia

IONA—Istituto Universitario Orientale di Napoli, Annali

Isr. EJ—Israel Exploration Journal, Jerusalem

JAAR—Journal, American Academy of Religion

JAOS—Journal of the American Oriental Society, New Haven, Conn.

JBL—Journal of Biblical Literature, Philadelphia

JBR—Journal of Bible and Religion, Brattleboro, Vt.

JCS—Journal of Cuneiform Studies, New Haven, Conn.

JJLP—Journal of Jewish Lore and Philosophy

JKF—Jahrbuch für kleinasiatische Forschung, Istanbul

JNES—Journal of Near Eastern Studies, Chicago

JQR AV—Anniv. volume Jewish Quarterly Review, Philadelphia

JRH—Journal of Religious History, Sidney, Australia

JSS—Journal of Semitic Studies, Manchester

JTC—Journal of Theology and Church, New York

JTS—Journal of Theological Studies, N.S., Oxford/London

Jud.—Judaica, Beiträge etc., Zurich, 1945

Judaism, New York

KBF—Karl Barth. Festschrift, Zurich, 1956

KD—Kerygma und Dogma, Göttingen

KRS—Kirchenblatt für die Reformierte Schweiz

LD—Lectio Divina, 1946 ff.

Leshonenu, Jerusalem

LKF—L. Köhler. Festschrift

LMH—Lutherische Monatshefte, Hamburg

LTQ—Lexington Theological Quarterly, Kentucky

LXX—Septuagint Version of the Bible

Lum.—Lumen. Revista . . . Seminário de Vitória

MAB—Miscellanea Academica Berolinensa. Deutsche Akad. d. Wissensch., Berlin

MACO—Miscellanea Alfredo Card. Ottaviani, Rome, 1969

MDO—Mitteilungen der deutschen Orientgesellschaft, Berlin

MEAH—Miscelanea de Estudios Arabes y Hebraicos, Granda

MHA—Museum Ha'aretz Annual

MHSS—M.H. Segal, Studies on the Bible presented by J. Grintz and J. Liver, Jerusalem, 1965

MIOR—Mitteilungen des Instituts für Orientforschung, Berlin

MKNAW—Mededelingen. Koningl. Nederlandsche Akad. van Wetensch.

MM—R.J. Christen, Monotheism and Moses, Lexington, Mass., 1969
Molad, Tel Aviv
MT—Masoretic text
MUSJ—Mélanges de l'Université St. Joseph, Beirut
NEB—The New English Bible, ed. G.R. Driver et al., New York, 1971
NGS—M. Noth, Gesammelte Studien zum Alten Testament, Munich, 1957
NGT—Nederduitse Gereform eerde Teologiese Tyskrif, Capetown
NTT—Nederlands Theologisch Tijdschrift, Wageningen
Numen, Leiden
NV—Nova et Vetera, Fribourg
NZSTR—Neue Zeitschrift für systematische Theologie und Religions Wissenschaft, Berlin
OA—Oriens Antiquus, Rome
Orient, Paris
Or. Suec.—Orientalia Suecana, Uppsala
OTWSA—Ou-Testamentiese Werkgemeenskap van Suid-Afrika
Oud. St.—Oudtestamentliche Studien, ed. PAH. de Boer, Leiden
PCR—Palestra de Clero, Rovigo
PdV—Parola de Vita, Rome
PEF QS—Palestine Exploration Fund. Quarterly Statement, London
PSF—P. Schebesta Festschrift (Studia Inst. Anthropos 18), Vienna, 1963
Psy. Q.—Psychological Quarterly
RAC—Reallexikon für Antike und Christentum, 8 vols to date, Stuttgart, 1950-1972
R. Ass.—Revue Assyriologique, Paris
RB—Revue Biblique, Paris
RBA—Revista Biblica. Rafael Calzada, Argentina
RCAJ—Royal Central Asian Journal, London
RCB—Revista di Cultura Biblica, NS, São Paulo
RCMM. See MM
RDT—Revue Diocésaine de Tournai
Ref. TR—Reformed Theological Review, Melbourne
Rev. TP—Revue de Théologie et de Philosophie, Geneva, Lausanne
RGS—Rad (G. von), Gesammelte Studien Zum AT, Munich, 1958
RH—Repue Historique, Paris
Rhema
RHMH—Revue d'Histoire de la Médecine Hébraique, Paris
RHPR—Revue d'Histoire et de Philosophie Religieuses, Strasbourg
RHR—Revue de l'Histoire des Religions, Paris
RIL—Rendiconti Istituto Lombardo (Lettere), Milan

RMI—Rassegna Mensile di Israel, Rome

RsBs—Recherches Bibliques, Brussels

RSR—Recherches de Science Religieuse, Paris

R. Thom.—Revue Thomiste, Toulouse, Brussels

SAJF—Schalom . . . Alfred Jepsen Festschrift, ed. K. -H. Bernhardt, Berlin, 1971

SAWL—Sitzungsberichte, Akademie der Wissenschaften, Leipzig

SBE—Semana Biblica Española, Madrid

SBF—Studi Biblici Franciscani

SBG—Sefer Ben Gurion, Jerusalem, 1964

SBO—Studia Biblica et Orientalia, Rome, 1959

Scripture, Ware (England)

Script. Hier.—Scripta Hierosolymitana, Jerusalem

Sef.—Sefarad, Madrid

Sem.—Semitica, Paris

SJLC—Studies on Jewish Life and Culture, Tokyo

SJT—Scottish Journal of Theology, Edinburgh

SM—Sacramentum Mundi, Fribourg

SOTSB—Society for Old Testament Study, Booklist.

SRHJ—S. Baron, A social and religious history of the Jews, New York, 1952-73, 15 vols. to date

St.B.—Stuttgarter Bibelstudien, Stuttgart

Sti.Zt.—Stimmen der Zeit. Fribourg

Streven, Brugge (Belgium)

STUB—Schweizer Theologische Umschau., Bern

Stu. Th.—Studia Theologica. Aarhus, Lund

Tabor

Tarb.—Tarbiz, Jerusalem

Targ.—Targum

TB—Tyndale Bulletin, Cambridge

TE—Theologia Evangelica

TEH—Theologische Existenz Heute, Munich

TG—Theologie und Glaube, Paderborn

THAT—Theologisches Handwörterbuch zum AT. ed. E. Jenni, vol. 1, Munich, 1971

Theol. Arb.—Theologische Arbeiten, Elberfeld

Theol. Q.—Theologische Quartalschrift, Tübingen

Theol. R.—Theologische Rundschau, Tübingen

Theol. Rev.—Theologische Revue, Milnster i.w.

Theol. Z.—Theologische Zeitschrift, Basel

TLZ—Theologische Literaturzeitung, Berlin

Torah—The Torah. A New Translation, Philadelphia, 1962

TP—Theologie und Philosophie, Fribourg

Trad.—Tradition, New York

TS—La Terre Sainte, Jerusalem

TT—Tijdschrift voor eologie

TU—Texte und Untersuchungen, ed. K. Aland, F.S. Cross, Berlin, 1959

TVF—T. Vriezen Festschrift, Studia Biblica et Semitica, Wageningen, 1966

Ug.—Ugaritic

Ug.a—Ugaritica

VC—Veritatem in Caritate (Protest. Theol. Faculteit), The Hague

VD—Verbum Domini Commentarii . . . de re biblica, Rome

VT—Vetus Testamentum, Leiden

V Theol.—Vox Theologica, Assen

VTS—VT Supplements

VV—Verdad y Vida, Madrid

WBT—Wiener Beiträge zur Theologie

4.WCJS—Fourth World Congress of Jewish Studies, Jerusalem

WDB—Wort und Dienst, Bethel

Wd O.—Welt des Orients, Göttingen

WG—E. Auerbach, Wüste und Gelobtes Land, 2 vols., Berlin, 1936; vol. 1: 2nd ed., 1938

WRF—W. Rudolph Festschrift. Verbannung und Heimkehr, ed. A. Kuschke, Tübingen, 1961

WTF—D. Winston Thomas Festschrift. Words and Meanings, ed. P. Ackroyd, B. Linders, London, 1968

WTJ—Westminster Theological Journal, Philadelphia

WW—Wort und Wahrheit, Vienna

WZKM—Wiener Zeitschrift für die Kunde des Morgenlandes

YKJV—Y. Kaufmann, Jubilee Volume, ed. M. Haran, Jerusalem, 1960

ZA—Zeitschrift für Assyriologie und Vorderasiatische Archäologie, Berlin

ZAW—Zeitschrift für die Alttestamentliche Wissenschaft, Berlin

ZDMG—Zeitschrift der Deutschen Morgenländischen Gesellschaft, Wiesbaden

ZDPV—Zeitschrift des Deutschen Palästinavereins, Wiesbaden

ZEE—Zeitschrift für Evangelische Ethik, Gütersloh

ZTK—Zeitschrift für Theologie und Kirche, Tübingen

Notes and Bibliography

Additions to the original notes are bracketed.

⚡⚡⚡⚡⚡⚡⚡⚡⚡⚡⚡⚡⚡⚡⚡⚡⚡⚡⚡⚡⚡

1. [Historiography:
   R.C. Dentan, ed., The idea of history in the ancient Near East, New Haven, 1955; E. Speiser, The biblical idea of history in its common Near Eastern setting, Isr.E.J. 7(1957): 201-16; C. DeWit, Egyptian methods of writing history, Ev.Q. 28 (1956): 158-69; [O. Eissfeldt, Historiography in the OT (Germ.), Berlin, 1948; C.R. North, The OT interpretation of history, London, 1946; J. Pedersen, Israel, its life and culture, 4 vols., Copenhagen, 1959; E. Auerbach, The great revision of the biblical books (Germ.), VT, Suppl. 1, pp. 1-10. Copenhagen, 1953; J. Bright, Early Israel in recent history writing: A study in method, Chicago, 1956; S. Hermann, Recent works on the history of Israel (Germ., on Bright, Smend, Weiser), TLZ 89 (1964), col. 813-24; S. Mowinckel, Israelite historiography (on Hölscher, Noth, v. Rad, Rost), ASTI 2 (1963): 4-26; R. de Vaux, Method in the study of early Hebrew history (in Hyatt), pp. 15-29; K.A. Kitchen, Historical method and early Hebrew tradition TB 17 (1966): 63-97; cf. ZAW 79 (1967): 108 by G. Fohrer; G.E. Mendenhall, Biblical history in transition, ABANE, pp. 32-53; D.J. Eiseman ed. Peoples of OT Times, Oxford, 1973.]

2. [D.B. Bedford, The literary motif of the exposed child, Numen 14 (1967): 209-28; G. Binder, The exposition of the royal child, Cyrus and Romulus (Germ.), Rhema 8-11 (1962-65): 74-80.]

3. [On the stay in Egypt, cf. N.H. Tur-Sinai (Germ.), Bib. Or. 18, 1/2 (1961): 16-17; H.H. Rowley, AICO, 20 (Louvain, 1940): S. Hermann (Germ.), St.B. 40 (1970): 7-110; A. de Buck, BVH; cf. note 49.]

4. What is especially naive in this case is that the generations, in order to reach the figure 430, are not reckoned at the birth of the next generation, but added according to the full amount of their life span:

Levi	137	(some 80 of this after the immigration)	see Exod. 6:16
Kehat	133		Exod. 6:18
Amram	137		Exod. 6:20
Moses	80	(up to the exodus)	Exod. 7:7
Total	430		

5. [Cf. D. Redford, VT 13 (1963): 401-18; H. Cazelles and J. Leclant, Pithom (Fr.), DBS 8 (1967): 1-6; E. Uphill, JNES 27 (1968): 291-316; 28 (1969): 15-39.]

6. [For the date, cf. AGEP, p. 445; J. Černy, Bib. 40 (1959): 75-82; W. Helck, as to Redford: VT 15 (1965): 35-48.]

7. [R. Giveon, The Shosu Bedouins of the Egyptian documents (Fr.), Leiden, 1972;

F. Gabrieli, ed., The ancient Bedouin society (It.), Rome, 1959; H.v. Wissmann, F. Kussmaul, W.M. Watt, Badw, EI, 1 (1960): 872-92; on the Negev, E. Elath, RCAJ 45.2 (1958): 123-40; cf. W.L. Reed, Enc. 26.2 (1965): 143-53; E. Marx, Bedouin of the Negev, Manchester, 1967; S. Nyström. Bedouin ways and Yahwism (Germ.), Lund, 1946; M. Ben-Gavriel, The nomadic ideal in the Bible (Germ.), Sti. Zt. 171 (1962): 253-63.]

8. There must of course have been more than two; the second half of the verse, which contains this statement and the two names, is a clumsy later addition.

9. The text has "on the two stones," *ha-'obhnayim*. That does not make sense, not even when one interprets them as birthstones, for one cannot recognize sex by these. I propose to read *'ebharum; 'ebher* denotes "limb" in general and the male organ in particular. [Cf. H. Brongers (Dutch) NTT 20 (1965): 241-49.]

10. As a continuation of the story of the midwives, the text has *le-bhath par'oh*. In verse 10 I see the continuation of verse 6; in that case the daughter of Pharaoh is the subject of the sentence (which otherwise would have to change), and I therefore read *le-bheth par'oh*. The word *wa-yigdal* at the beginning of the sentence fits better with this interpretation; otherwise one would expect *wa-yiggamel*, "he was weaned."

11. [On the name, cf. J. Griffiths, JNES 12 (1953): 225-31; H. Baer, Mahanayim (Heb.) 115 (1967); on the birth, cf. also E. Lacocque (Fr.), VC 6, 3-4 (1961): 111-20); A. Horef, Mahanayim, 115; B. Childs, JBL 84 (1965): 109-22.]

12. [Cf. H. Gunneweg, ZTK 61,1 (1964): 1-9; R. DeVaux, Er. Isr. 9 (1969): 28-32.]

13. Read with Syr. *wa-yelekh* instead of *wa-yeshebh* which has crept in from the continuation through dittography.

14. [Cf. W.F. Albright, CBQ 25 (1963): 1-11; A. Cody, Bib. 49 (1968): 153-66; B. Mazar, Er. Isr. 7 (1964): pp. 1-5.]

15. The "testimony" about Moses that Robert Eisler and Hubert Grimme have gathered from Sinai inscriptions discovered by Sir Flinders Petrie bears witness to the two authors' imagination only. [On the Sinai inscriptions, cf. A. Gardiner, T.E. Peet, J. Černy, vol. 2. Translations and commentary (London, 1955). On the historiography of Moses, cf. E. Osswaldt, The image of Moses in British OT scholarship since Jul. Wellhausen (Germ.), Berlin, 1962; C. Keller, About the [present] state of research on Moses (Germ.), Theol. Z. 13 (1957): 430-41; H. Schmid (Germ.), Jud. 21,4 (1965): 194-221; R. Smend, The image of Moses as conceived from Heinr. Ewald to Martin Noth (Germ.), Tübingen, 1959; R. Thompson, Moses and the Law in a century of criticism since Graf, Leiden, 1970. In addition to "literary criticism" there are now also "tradition history," "form-criticism," and "redaction criticism." F. Schnutenhaus, The origins of the Moses traditions (Germ., diss.), Heidelberg, 1958; W.M. Wilson, The Mosaic faith . . . the nature of Israel's earliest faith (diss.), Nashville, 1963; G. Widengren, GHD, pp. 21-47; critical survey.]

16. [Cf. ANET, pp. 18-22.]

17. Freud's complete ignorance of the Bible is clearly shown in that he has overlooked the *only* passage which might favorably explain his theory, Exod. 2:19: "An Egyptian delivered us." But here that means only a man in Egyptian clothing.

18. [Abd el-Moḥsin Bakir, Slavery in Pharaonic Egypt (diss.), Suppl. ASAE 18 (1952); A. Badawy, (Fr.) Cah. Hist. Eg. 4,3 (1952): 167-93; W. Starck, Slavery in the light of ancient Near Eastern and OT law (Germ., diss.), Vienna, 1965.]

19. [Cf. J. Baker, Exp.T. 76 (1964): 307-08; A. Ohlmeyer, BK 12 (1957): 98-111; D.N. Freedman, Bib. 50 (1969): 245-46; P.H. deBoer, Oud. St. 14 (1965): 153 f.; E. Young, The call of Moses, WTJ 29 (1967): 117-35; 30: 1-23; H. Seidel, The experience of solitude in the OT (Germ., diss.), Berlin, 1969.]

20. [For Heb. *seneh,* cf. Accad. *sinu;* Arab. *sanan,* "blackberry bush"; for Heb. *shen,* "tooth", cf. Accad. *sinnu;* Syr. *shenna;* Arab. *sinn;* Eth. *san;* cf. in Deut. 33: 16, MT *seneh,* "Sinai"; *har,* "Sinai'", "the mountain in midbar Sinai"(?).]

21. [E. Pascal, The angels in the pre-exilic literature of the OT (Fr., diss.), Rome, 1965.]

22. [Among recent studies about the tetragrammaton are:
On the name: R. Abba, JBL 80, 4 (1961): 320-28); E.C. MacLaurin, VT 12 (1962): 439-63; A.M. Besnard (Fr.), LD 35 (1962): 7-198; F.M. Cross, HTR 55 (1962): 225-59; D.N. Freedman, JBL 79 (1960): 151 f., and S. Mowinckel, HUCA 32 (1961): 121-33; H. Kosmala, ASTI 2 (1963): 103-06; J. Lindblom, ASTI 3 (1964): pp. 4-15; W. von Soden (Germ.), WdO. 3,3 (1966): 177-87: YHWH is a "prefigurating stative"; J. Gray JNES 12 (1953): 278-83; A. Vincent, L'ami du clergé, 63 (1952): 625-31; G.R. Driver, JBL 73 (1954): 125-36; R.A. Barclay, GUOST 15 (1955): 44-47; H. Chamiel, BM 1 (1956): 86-89; J. Vergote, ETL 39 (1963): 447-52; R. Giveon, VT 14 (1964): 244; S. Hermann (Germ.), 4 WCJS (1967), 1:213-16; K. Kohler, JJLP 1 (1919): 19-32; reprint (1969); R. deVaux, GHD, pp. 48-75: critical survey; J. Kinyongo, Origin and significance of the divine name Yahwe (diss.), Rome, 1966-67.
On the character of the deity: cf. W. Gerhardt (Germ.), Numen 13 (1966): 128-43; J.P. Hyatt, JBL 86,4 (1967): 369-77; H. Schmid (Germ.), Jud. 25,3-4 (1969): 257-66; M. Buber, MM, pp. 88-96; D. Broadribb (Esperanto), Biblia Revuo 6,3 (1970): 162-63; R. Hillmann, Water and mountain: Cosmic contacts between the Canaanite weather-god and Yhwh (Germ., diss.), Halle, 1965.
On the pronunciation, O. Eissfeldt (Germ.), ELW 2: 81-97; W. Vischer (Germ.), Theol. Z. 16 (1960): 259-67; summaries: R. Mayer (Germ.), BZP 2 (1958): 26-53; R. Criado, An investigation about the value of the divine name in the OT, Madrid, 1952; cf. note 24.]

23. Buber-Rosenzweig, Die Schrift und ihre Verdeutschung, Berlin, 1936, pp. 184-210.

24. [J. Lindblom, ASTI 3 (1964): 4-15; O. Eissfeldt (Germ.), FF 39 (1965): 298 f., and ELW 4: 193-98; J. Brinktine (Germ.), TG 42 (1952): 173-79; E. Schild, VT 4 (1954): 296-302; L. von Pákozdy (Germ.), Jud. 11 (1955): 193-208; M. Allard (Fr.), RSR 45 (1957): 79-86; E. Schulze (Germ.), Jud. 11 (1955): 209-16; L. Rougier (Fr.), Bulletin Renan 93 (1962): 1-3; B. Albrektson, WTE, pp. 15-28.]

25. Compilations of such interpretations are found in H. Gressmann, Mose und seine Zeit; Göttingen, 1913; J. Hehn, Die biblische und babylonische Gottesidee, Leipzig, 1913; H. Torczyner, Die Bundeslade, Berlin, 1922.

26. [YHWH occurs about 6823 times in MT; *'elohim* 305 times. For the correct pronunciation *Yahweh,* cf. Exod. 3:14 (Heb. *ehyeh*), Greek *iaouai,* (Clemens

Alexandrinus, ca. 150- before 215), Stromata, V., 6:34; see G.R. Driver, ZAW 46 (1928): 7-25; Thierry, Oud. St. 5 (1942): 30-42; M. Noth, The Israelite personal names, chap. 3 (Germ.), Hildesheim, 1966; reprint 1928 ed.; A. Murtonen, Treatise on OT divine names, Helsinki, 1952; cf. Ug.hwt- "speech"; C.J. Labuschagne, The incomparability of Yhwh in the OT (diss.), Leiden, 1966. On *'el, 'elohim,* cf. also A. Gil Theotonio, MEAH 7,2 (1958); 45-75; F. Zimmermann, VT 12 (1962): 190-95; K. Nakanishi, SJLC 4 (1966): 16-23; O. Eissfeldt, JSS 1 (1956): 25-37; ELW 3: 386-97; A. Draffkorn, JBL 76 (1957): 216-24; R. deVaux, (Fr.), Ug.a 6 (1969): 501-17; M.H. Segal, VT 6 (1956): 124; art. *'elohim,* EM (Heb.), 1 (1955), col. 297-321; S. Geositz, The divine name 'elohim, (Germ., diss.), Vienna, 1953; G. Johannes, Formulations expressing incomparability in the OT (Germ., diss.), Mainz, 1968.]

27. See in particular Hehn, p. 229, and Driver, *ZAW* (1928).

28. [For Abram-Abraham, cf. also Arab. *ruham,* "multitude." The syllable -*ha*- is "a secondary extension . . . common in Aramaic;" Abram or Abiram, "the father is exalted," E.A. Speiser, Genesis, New York, 1964, 124.]

29. a. In the phrase "all the men" another version of the story is obvious that has not been told in our text. According to it, the king wants to kill not only Moses but also an entire group of men who intrigue against the king in his house. This version roughly corresponds to the account we find in Josephus. b. In the text "his sons," but following verse 25 it is *one* son only.

30. "And Aaron" is an addition, shown by the singular of the verb. For the systematic insertion of Aaron see below.

31. [B. Rothenberg (Fr.), BTS 32 (July 1960): 4-14; HL 95 (1963): 7-14; 19-23; H. Bar Deroma, PEF QS 96 (1964): 101-34; Studies on the Bible III (Heb.), Kadesh Barnea, Jerusalem, 1967; E. Edel, ZA 50 (1952): 253-58; M. Dothan, Isr. EJ 15 (1965): 134-51.]

32. The essential part has been suggested by Eduard Meyer in *Die Israeliten und ihre Nachbarstämme* (1906), p. 59.

33. [J. Morgenstern, HUCA 34 (1963): 35-70; H. Junker (Germ.), FNF, pp. 120-28; J. Blau (Heb.), Tarb. 26 (1956): 1-3; H. Kosmäla, VT 12 (1962): 14-28; Y. Braslavi (Heb.), BM 17 (1963): 108-15; L. Rivera (Span.), RBA 25 (1963): 129-36; H. Schmid (Germ.), Jud. 22 (1966): 113-18; cf. also M. Spira, The estimation of sex in the OT (Germ., diss., Institute for the History of Medicine), Munich, 1964.]

34. The interpretation of the old commentators that Moses was attacked because he failed to circumcise his son is an impossible, forced explanation intended to cover up the mythological character of the story. It does not explain Zipporah's obscure words about the blood bridegroom. And, after all, why should Moses not have circumcised his son at the right time in Midian? "He hastened," they say, "to fulfill God's command." But if the child was recently born, Zipporah could not have traveled.

35. It is well known that there are two other accounts about the introduction of circumcision among the Israelites. One, Josh. 5:2-3, 8-9, belongs to E and explains circumcision as an assimilation to the Egyptian custom; the other, Gen. 17:10-27, comes from P and explains circumcision as "a sign of the covenant," which it assigns to the pre-Mosaic period of the patriarchs.

[Cf. J.M. Sasson, JBL 85,4 (1966): 473-76; E. Isaac, Anthropos 59 (1964): 444-56;

H. Schlossmann, Psy.Q. 35,3 (1966): 340-56; E. Junes (Fr.), RHMH 16 (1953): 35-57; 17: 91-104; 18: 159-68; I. Jakobovits (Fr.), RHMH 82 (1968): 161-74; J. Licht (Heb.), EM 4, col. 894-901; R. Schwarzenberger, The significance and history of circumcision in the OT (Germ., diss.), Vienna, 1964.]

36. [H. Eising (Germ.), HJF, pp. 75-87; G. Hort, ZAW 69 (1957): 84-103; F. Dummermuth (Germ.), ZAW 76 (1964): 323-25; D. McCarthy, JBL 85 (1966): 137-58; R. Friebe, Form and historical origins of the cycle of plagues (Germ., diss.), Halle-Wittenberg, 1967-68.]

37. [On the treaty background of yada', e.g., Exod. 6,7;10,2f;16,6; cf. H. Huffmon, BASOR 181 (1966): 31-37.]

38. [On pasah, "to protect," cf. E. Testa (It.), Eunt Doc. 10 (1957): 281-84; G. Rinaldi (It.), BO 11 (1969): 158. On the terror, cf. S. Morenz, Studies in the history of religions, suppl. to Numen, Leiden, 1969, pp. 112-25.]

39. [Cf. S.I. Curtiss, Primitive Semitic religion to-day, Chicago, 1902, German trans. W.W. Graf Baudissin, Leipzig, 1903; J. Henninger (Germ.), PSF, pp. 279-316; G. Ryckmans (Fr.), The pre-Islamic Arab religions, Louvain, 1960.]

40. [Cf. G. Coats, VT 18 (1968): 450-47.]

41. Ed. Meyer, Israeliten, pp. 11-13.

42. [D. Redford, VT 13 (1963): 401-18; H. Cazelles, J. Leclant (Fr.), DBS 8,42 (1967): 1-6; E. Uphill, JNES 28 (1969): 15-39; S. Achituv, EM 6, col. 639-41.]

43. [B. Childs, VT 20 (1970): 406-18; D. Michel, Israel's faith in its changes (Germ.), Berlin, 1968: 33-49; L.S. Hay, JBL 83 (1964): 397-403; R. Schmid (Germ.), Theol. Z. 21 (1965): 260-68; N. Snaith, VT 15 (1965): 395-98; D. Ashbel (Heb.), BM 18 (1964): 71-76; G. Botterweek (Germ.), BL 8 (1967): 8-33; W. Krebs (Germ.), Altertum 12 (1966): 135-44, and A. Galanopoulos, Tsunami (Germ.), Altertum 13 (1967): 19; D. Nicovich, B. Heezen, Submarine geology and geophysics, Colston Papers 77 (London, 1965): 415-53; F. Spadafora (It.), AB, pp. 25-31; F. Eakin, JBL 86 (1967): 378-84; K. von Rabenau (Germ.), Theol. Versuche, ed. P. Wätzel, East Berlin, 1966, pp.7-29; G. Coats, LTQ 4,1 (1969): 22-32; E. Lauha (Germ.), VT, Congr. Vol. (1962), pp. 32-46.
      On the Sea of Reeds, cf. M. Copisarow, VT 12 (1962): 1-13; J. Towers, JNES 18 (1959): 150-53; C. Becker, EI 1: 931-33; S. Loewenstamm, EM 3, col. 695-700. On the sea in general, O. Eissfeldt, Studia Or. J. Pedersen (1953), pp. 76-84, and ELW, 3:256-64; W. Beyerlin (Germ.), Christiana Albertina 3 (1967): 21-27; A. Hermann, Drowning (Germ.), RAC 6, col. 370-409; O. Kaiser, The mythical significance of the sea in Egypt, Ugarit and Israel (Germ.), Berlin, 1959.]

44. [Cf. G. Ramey, The horse and chariot in Israelite religion (diss., S. Baptist Theol. Sem.), 1968). On the terms hosi and he'elah, cf. J. Wijngaards, VT 15 (1965): 91-102.]

45. The words wa-yehi he-'anan we-ha-ḥoshekh are completely unintelligible, but they are likely to be the remnant of a short sentence which had the meaning given above.

46. Gressmann did not succeed in making it likely that the Sea of Reeds is identical with the Gulf of Akaba or with the Gulf of Suez. The passages listed by him (1 Kings 9:26; Jer. 49:21; Exod. 23:31) show at most that the Gulf of Akaba was designated as a "Sea of Reeds" also, but in Exod. 10:19 yam suf can denote the Gulf of Suez only.

47. [F.M. Cross, D.N. Freedman, JNES 14 (1955): 237-50; J. Watts, VT 7 (1957): 371-80; N. Lohfink (Lat.), VD 41 (1963): 277-89; also (Germ.) in Freiheit u. Wiederholung, Frankfurt, 1965, pp. 174-98; G. Coats, CBQ 31 (1969): 1-17; F.M. Cross, JTC 5 (1968): 1-25; P. Craigie, VT 20 (1970): 83-86; E. Good, VT 20 (1970): 358-59.

Following Exod. 15:20 Miriam used a tambourine (thus NEB) to accompany her song; cf. E. Gerson-Kiwi (Fr.), DBS (1957), col. 1411-68; B. Bayer, EM 5, col. 755-82; J. Dyson, The musical instruments of the Bible (diss., Baylor Univ., 1955); D. Wohlenberg, Cult music in Israel (Germ., diss.), Hamburg, 1967; E. Wellesz, Ancient and oriental music, New Oxford history of music, vol. 1, New York, 1957; E. Gerson-Kiwi, The music of the Bible (Germ.), Düsseldorf, 1961.]

48. By this, the conclusions Buber drew from this song (in *Königtum Gottes*) about the age of the theocracy are shown to be wrong.

49. [M.B. Rowton, PEF QS 85 (1953): 46-60, and H.H. Rowley, HSN, pp. 195-204; Or. Suec. 4 (1955): 77-86; G. Fohrer, Tradition and history of the Exodus (Germ.), Berlin, 1964; O. Eissfeldt, CAH 2 (1965), chap. 26, and K.A. Kitchen, TB 17 (1966): 63-97; in particular, *literary:* V. Fritz, Israel in the desert (Germ.), Marburg, 1970; J. Gray, VT 4 (1954): 148-54; E. Galbiati, The literary structure of the Exodus (Span.), Alba, 1956; S. Loewenstamm, The Exodus from Egypt, a literary study (Heb.), Jerusalem, 1960; idem, The tradition of the Exodus from Egypt (Heb.), Jerusalem, 1965; idem (Heb.), BM 1,13 (1962): 121-25; P. Harner, JBL 85 (1966): 233-36; J.M. Schmidt (Germ.), ZAW 82 (1970): 1-31; *geographical:* H. Cazelles (Fr.), RHPR 35,1 (1955): 51-58; idem, RB 62,3 (1955): 321-64; idem BSFE. Réunions trim. 42, Paris, 1965, pp. 12-18; J. Simons (Dutch), Streven 9,2 (1956): 812-19; J. Prado, Sef. 17,1 (1957): 151-68; P.J. Smith (Dutch), GTT 60 (1960): 26; M. Haran, in Er. Isr., Archaeologic Studies X, Jerusalem, 1971, pp. 138-42; A. Charbel (Port.), RCB 4,8 (1967): 84-103; *historical:* S. Yeivin (Heb.), Tarb. 30 (1960): 1-7; H.H. Rowley (v.s.); E. Drioton (Fr.), RHPR 35,1 (1955): 36-49; J.A. Soggin (It.), Protestantesimo 15 (1960): 222-25, and CAO, Bible et Orient, 1955; C. de Wit, The date etc. of the Exodus, London, 1960; J. Leibovich (Fr.), Isr. EJ 3 (1953): 99-112; A. Murtonen, Stu. Th. 8 (1954): 133-37; R. North, AER 134 (1956): 161-82; F. Blaess, ATR 27 (1957): 99-106; R. Giveon 4 WCJS 1 (1967): 193-96; A. Ibáñez Arana (Span.), Lum. 17 (1968): 193-213; A. Weiser (Heb.), Sinai 54 (1963): 105-09. Further: D. Daube, The exodus pattern in the Bible, London, 1963; J. Solari, Bible Today 1 (1962): 294-301; M. Zer-Kavod, Karmelith 10 (1963): 112-16; S. Talmon, ABM, pp. 31-63. Philological, on *'alah-yarad:* W. Leslau, ZAW 74 (1962): 322; R. North, JKF 2,1 (1965): 343-57; on *nassel:* J. Radai, (Heb.), Sefer Yair Katz, Haifa, 1965, pp. 34-40. Dissertations: M. Harel, The route of the exodus of the Israelites from Egypt, New York, 1965; A. Gros, The theme of the route in the Bible (Fr.), Lille, 1954; H. Asmussen, On the dating of the exodus (Germ.), Kiel, 1960; H. Lubscyk, The theological significance of the exodus from Egypt in prophetic and priestly tradition (Germ.), Münster, 1960.]

50. See Auerbach, Wüste und Gelobtes Land, 1:82.
51. [Cf. S. Schwertner, The "promised land" . . . according to the early testimony of the OT (Germ., diss.), Heidelberg, 1966.]
52. Verse 26 does not belong to this account. Here YHWH is described as Israel's physician in theological terms which belong to another period and other literary strata. Perhaps this is the remnant of an account about the healing powers of the sacred springs of Kadesh.
53. [Cf. J.H. Grønbaek, Stu. Th. 18, 1-2 (1964): 26-45.]
54. Read *lekha* instead of *lanu*.
55. Added: and his people.
56. [E. Auerbach, Congr. Vol., VT XVII suppl. (1969): 37-63; H. Judge, JTS 7 (1956): 70-74; M. Fränkel, Bib. Or. 19 (1962): 213-16; H. Seebass, Moses, Aaron, Sinai and he Mountain of God (Germ., diss.), Bonn, 1961.]
57. See chap. 2.
58. [S. Lehming (Germ.), ZAW 73 (1961): 71-77; S. Loewenstamm, EM 5, cols. 57 and 456-58).]
59. The dating is that of the Babylonian calendar, in which the beginning of the year is in the spring and Nisan the first month. Since this calendar was introduced in Judah only in 605 after the battle of Carchemish, all the sections which point to this date are written down after 605; see Auerbach, VT2 (1952): 334-42.
60. Because of the subsequent double allusion that is the better reading, following 27:14.
61. [J. Coppens (Fr.), EE 34 (1960): 473-89; J. Ponthot (Fr.), RDT 11 (1956): 213-18; on *ṣappiḫith:* C. Rabin, BM 27 (1966): 151 f.]
62. [E. Sergent (Fr.), Archives de l'Instit. Pasteur d'Algérie 19,2 (1941): 161-92; X. Jacques (Fr.), Science et Esprit, Bruges, 20 (1968): 247-68.]
63. *Mose und seine Zeit.*
64. [Cf. LXX: *ártons toproï, kai kréa todeíles.*]
65. A later addition to this, with the intention of minimizing the contradiction to 4:20, is: "after he had sent her away."
66. Addition: "of whom the name of the one was Gershom, for he said, I have been a stranger in a strange land; 4. and the name of the other was Eliezer: for the god of my father was my help and delivered me from the sword of Pharaoh."
67. The further repetition of this sentence in this passage is impossible. We are assuming that it was placed here by mistake from the next verse. While otherwise 11b is unintelligible, it makes good sense to read *dabhar* instead of the word *debher*.
68. Instead of *wa-yiḳaḥ* it is better to read with Syr. and Targ. *wa-yaḳrebh*.
69. It is of course possible that there was a cult of the YHWH of Sinai in Midian and that Jethro was its priest. In that case we could understand more readily why Moses called him, and that there would be a way by which the Sinai stories could have penetrated into the Kadesh legends. We will find the problem again later.
    [On the Kenites and Midianites, cf. S. Abramsky, Er. Isr. 3 (1954): 116-24; R. de Vaux, loc. cit. 9 (1969): 28-32; F. du Buit, BTS 123 (1970): 2-5; H. Gunneweg (Germ.), ZTK 61,1 (1964): 1-9. Moses' father-in-law is described both as Midianite and as Kenite; cf. J. Liver, EM 4, col. 686-91.]

70. [Cf. F. Spadafora, M. Liverani, Moses . . . prophet and sacred legislator (It.), Bibl. Sanct. Later. 9 (1967): 604-49.]
71. The allusion in verse 23 that somewhere else the people "will go to their place in peace" proves this verse belongs to E.
72. Late addition: "for he had married a Cushite woman."
73. Addition in verse 3: "Now the man Moses was very meek, above all the men that were upon the face of the earth."
74. Instead of the unintelligible text, read with the Latin *bakhem nabhi'*. [Cf. W. O'Rourke Scripture 15,30 (1963): 44-55; F. Spadafora (It.), Tabor 20 (1956): 165-94, and in his Attualità Bibliche, Rome, 1964: 46-63, 63-75; A. Penna (It.), BO 12 (1970): 145-52; L. Perlitt, Moses as a prophet (Germ., diss. habil.), Heidelberg, 1969.]
75. Addition: "even manifestly and not in dark speeches."
76. [Cf. E.S. Hartom, EM 1, col. 33; S. Loewenstamm, EM 2, cols. 773-74.]
77. There is an addition, "and On ben Peleth ben Reuben," but this person is never mentioned again.
78. [J. Liver, Script. Hier. 8 (1961): 189-217; S. Lehming (Germ.), ZAW 74 (1962): 291-321; G. Hort, ABR 7 (1959): 2-26.]
79. The same applies to other springs and wells; the names Beersheba (Gen. 21:31), 'Esek (36:20), and Sitna (26:21) have the same connotation.
80. Meyer, *Die Israeliten*, p. 55.
81. [C. Lattey, CBQ 12 (1950): 277-91; E. Nielsen, ASTI 3 (1964): 16-27; A. Cody, A history of the OT priesthood, Rome, 1969; M. Noth, JSS 1 (1956): 327; R. de Vaux, HJF, pp. 265-73, and his Bible et Orient, Paris, 1967, pp. 277-85; A. Gunneweg, Levites and priests (Germ.), Göttingen, 1965; M. Rehm, Studies in the history of the pre-exilic levites (diss., Harvard University), 1967; H. Strauss, Studies of the traditions of the pre-exilic levites (Germ., diss.), Bonn, 1959.]
82. Meyer, *Die Israeliten*, p. 53.
83. [Or: "Their weapons are tools of lawlessness"; cf. *The Torah: A New Translation*, Philadelphia, 1962.]
84. Cf. Meyer, p. 89.
85. [B. Rothenberg, God's wilderness, London, 1961; A. Weiser (Heb.), Sinai 52 (1964): 289-98; E. Lákatos (Span.), RBA 28 (1966): 90-96; M. Harel (Heb.), BM 43 (1970): 458-60; O. Eissfeldt, TVF, pp. 62-70; V. Fritz, Israel in the wilderness . . . investigation . . . of the Yahwist (Germ., diss.), Marburg, 1970; H. Mallan, The theological significance of the wilderness in the OT (Germ., diss.), Kiel, 1963; on the accompanying deity: H. Preuss (Germ.), ZAW 80 (1968): 139-73; on *panim holekhim:* E. Speiser, JQR AV (1967): 451.]
86. [On the face: W. Boyd, SJT 13 (1960): 178-82; J. Reindl, The 'face of God' in the linguistic usage of the Bible (Germ., diss.), Freiburg, 1969; F. Nötscher, 'To see God's face' according to biblical and Babylonian views, 2d ed., Darmstadt, 1969; on the glory: T. Meger, The notion of divine glory in the Hebrew Bible (diss.), Louvain, 1965.]
87. "A journey of three days" repeated once more makes no sense and is surely copied incorrectly from the preceding text.
88. All references to the ark before this passage belong to the late Priestly Code.

89. [T. Worden, Scripture 5,4 (1952): 82-90; J. Dus (Germ.), Theol. Z. 20 (1964):
     241-51; G. Henton Davies, ASTI 5 (1966-67): 30-47; M. Haran, Miscellany in
     honor of Mazar, Er. Isr. Archaeolog. Studies 5 (1958): 83-90; O. Eissfeldt
     (Germ.), ELW 2: 282-305, and 3: 526-29; M. Buber, Essays L. Baeck, London,
     1954, pp. 20-25; E. Nielsen, VTS 7 (1960): 61-74; R. de Vaux (Fr.), Mém. A.
     Gelin, 1961, pp. 55-70, and Bible et Orient, pp. 261-76; L. Randellini (It.), SBF 13
     (1962): 163-89; W. McKane, GUOST 21 (1967): 68-76; on the end of the ark, cf.
     M. Haran, Isr. EJ 13,1 (1963): 46-58; O. Eissfeldt (Germ.), Altertum 14,3 (1968):
     131-45; J. Maier, The ancient Israelite ark (Germ.), Zerlin, 1965.]
90. It is a matter of indifference if, following tradition, the tables were really in the
     ark. It is striking that in historical accounts the tables are never mentioned, that
     is, whether the Philistines carried them off and then returned them. That the
     sources do not mention them tells against their presence in the ark. Only when
     the ark was placed in the Temple was an assurance given that nothing was in the
     ark but the two tables; but this statement now has little value.
91. H. Torczyner, *Die Bundeslade,* 1929.
92. For references see Torczyner, p. 38. [On the *parokheth,* cf. C.J. Gadd, Anatol.
     Stud. 9 (1958): 67; on the cherubim: R. de Vaux (Fr.), MUSJ 37,6 (1961): 93-124;
     E. Tsoref, BM 27(1966): 59-88; M. Haran, *vide supra;* W.F. Albright, BAR 1
     (1961): 95-97; M. Cassuto, R.D. Barnett, EM 4, col. 238-44; cf. also ANEP, p.
     212 f.]
93. It has been suggested that the repetition "let them that hate you flee" is a later
     expansion, this verse being a pentameter also. That is possible but cannot be
     proved.
94. This is still expressed clearly in the passage in Exod. 7:4, belonging to P, which
     calls the children of Israel YHWH's *ṣebha'oth.* [On *ṣebha'oth,* cf. O. Eissfeldt,
     MAB (1950), 2:128-50; ELW 3: 102-23; M.L. Burke, ARM 11 (1963): 136; M.
     Tsevat, HUCA 36 (1965): 49 f.; J. Crenshaw, ZAW 81 (1969): 156-75; M.
     Liverani, IONA 17 (1967): 331-34; V. Maag, LKF, pp. 27-52; J. Maier, The
     ancient Israelite sanctuary of the ark (Germ.), Berlin, 1965; Cf. B. Wambacq,
     The divine epithet Jahve Ṣeba'ot (Fr., diss.), Brussels, 1947; A.E. Glock, War-
     fare in Mari and early Israel (diss.), 1968-69.]
95. *Mose und seine Zeit,* pp. 445-48.
96. [I. Lewy, VT 9 (1959): 318-22; M. Noth, VT 9 (1959): 419-22; J. Petuchowski, VT
     10 (1960): 74; R. Gradwohl, Theol. Z. 19 (1963): 50-53; M. Barrelet, R. Ass. 48
     (1954): 16-27; U. Pestalozza, RIL 93 (1959): 349-81; S. Loewenstamm, Bib. 48
     (1967): 481-90; C. Schaeffer, AIBL (1966), pp. 327-38; F. Fensham, Isr. EJ 16
     (1966): 191-93; J. Sasson, VT 18 (1968): 380-87; S. Ryser, The Golden Calf (Fr.),
     Geneva, 1954; cf. also P. Maon, Mutual responsibility and guilt in the very
     ancient Biblical institutions (Fr., diss.), Louvain, 1964.]
97. [Cf. H.H. Rowley, The meaning of sacrifice in the OT, Manchester, 1951; E.
     Forster, The ancient views about the sacrifices (Germ., diss.), Innsbruck, 1953.]
98. Instead of the unintelligible *be-ra',* read with Samaritan *paru'a.*
99. This verse is so mutilated that only an approximate translation can be given and
     that only with the help of some textual corrections.
100. Literally, "You have filled your hand for YHWH." For this phrase, cf. Judg.
     17:12.

101. [On *ṣahek*; cf. M. Held JCS 15 (1961): 20.]
102. [Cf. S. Blank, Men against God: The Promethean element, JBL 72 (1953): 1-13; F. Hesse, Intercession in the OT (Germ., diss.), Erlangen, 1949; f. Judg. 17:12.]
103. [On divine justice: E. Beaucamp (Fr.), SBF 9 (1960-61): 5-55; J. Licht (Heb.), EM 6, cols. 678-85; J. Vella, The judicial justice of God (It., diss.), Brescia, 1964; A. Gamper, God as judge in Mesopotamia and the OT (Germ., diss., habil.), Innsbruck, 1966; W. von Soden, MDO 96 (1965): 41-59; Anthropos 61 (1966): 895.]
104. [E. Auerbach (Germ.), Congr. Vol. (1962); H. Cazelles (Fr.), MACO 1: 169-200; R. de Vaux, in G. Castellino, ed., Israel, Rome, 1966; A. Cody, A history of OT priesthood, An. Bib. 35 (1969): 1-216; R. Sklba, The teaching function of the pre-exilic priesthood (diss.), Rome, 1965; G. Tyner, The mosaic background of the priestly code (diss., S. Baptist Seminary), 1955; on *sedek*, cf. K. Koch, Sedek in the OT. A study in tradition-history (Germ., diss.), Heidelberg, 1953; on *ṣedaḳah*, cf. F. Breukelmann (Germ.), Justice, V Theol. 32 (1961): 42-57.]
105. And yet there may be some truth in the matter. For adherence to the outlived notions and formulas of early antiquity becomes more and more marked in the priesthood deriving its descent from Aaron, in contrast to the Jahwist and Jeremiah, who are the descendants of Moses.
106. [The Abisha-Scroll in Deut. 33:9 has *lo' ra'ithi;* read *lo' re'ithim,* "I have not seen them."]
107. In Mose und seine Zeit, pp. 212 ff.
108. [Edw. Robertson, VT 14 (1964): 67-74; E. Lipinski, VT 20 (1970): 495-96; Z. Karl, 'Al hag ha-mikra' (Heb.), TA 3 (1952): 1-15; N.H. Tur-Sinai (Heb.), EM 1 (1955), cols. 179-183; on the etymology: ' *-t* cf. Press, ZAW 51 (1933): 229, or *'rr-tmm* cf. Festschrift J. Hempel, Berlin, 1961, p. 101, 318.]
109. [Cf. F. Haulotte, The symbolism of the clothing according to the Bible (Fr.), Paris, 1966.]
110. [Genizah fragment E263 reads *kohen* instead of MT *ha-kohen.*]
111. [On the alphabet: D. Diringer, Biblical scripts in P. Ackroyd, C. Evans, ed., Cambridge History of the Bible, Cambridge, 1970: 11-29; on the origins: D. Diringer, CHM 4,1 (1957): 40-58; J. Friedrich (Germ.), SBO 3 (Rome, 1959): 85-103; F.M. Cross and T. Lambdin, BASOR 160 (1960): 21-26; M. Lambert (Fr.), AICO (Moscow, 1960) 1: 187-89; S. Rin (Heb.), Leshonenu 26 (1962): 56-61; D. Diringer (Heb.), MHA 6 (1964): 51-62; B. Delavault in S. Moscati (Fr.), The Phoenicians, Archeologia 20 (Paris, 1968); M. Pope, Antiquity, Gloucester, 40 (1966): 17-23; on the beginnings of the Greek alphabet: S. Segert (Germ.), Klio 41 (1963): 38-57; G.R. Driver, From pictograph to alphabet, London, 1954; H. Jensen, Sign, symbol and script (trans.), London, 1970; I. Gelb, From the cuneiform script to the alphabet (Germ.), Stuttgart, 1958; K. Földes-Papp, From the pictograph on the rock to the alphabet. A history of script (Germ.), Stuttgart, 1966; O. Eissfeldt, in G. Pfohl, The alphabet (Germ.), Darmstadt, 1968, pp. 214-20; S. Mercer, The origin of writing and our alphabet, London, 1959; J. Friedrich (Germ.), A history of script (Heidelberg, 1966); F.M. Cross (Heb.), The origin of the alphabet and its beginning development (Jerusalem, 1965); J. Croatto, Origin and development of the alphabet (Span.), Buenos Aires, 1968.]
112. [G. Lippold (Germ.), in D.M. Robinson, Studies . . . on his 70th birthday, 1951,

pp. 648-54; W.B. Kristensen (Dutch), MKNAW, Letterk. 16,14 (1953): 591-610; S. Bertman, HR 3 (1964): 323-27; K. Joines, JBL 87 (1968): 245-56; M. Haran (Heb.), EM 5, cols. 826-27; on the serpent in ancient Near Eastern art: M. Erlenmeyer (Germ.), AO 23 (1970): 52-62; K. Joines, The serpent in the OT (diss., S. Baptist Theol. Sem.), 1967.]

113. [A. Jirku (Germ.), ZDPV 67 (1945): 43-45, and his From Jerusalem to Ugarit (Germ.), Graz, 1966, pp. 347-49; M. Haran (Heb.), EM 5, cols. 57-58.]

114. [On the ephod: M. Haran (Heb.), Tarb. 24,4 (1955): 380-91; G. Dahl, AnTR 34 (1952): 206-10; K. Elliger (Germ.), VT 8 (1958): 19-35; CAD 4 (1958): 183; I. Friedrich, Origin and character of ephod and hoshen in the light of the ancient East (Germ., diss.), Vienna, 1963; also WBT 20 (1968): 5-80; on the teraphim, linguistic: H. Hoffner, BS 124 (1967): 230-38; F. Baumgartner, Teraphim (Germ., diss.), Vienna, 1960.]

115. [Cf. also F. Dummermuth (Germ.), Theol. Z. 17 (1961): 240-48.]

116. The same conclusion, although it cannot be used for our purpose, results from the reference in Ezekiel (21:26).

117. [M. Haran (Heb.), Tarb. 25 (1955): 11-20; MHSS, pp. 33-41; Script. Hier. 8 (1961): 272-302; JSS 5 (1960): 50-65; HUCA 36 (1965): 191-226; YKJV, pp. 20-42; cf. also M.H. Segal, Tarb. 25 (1956): 231; G. Widengren, Numen 7 (1960): 1-25; R. de Vaux, Mélanges A. Gelin, Le Puy, 1961, pp. 55-70; G. von Rad (Germ.), RGS, pp. 109-29; F.M. Cross, BAR 1: 201-28; S. Lehming (Germ.), HHF, pp. 110-32; V. Rabe, JNES 25 (1966): 132-34; F. Sole (It.), PCR 45 (1966): 864-75; Y. Kaufmann, Maʿalot 5,4 (Tel Aviv, 1967): 51-58; G.R. Brinke, The symbolism of the Tabernacle (Germ.), 1956; M. Görg, The Tent of Meeting (Germ., diss., incl. survey of 160 years of research), Bonn, 1967; V. Rabe, The Temple as tabernacle (diss., Harvard University), Boston, 1962; J.A. Scott, The pattern of the Tabernacle (diss.), Philadelphia, 1965.]

118. The information is reliable, otherwise the reason for Solomon going to Gibeon for the coronation sacrifices would be quite unintelligible (1 Kings 3:4).

119. [Geographical: J. Koenig (Fr.), RHPR 43 (1963): 2-31; 44 (1964): 200-35; RHR 167,2 (1965): 129-55; CO 10 (1966): 113-23; RHR 166 (1964): 121-41; Francès, Lugans (Fr.), TS 9 (1963): 284-89; R. Cargnelli (It.), RMI 36 (1970): 24-30; historical: J. Gray, VT 4 (1954): 148-54; T. Reik, Midstream 5,3 (1959): 5-24; F. Dattler (Port.), RCB 6 (1969): 99-102; W. Beyerlin, Origins and history of the oldest Sinaitic traditions (trans.), Oxford, 1965; literary: P.B. Harner, JBL 85,2 (1966): 233-36; O. Eissfeldt (Germ.), ZAW 73 (1961): 137-46; TLZ 91 (1966): 1-6; ELW 4: 209-14; SAWL 113,1 (Berlin, 1961): 31; ELW 4: 12-20; (the oldest account); M. Haelvoet, ETL 29 (1953): 374-97; G. Rinaldi (It.), Pd V 7 (1962): 345-51; H. Gese (Germ.), ZAW 79 (1967): 137-54; N. Loss (It.), Salesianum, Turin 29 (1967): 669-94; J. García Trapiello (Span.), Stadium, Madrid, 9 (1969): 239-56; M. Haelvoet (Fr.), The Theophany of the Sinai, Brussels, 1953; H. Seebas, Moses and Aaron: Sinai and Mountain of God (Germ.), Bonn, 1962; K.H. Walkenhorst, The Sinai in the liturgical understanding of the deuteronomistic and priestly traditions, (Germ.), Bonn, 1969; theological: H. Huffmon, CBQ 27 (1965): 101-13; M.H. Segal, JQR AV (1967), pp. 490-97; cf. also Martin Buber, Moses, Oxford, 1946; philological: J. Craviotti (Span.), RBA 30 (1968): 77-135; 31 (1969): 1-9; R. Tournay, VT 7 (1957): 411-13; H. Cazelles,

VT 8 (1958): 103; M. Greenberg, JBL 79 (1960): 273-76; further: H. Skrobucha (Germ.), Sinai, Olten, 1959; D. Correa Gomez, On the significance of Mt. Zion in' S. Scripture (Lat., diss.), Rome, 1961, cf. also in Franciscanum, Bogotá, 1961; R. Aron, The god of the origins, of the caves at Sinai (Fr.), Paris, 1964; Y. Kaufmann, Knowing the Bible: Sinai (Fr.), (trans.), Paris, 1970; G. Gerster, Sinai: Land of revelation (Germ.), 2d ed., Zurich, 1970.]

120. [On the biblical theophany, cf. J. Lindblom, HUCA 32 (1961): 91-106; as to Exod. 34:6f: R.C. Dentan, VT 13 (1963): 34-51. S. Loewenstamm SBG 508; as to Judg. 7:16 f.: H. Müller (Germ.), VT 14 (1964): 183-91; as to Exod. 19 f.: F. Dummermuth (Germ.), Theol. Z. 21 (1965): 1-21; as to the Tabernacle: A. Pieper, Theol. Q. 55 (1958): 1-15; others: A. Dubarle (Fr.), Vie Spirituelle, Paris, 119 (1968): 11-23; J. Jeremias, Theophany: The history of an OT literary species (Germ., diss.), Neukirchen, 1965.]

121. The next six words are inserted and anticipate verse 20.

122. [Cf. F. Schnutenhaus (Germ.), ZAW 76 (1964): 1-22.]

123. Verse 13 is an interpolation: Moses cannot first ascend the mountain and then speak to the elders. He goes up only in verse 15.

124. Since in the addition verse 13, which is inserted with regard to 32:17-18, Joshua is suddenly made to go up the mountain with Moses, the plural is used here.

125. [Arab. *ard es-Sini*; cf. L. Woolley and T.E. Lawrence in PEF QS 46 (1914).]

126. [S. Wagner (Germ.), ZAW 76 (1964): 255-69; D. Silver (Heb.), BM 32 (1968): 65-74.]

127. At the name Hebron we find two glosses in the text; the first is a short legend: "there were Ahiman, Sheshai and Talmai, the descendants of Anak"; the second, a historical note: "Hebron was built seven years before Tanis (Zoan) in Egypt." According to Eduard Meyer that would be 1677 B.C. The information may be right; it cannot be checked, however.

128. [S. Vries, JBL 87 (1968): 51-58; P. Termos Ros (Span.), SBE 26 (1969): 387-95; G.W. Coates, Rebellion in the wilderness: The murmuring motif in the wilderness traditions of the OT, Nashville, 1968; cf. also F. Hesse, The problem of obduracy in the OT (Germ.), Berlin, 1955.]

129. For details see Auerbach, Wüste und Gelobtes Land, 1: 87-89. [On the Negev, cf. Y. Aharoni in Archaeology and the OT, ed. D.W. Thomas, Oxford, 1963, pp. 385-403, and Y. Aharoni, The land of the Bible. A historical geography, Philadelphia, 1966.]

130. Auerbach, WG 1: 84.

131. [On the external sources cf. S. Waterhouse, Syria in the Amarna age (diss., Univ. of Michigan), 1965, and on the Merneptah stela: ANET, cols. 376-78, and J. Murtagh, Scripture 15 (1968): 20-23.]

132. [N. Glueck, BAR 2: 51-58; J. Prado (Span.), EE 34 (1960): 557-67; B. Cresson, Israel and Edom. A study of the Edom bias in the OT religion (diss.), Durham, 1964.]

133. [Also known as the Moabite Stone.]

134. [Cf. G.A. Cooke, *Handbook of North Semitic Inscriptions*, Oxford, 1903, p. 3; E. Ullendorff in D.W. Thomas, *Documents from O.T. Times*, London, 1958, p. 196; Donner-Röllig, Kannaanäische und aramäische Inschriften, Wiesbaden 1962-64, 1:33; 2:168. Cf. also J.C. Gibson, *Textbook*, Oxford, 1971- .]

135. [R. de Vaux, Bible et Orient, 1967, pp. 118-27; S. Achituv (Heb.), EM 5, cols. 1017-18; on the Heshbon Song: P. Hanson, HTR 61 (1968): 297-320.]
136. Although Jephthah states (Jud. 11:26) that Israel has been dwelling in this stretch of territory for 300 years, that is useless for calculating the period of Moses, because the calculation is based on a chronology found in much later supplements (see E. Auerbach, WG).
137. [A.H. Van Zyl, The Moabites, Leiden, 1960; N. Donner (Germ.), MIOR 5 (1957): 155-84; re the 8th cent. B.C.; J.A. Thompson, ABR 5 (1956): 121-43; W.F. Albright, BASOR 163 (1961): 52; J. Liver (Heb.), EM 4, cols. 707-23; on the Ammonites, cf. G. Landes, BA 24 (1961): 66-86, and BAR 2: 69-88; R. Hentschke (Germ.), ZDPV 76 (1960): 603-23; H. Graf Reventlow, ZDPV 79 (1963): 127-37.]
138. Verse 4b is an addition, as YHWH cannot speak of himself in the third person.
139. See Auerbach, WG, 2d ed., 1:142;
[cf. N. Habel, Yahweh versus Baal. A conflict of religious cultures, New York, 1964; M. Mulder, Baal in the OT (Dutch, diss.), The Hague, 1962; F. Eakin, The relation of Yahwism and baalism during the pre-exilic period (diss.), Durham, 1964.]
140. [Hebrew Pinḥas, a name of Egyptian origin, i.e., P'-nhsy, 'the Nubian.'']
141. [G.R. Driver, AAN, pp. 128-43; G. Gerleman, THAT 1, cols. 600-21; L. Wächter, Death in the OT (Germ., diss. habil.), Rostock, 1964.]
142. Verse 7a could not possibly belong to the old account. The precise statement of age elsewhere usually derives from P. The number of 120 years is not only improbable in itself but contradicts all other presuppositions in the stories. If that were right, Moses would have been an old man of eighty years at the exodus from Egypt (P in Exod. 7:7), an impossible thought! How old indeed would his father-in-law have been when he visited him in Kadesh and gave him sound advice? If Moses was forty years old at the commencement of his work, he died at eighty years, old and tired of life. If verse 7a is deleted from the old account, verse 7b must be placed before verse 6 which, in any case, is natural. Verse 6 is a clear and fitting conclusion of the account.
143. [Introductory: J. Stamm, M.E. Andrew, The Ten Commandments in recent research, London, 1967; J. Stamm (Germ.), Theol. R. 27 (1961): 189-239; 281-305; E. Zenger (Germ.), Theol. Rev. 64 (1968)j; 189-98; G. Chiaradia, Introduction to the decalogue (It.), Genoa, 1969; S. Goldman, The Ten Commandments, semi-critical introduction by M. Samuel, Chicago, 1963; historical: A.S. Kapelrud, Stu. Th. 18,2 (1964): 81-90; H. Cazelles (Fr.), Er. Isr. 9 (1969): 14-19; H.H. Rowley, Men of God, Edinburgh, 1963, pp. 1-36; A.I. Patrick (Fr.), ALBO 4,15 (1964): 241-51; cf. B. Celada, CBS 23 (1966): 352-57; cf. G. Fohrer, ZAW 79 (1967): 115; A. Jepsen (Germ.), ZAW 79 (1967): 277-304; S. Lustig, Shema'tin, (Heb.), New York, 1969, pp. 7-15; cf. also S. Baron, SRHJ, 2d ed., New York, 1952, 1: 49 f., 227; Index vol. (1960), pp. 38-39; J. Schreiner, The Ten Commandments in the life of God's people (Germ.), Munich, 1966; literary: Cyr. Gordon, Christianity Today 8,14 (1964): 625-28; M. Kline, WTJ 16,1 (1953): 1-27; W. Kessler (Germ.), VT 7 (1957): 1-16; M. Perath, BM 1 (1956): 100-02; P. Van den Berghe (Dutch), CBG 8 (1962): 37-48; cf. pp. 171-88; P. Mamie (Fr.), NV 37 (1962): 277-83; 38 (1963): 216-24; G. Botterweck (Germ.), Concilium 1 (1965): 392-401; E. Pfeiffer (Germ.), LMH. Literaturheft (1963), pp. 1-7; H. Gese

(Germ.), ZTK 64 (1967): 121-38; H. Haag (Germ.), Anima 19, 2 (1964): 120-28,
and (It.), BO 9 (1967): 3-12; on the number ten: H. Brongers (Germ.), TVF, pp.
30-45; others: S. Buckley, IJT 16 (1967): 106-20; H. Cazelles, SM 1 (1967):
382-84; H. Gese, 4 WCJS 1 (1967): 155-59; D. Gonzalo Maeso (Span.), CBS 24
(1967): 323-39; N. Lohfink, in his Bibelauslegung, Frankfurt, 1969, pp. 129-57;
on the conclusion: W.L. Moran, CBQ 29 (1967): 543-54; on New Testament
parallels: R. Aldrich, Bib. Sacr. 118 (1961): 251-88; on the ritual decalogue,
Exod. 34:10-26: J. Guillén Torralba (Span.), EB 20 (1961): 407-21; H. Kosmala,
ASTI 1 (1961):; 31-61; on single commandments: (1) W.H. Schmidt (Germ.),
TEH 165 (1969): 5-55, and The first Commandment, Munich, 1969; WW 25
(1970): 402-10; N. Lohfink (It.), BO 7 (1965): 49-60; (1 & 2) B. Jacob, Judaism 13
(1964): 3-18; R. Knieriu (Germ.), ZAW 77 (1965): 20-39; T. Vriezen (Fr.), RsBs 8
(1967): 35-50; E. Zenger (Germ.), ZDMG, suppl. 1 (1969): 334-42; (2) S. du Tor
(Afr.), OTWSA, (1969): 101-10; W. Zimmerli (Germ.), God's Revelation. Essays, Munich, 1963, pp. 234-48; W. Vischer, KBF, pp. 764-72; J. Dus (Germ.),
CV 4 (1961): 37-50; J. Ouelette (Fr.), RB 74 (1967): 504-16; J. Wijngaards, IJT 18
(1969): 180-90; G. Gismondi (It.), in L. Babbini, Man and the decalogue, Genoa,
1969, pp. 99-133; (5) J. Gamberoni (Germ.), BZP 8,2 (1964): 161-90; G. Han
(Lat.), On the commandment of filial piety in the decalogue (diss.), and VV 25
(1967): 435-66; also Jerusalem, 1961; (6) A. Jepsen (Germ.), ELKZ 2,13 (1959):
384 f.; U. Neuenschwander (Germ.), STUB 31 (1961): 89-103; (6 & 10) D.
Flusser, Textus 4 (1964): 220-24; (8) H. Stoebe (Germ.), WDB 3 (1952): 108-26;
A. Alt (Germ.), AKS, 1:333-40; (9) K. Lüthi (Germ.), KRS (1955): fasc. 15; (10)
Cyr. Gordon, JBR 31 (1963): 208-09; on the commandments, cf. also M.D.
Cassuto (Heb.), EM 2: cols. 590-96; ethical: (1) Soisalon-Soininen (Germ.), ZEE
13,3 (1969): 146-53; D. Gonzalo Maeso (Span.), CB 15 (1958): 327-37; J. Hyatt,
Enc. 26,2 (1965): 199-206; J. Schreiner (Germ.), Diakonia 3 (1968): 98-117; R.S.
Wallace, The Ten Commandments: A study of ethical freedom, Edinburgh,
1965; legal: Auerbach, The Ten Commandments — a general form of law in the
Bible (Germ.), VT 16 (1966): 255-76; cf. G. Fohrer, Regarding OT theology and
history (Germ.), Berlin, 1969; others: H. Graf Reventlow, Commandment and
Preaching in the Decalogue (Germ.), Gütersloh, 1962; E. Nielsen, The Ten
Commandments in new perspective (trans.), London, 1968; C. Quin, The Ten
Commandments, London, 1952; J.L. Koole, The Ten Commandments (Dutch),
Bern, 1964; J. van den Bergh, The thora in the thora (Dutch), Aalten, 1963; K.
Kinoshita, A study of the decalogue (diss.), New York, 1963.]

144. Cf. Gressmann, Mose, pp. 471 f.
145. Festschrift for Heinrich Loewe, Tel Aviv, 1939.
146. Cf. K. Bunding, The norms and their transgressions (Germ.), 4 vols, 1872-1920.
147. [On *pāḵad*, cf. example on Exod. 20:5: rendered by "visit guilt" (Torah) or
     "punish" (NEB); cf. J. Hooser, The meaning of the Hebrew root *pāḵad* in the
     OT (diss., Harvard University), Cambridge, 1962; on the problem of theodicy,
     cf.: M. Sekire (Fr.), Orient 1 (1960): 23-34; K. Koch (Germ.), ZTK 52 (1955):
     1-42; P. Merusi, The concept of divine causality with the Hebrews (Lat., diss.),
     Rome, 1954; cf. H. Gevaryahu (Heb.), BM 2 (1962): 87-93.]
148. [Cf. W. Schottroff, The root *zkr* in the OT (Germ., diss.), Mainz, 1961.]
149. [On the *gēr:* L. Muntingh (Dutch), NGT 3 (1962): 534-58; E. Neufeld, HUCA 26

(1955): 391 f.; I.A. Seeligmann, EM 2, cols. 546-49.]

150. In the masoretic text there io no sign of separation between the first and second commandments.

151. "Trage nicht seinen Namen auf den Wahn."

152. Jerome of Cardia, in Diodorus XIX, 94.

153. [J. Hoftijzer (Dutch), NTT 14,4 (1960): 24i-63; G. Fohrer (Germ.), TLZ 91 (1966): cols. 80i-16; 893-904, and his A history of Israelite religion (Germ.), Berlin, 1969 (cf. on the theory of an amphyctiony); H. Orlinsky, AAN, pp. 375-87, and OA 1 (1962): 11-20 regarding the period of the judges; as to Mari: A. Malamat, JAOS 82 (1962): 143-50, and Anthropos 61 (1966): 896, also M. Noth (Germ.), AIPHOS 13 (1953): 433-44, and NGS, pp. 142-55; R. Smend, Yahweh war and tribal confederation (trans.), Nashville, 1970, (Alt, v. Rad, Noth tradition); Z. Kallai, The allotments of the tribes of Israel and their boundaries (diss.), Jerusalem, 1962; on the covenant, cf. also: G.E. Mendenhall, BA 17,3 (1954): 50-76, and BAR 3: 25-53; also his Law and covenant in Israel and the ancient Near East, Pittsburgh, 1955; cf. the review by H.H. Rowley in SOTSB (1955); D.J. McCarthy, CBQ 27,3 (1965): 217-40, his Treaty and covenant (diss.), Rome, 1963, and his The divine covenant in the OT (Germ.), Stuttgart, 1966; W.L. Moran's review of K. Baltzer (Germ.), The covenant formulary, 1960, Bib. 43 (1962): 100-106; surveys: F. Nötscher (Germ.), BZP 9,2 (1965): 181-214; F. Vattioni (It.), IONA 17 (1967): 181-232; R. Martin-Achard, (Fr.) Rev. TP 11 (1968): 88-102; G. Baena (Span.), EB 29,1-2 (1970): 5-54; others: A. Jepsen, Berith (Germ.), WRF, pp. 161-79; W. Eichrodt, Int. 20 (1966): 302-21; H. Cazelles, VT 8 (1958): 104; SM 1 (1967): 642-52; 2 (1968): 18-23; G.M. Tucker, VT 15 (1965): 487-503; J.A. Thompson, Ref. TR 18 (1959): 65-75; ABR 8 (1960): 38-45; JRH 3 (1964): 1-19; E. Kutsch (Germ.), BZAW 105 (1967): 133-43, and ZDMG suppl. 1 (1969): 356-61; philological: W.F. Albright, BASOR 121 (1951): 21; E. Kutsch (Germ.), Archaeology and OT, 1970, pp. 165-78; J. Fitzmyer, JAOS 81 (1961): 187; O. Loretz, VT 16 (1966): 239-41; F. Vattioni, Biblos Press (Rome, 1965): pp. 112-16; theological: J. Cadier (Fr.), ETR 31,4 (1956): 10-30; on hesed: J. Anandale, TE 3 (1970): 67-74, and N. Glueck, Hesed in the Bible, trans. A. Gottschalk, ed. E.L. Epstein, Cincinnati, 1967; others: D.N. Freedman, Int. 18 (1964): 419-31; J. Faur, Trad. 9,4 (1967): 33-55; L. Perlitt, Covenant theology in the OT (Germ.), Neukirchen, 1969; K. Baltzer, The covenant formulary in OT Jewish and early Christian writings (trans.) (diss.), Philadelphia, 1971; Rud. Schmid, The covenant sacrifice in Israel (Germ., diss.), 1963; D.R. Hillers, Covenant: the history of a Biblical idea, Baltimore, 1969.]

154. [Ch. Virolleaud (Fr.), AIBL (1956), p. 56; Cyr. Gordon, ABM: 1-9; E. Speiser, JBL 79 (1960): 157-63; E. Dhorme, ETR 34 (1959): 78-100; N. Walker, VT 4 (1954): 434; S. Loewenstamm, EM 3 (1) cols. 938-40; (2) cols. 940-43; G.A. Danell, Studies in the name Israel in the OT, Uppsala, 1946; A. Hulst (Dutch), What does the name Israel in the OT mean?, The Hague, 1962.]

155. See Auerbach, Wüste und Gelobtes Land, 1:80

156. [Cf. J. Curtis, JBR 33 (1965): 247-49; M. Noth on Reuben, EBB 6 (1965): 268-71; Simeon, EBB, pp. 697-99; Zebulun, EBB, pp. 1369-71.]

157. [M. Greenberg, The Hab'piru, New Haven, 1955; R. de Vaux (Fr.), RB 63 (1956): 261-67; JNES 27,3 (1968): 221-28; E. Dhorme (Fr.), RH 78,2 (1954):

256-64; M. Kline, WTJ 19 (1956): 1-24; 170-84; 20 (1957): 46-70; A. Pohl (Germ.), WZKM 54 (1957): 157-60; M. Gray, HUCA 29 (1958): 135-202; T. Säve-Söderbergh, Or. Suec. 1, 1-2 (1952): 5-14; A. de Buck (Dutch), BVH, pp. 1-16; J. Bottéro (Fr.), The problem of the Habiru at the 4th international gathering of Assyriologists, Paris, 1954, all known texts.]

158. [Cf. W. Beltz, The Caleb tradition (Germ., diss.), Budapest, 1966.]

159. [R. de Vaux, HMF, pp. 108-34: on the origins.]

160. [Cf. T. Dothan, Ant. Sur. 2 (1957): 151-64; B. Rahtjen, JNES 24 (1965): 100-104; B. Rahtgen, The Philistine amphyctiony (diss.), New Jersey, 1964.]

161. *Das System der Zwölf Stämme Israels,* 1930.

162. [K. -D. Schunk, Studies on the origins and history of an Israelite tribe (Germ.), Berlin, 1963; cf. also S. Yeivin, EM 2: cols. 263-81.]

163. [H. Brichto, The problem of "curse" in the Hebrew Bible, Philadelphia, 1968; cf. also: J. Scharbert (Germ.), Bib. 89 (1958): 1-26; C.A. Keller, THAT 1: cols. 236-40; on blessing, cf. A. Murtonen, VT 9 (1959): 158-77, 330; C.A. Keller and G. Wehmeier, THAT 1: cols. 353-76; S. Gevirtz, Curse motifs in the OT and in the ancient Near East (diss.), Chicago, 1959; G. Wehmeier, The blessing in the OT . . . the root *brk* (Germ., diss.), Basle, 1970.]

164. J. Wilson, E. Speiser, Authority and law in the ancient orient, JAOS, suppl. 17 (1954); P. Collela (It.), in G. Rinaldi, ed., Centuries over the world, Turin, 1955; G. Mendenhall, BAR 3 (1970): 3-24; G. d'Ercole, in G. Castellino, ed., Israel 1 (Rome, 1966); H. Cazelles (Fr.), DBS 5 (1952): 498-512; on apodictic law: G. Fohrer (Germ.), KD 11 (1965): 49-74; S. Hermann (Germ.), MIOR 15 (1969): 149-61; K.R. Sauber, Abstraction in Israelite law (Germ., diss.), Göltingen, 1950; H.J. Boecker (Germ.), Forms of speech in OT law (diss.), 2d ed., Neukirchen, 1970; G. Liedke, Form and intention of OT legal clauses (Germ., diss.), Neukirchen, 1971; A.C. Phillips, Ancient Israel's criminal law, Oxford, 1970; E. Gerstenberger, Essence and origins of apodictic law (Germ., diss.), Neukirchen, 1965; Z.W. Falk, Hebrew law in Biblical times, Jerusalem, 1964.]

165. This holds good especially for the ancient legal dicta that Alt in *Ursprünge des altisralitischen Rechts* (1934) called "apodictic law."

166. For a recent reference, see Y. Kaufmann, *Tole doth ha-emunàh ha-yisraelith,* Tel Aviv, 1938, vol. 3.

167. [W. Zimmerli (Germ.), SAJF (1971), pp. 86-89; W. Vischer (Germ.), KBF, pp. 764-72; W. Schmidt (Germ.), WW 23 (1968): 209-16; H. Schrade, The hidden god. The image and conception of the deity in Israel and the ancient East (Germ.), Stuttgart, 1949; K. -H. Bernhardt, God and image. A contribution to the reasoning and interpretation underlying the prohibition of images in the OT (Germ.), Berlin, 1956; J. Hempel, The image in Bible and divine worship (Germ.), Tübingen, 1957; D.R. Hunsberger, Theophoric names in the OT and their theological significance (S. African diss.), 1919.]

168. [A. Botterweck (Germ.), TQ 134 (1954): 134-47; R. North, Bib. 36 (1955): 182-201; A.R. Hulst (Germ.), TVF, pp. 152-64; cf. also J.Z. Lauterbach, Rabbinic Essays, Cincinnati, 1951, pp. 437-70; on the number seven in Ugarit, cf. A.S. Kapelrud, VT 18,4 (1968): 493-99; C.W. Kiker, The Sabbath in the OT cult (diss.), ca. 1968; E. Jenni, The theological foundation of the Sabbath commandment in the OT (Germ.), Zurich, 1955; G. Yamashiro, A study of the Hebrew

word Shabbath in Biblical and Talmudic literatures (diss., Harvard University), 1955.]

169. The word *na'af* has a more comprehensive meaning than "to commit adultery."

170. [H.H. Rowley, From Moses to Qumran, London, 1963, pp. 33-63; also in ZAW 69 (1957): 1-21; others: RCMM, pp. 79-88; W.F. Albright, RCMM, pp. 61-67, and his The Bible after twenty years of archaeology, Pittsburgh, 1954; N. Snaith, ALUOS 5 (1966): 100-13; D. Baly, HMF, pp. 253-78; H. Orlinsky, HMF; J. Barr, GUOST 17 (1959): 52-62; J. Hempel, HHF, pp. 56-66; cf. also T. Meek, RCMM, pp. 68-77; psycho-analytic: A. Peto in The psycho-analytic study of society. (New York, 1960), 1: 311-76; H. Boesche, The polemics against the veneration of other deities besides YHWH in ancient Israel (Germ., diss.), Göttingen, 1962; on the one-ness of God, cf. C. Gordon, JNES 29,3 (1970): 198-99; G.A. Knight, Exp. T. 79 (1967): 8-10; O. Lehman, TU 73 (1959): 557-61; A.R. Johnson, The one and the many, 2d ed., Cardiff, 1961; C. Labuschagne, The incomparability of Jhwh in the OT, Leiden, 1966.]

171. For example P. Volz, *Mose* (1907); cf. 2d. ed. (1932).

172. [E. Dhorme (Fr.), Hommage á W. Vischer, Montpellier, 1960, pp. 46-54; J. Quinlan (Dutch), TT 7,1 (1967): 43-62; A.G. Blanco (Span.), CBG 221 (1968): 195-214; P. Mesnard (Fr.), R. Thom. 52 (1952): 473-90; A. Caquot (Fr.), Sem. 6 (1956): 53-68; G.R. Driver, PEF QS 91 (1959): 55-58; H. Wohlstein (Germ.), ZDMG 113 (1963-64): 483-92; ZDMG 117 (1967): 223-31; J. Fichtner (Germ.), FBF, pp. 24-40; E. Langton, Essentials of demonology. A study of Jewish and Christian doctrine, London, 1949; A. Jirku (Germ.), From Jerusalem to Ugarit, Graz, 1966, pp. 1-110; on the symbolism of blood, cf. also D. McCarthy, JBL 88 (1969): 166-76; G. Kiefer, The blood in the cult of the Old Covenant (Germ., diss.), Trier, 1966, cf. also A. Saphir, The mysterious wrath of Yahweh (diss., Princeton Theol. Sem.), 1964; in general, cf. M. Eliade (Fr.), Images and symbols, Paris, 1952.]

173. [C. Catanzaro, CJT 9 (1963): 163-73; J. Piña (Span.), CB. Serie negra 2 (1960): 5-52; on Buber: T. Vriezen (Germ.), Theol. Z. 22 (1966): 1-11; others: D. Morgan, Judaism 5 (1956): 31-45; I. Heinemann, EM 1: cols. 121-22; C. Wiéner (Fr.), Studies on the love for God in the Old Testament, Paris, 1957.]

174. [Cf. M.A. Klopfenstein, The lie according to the Old Testament: Its notion, significance, etc. (Germ.), Zurich, Frankfurt, 1964.]

175. [Cf. C. Wallace, Several animals as symbols in the Old Testament (diss.), Basel, 1961.]

176. [On anthropomorphism: E. Yamauchi, BS 125 (1968): 29-44; J. Barr, VT, suppl., 7 (1960): 31-38.]

177. [Regarding the Bible, cf. S. Plath, Fear of God: the term *yare'* in the OT (Germ.), Stuttgart, 1963; J. Becker, Fear of God in the OT (Germ.), (diss., Rome), 1965; cf. also I. Heinemann, EM 3: col. 768-70.]

178. [NEB on, for example, Exod. 6:3, renders Heb. *shadday*, "almighty"; cf. on the etymology: M. Weippert (Germ.), ZDMG 36,1 (1961): 42-62; E.C. MacLaurin, ZDMG 3 (1961): 99-118; F.M. Cross, HTR 55 (1962): 244-50; others: L. Bailey, JBL 87,4 (1968): 434-38; J. Ouelette, JBL 88 (1969): 470 f.; N. Walker, ZAW 72 (1960): 64 f.]

179. [On some mythological aspects, cf. B. Mazar (Heb.), Molad 22/195/6 (1964): 578-82; J. Gray, GUOST 14 (1953): 47-57; G. Widengren, in S.H. Hooke, ed., Myth, ritual and kingship, Oxford, 1958, pp. 149-203; A. Hoguth, Mythological elements in the OT: A study of the history of motifs (Germ., diss.), Freiburg, 1965; cf. also J. Gray, The legacy of Canaan, London, 1957; E. Auerbach, Moses, p. 230 against Y. Kaufmann (Fr.), Evidences 13,92 (1962): 5-12.]

180. [On the Book of the Covenant and the Holiness Code, cf. Eissfeldt-Ackroyd, Introduction, pp. 212-19, 233-39.]

181. [O. Eissfeldt (Germ.), NZSTR 9 (1969): 8-27; R. de Vaux, Concilium 5, 12 (1969): 729-35; on Benjaminite heathendom: J. Dus (Germ.), CV 6 (1963): 61-80; others: R. Rendtorff (Germ.), TLZ 88 (1963): cols. 735-46; E. Zenger (Germ.), TP 43 (1968): 338-59; A. Glock, CTM 41 (1970): 558-605; H.H. Rowley, The faith of Israel, London, 1956; W.F. Albright, New horizons in Biblical research, London, 1966, chaps. 1-2; G.W. Ahlström, Aspects of syncretism in Israelite religion, Lund, 1963; C. Westermann, The relation of the Yahweh faith to the non-Israelite religions (Germ.), Munich, 1964, pp. 189-218; S. Segert in Miscellany in honor of G. Rinaldi, Studies on the Orient and the Bible (It.), Genoa, 1967, pp. 155-61; G. Fohrer (Germ.), Studies in OT theology and history (1949-66), BZAW 115 (1970), 10: 1-372; S. Wagner, Religious nonconformity in ancient Jewish life (diss., Ann Arbor), 1965; on the relevance of religious studies: S. Sandmel, JAAR 35 (1967): 372-78, and his, Alone on top of the mountain, Garden City, N.Y., 1973; I.O. Lehman, EBB 1:213-19; A Néher, Moses and the vocation of the Jewish people, New York, 1959.]

182. [Cf. A. Gelin, The poor of Yahweh (Fr.), Paris, 1954; E. Kutsch, 'Anawah (humility). A contribution to the theme of God and man in the OT (Germ., diss.), Mainz, 1960.]

Subject Index

Name Index

Elias Auerbach (1882-1972) was a physician, lecturer and eminent Israeli authority on biblical history. He was born in Germany, but went to Israel as a young man. His book *Wuste und Gelobtes Land,* a history of Israel from its beginning to the return from Babylon, was published in 1938.

Robert A. Barclay (1901-1971) was senior lecturer in the Old Testament and comparative religion at the University of Leeds.

Israel O. Lehman, curator of manuscripts and special collections at Hebrew Union College, Cincinnati, received his B.Litt. (1947), M.A. (1948), and Ph.D. (1960) degrees from the University of Oxford. He is a fellow of the Royal Asiatic Society. His book, *Miniatures of God,* was published in 1970-71.

The manuscript was edited by Marguerite C. Wallace. The book was designed by Joanne Kinney. The typeface for the text is Times Roman, designed under the supervision of Stanley Morison about 1932; and the display face is Columna designed by Max Caflisch about 1955.

The text is printed on Nashoba Text paper and the book is bound in Columbia Mills' Title Linen oven binders' boards. Manufactured in the United States of America.